THE WHITE MOUNTAINS FROM NORTH CONWAY.

INCIDENTS

IN

WHITE MOUNTAIN HISTORY:

CONTAINING

FACTS RELATING TO THE DISCOVERY AND SETTLEMENT OF THE MOUNTAINS, INDIAN HISTORY AND TRADITIONS, A MINUTE AND AUTHENTIC ACCOUNT OF THE DESTRUCTION OF THE WILLEY FAMILY, GEOLOGY AND TEMPERATURE OF THE MOUNTAINS;

TOGETHER WITH

Many Interesting Anecdotes

ILLUSTRATING

LIFE IN THE BACK-WOODS.

BY

BENJAMIN G. WILLEY.

———◆———

HERITAGE BOOKS
2024

HERITAGE BOOKS
AN IMPRINT OF HERITAGE BOOKS, INC.

Books, CDs, and more—Worldwide

For our listing of thousands of titles see our website
at
www.HeritageBooks.com

A Facsimile Reprint
Published 2024 by
HERITAGE BOOKS, INC.
Publishing Division
5810 Ruatan Street
Berwyn Heights, MD 20740

Entered according to Act of Congress, in the year 1855, by
Benjamin G. Willey,
In the Clerk's Office of the District Court
of the District of Massachusetts

Stereotyped by
Hobart & Robbins
New England Type and Stereotype Foundery
Boston

— Publisher's Notice —
In reprints such as this, it is often not possible to remove blemishes from the original. We feel the contents of this book warrant its reissue despite these blemishes and hope you will agree and read it with pleasure.

International Standard Book Number
Paperbound: 978-0-917890-48-2

PREFACE.

ALMOST invariably the question is asked me, on an introduction to a stranger, "Are you a connection of the family destroyed at the White Mountains?" and, on learning that I am, the question is almost certain to follow, "What were the facts in regard to their destruction?"

The frequency of the inquiry, and the apparent interest with which the narration of that fearful scene has been listened to, have led me to suppose that a particular account of that terrible storm, and the destruction of my brother's family, would be interesting to the public. Travellers have long needed a Book of the Mountains; and so pressingly have I been urged to undertake such a book, that the above fact, the abundance of material, and the thought that I might *benefit* myself, and supply an existing want, has induced me to undertake the task. How I have succeeded others will judge. It was not undertaken as a literary effort, but a simple narration of facts. Are they intelligible? is my only inquiry. When I commenced, there was no book on the White Mountains, save a small work by Mrs. Crawford, widow of the late Ethan A. Crawford. That was out of print, and had been so for years. When my manuscript was nearly completed, a small book on the White Mountains came out, by Mr. John H. Spaulding; but it does not conflict with mine.

I am under great obligations to the Rev. Daniel Goodhue, formerly of Gilead, Me., now of Andover, N. H., for the large amount of matter which he furnished me concerning the history of the eastern side of the mountains. Joel Winch, Esq., of Bethlehem, has also my hearty thanks for matter furnished by him. The kindness of the Hon. N. B. Baker, of Concord; E. J. Lane, Esq., of Dover; B. B. French, Esq., Washington, D. C.; Gen. Samuel Fessenden, of Portland; James Willey, Esq., of Conway; Rev. Samuel Souther, of Fryburg, and others, who have assisted me with books and material, is gratefully remembered. My son, Mr. S. T. B. Willey, has also been of great assistance to me in arranging and writing much of the book.   B G W.

EAST SUMNER, ME., *Sept.*, 1855.

CONTENTS.

CHAPTER I.

THE MOUNTAINS.

The extent and location of the mountains.— Their height and the great distance at which they are seen.— The Indian names.— The origin of these names.— Dr. Belknap's description.— The early visitors.— Vines' and Gorge's visit.— Josselyn's account of his visit.— The central group of mountains.— Heights of different summits.— Gate of the Notch.— Notch.— Mount Webster.— Giant's Grave.— View from Giant's Grave.— The tops of the mountains.— The foliage on their sides.— The vegetation on the higher summits.— The shadows of clouds.— Insects on the mountains.— Birds.— The dead trees.— The mountains during a storm — as seen by moonlight — as seen in winter.— The sides.— View from the summit of Mount Washington.— View at sunrise.— Indian tradition, ... 13

CHAPTER II.

MOUNTAINS CONTINUED.

The many objects of interest.— The great gulf.— Oakes' gulf.— Tuckerman's ravine.— Snow cavern.— Source of the many springs on the mountains.— Saco and Merrimac rivers.— Ellis and Peabody rivers.— Cascades.— Silver cascades.— The flume.— The devil's den.— Crystal falls.— Glen Ellis falls.— Ammonoosuc.— Falls of the Ammonoosuc.— Franconia mountains. — Mount Lafayette. — Eagle cliff. — Cannon mount. — Old Man of the Mountains.— Profile lake.— Optical illusions from Cannon mount. — Echo lake. — The basin.— The flume.— The pool.— Narrow escape from a fall into the pool, 28

CHAPTER III.

THE INDIANS.

The Uncertainty of the many traditions.— The superstitions of the Indians.— Probable cause of those superstitions.— Tradition of a flood.— Great treasures of gold and gems.— Search for treasures.— The particular tribes inhabiting the mountains.— Indian relics in Conway — In Ossipee — in Fryburg — The Sokokis.— Their destruction by the pestilence.— Account of Vines of his visit to them.— Squando.— Death of his child.— Assacumbuit.— Visit to France. — Destruction of Haverhill. — Polan. — Whittier's verses on his burial.— Chocorua.— His curse.— Anasagunticooks.— Their chiefs.— Hon. Enoch Lincoln's interest in Indians of this region.— Visit of Gov. Lincoln to Natalluck.— Indian myth.— The little Indian infant.— Curious marriage custom, ... 42

CHAPTER IV.

COÖS COUNTY.

Coös as a farming county.— The opinion of Hon. Isaac Hill.— Dr. Dwight's account of the climate.— The many and peculiar shapes of towns.— Kilkenny.— Pilot and Willard mountains.— Story of Willard and his dog.— Randolph.— Extensive views from Randolph.— Ascent of Mount Jefferson.— Great danger in a storm.— View from Jefferson.— Jefferson.— Beautiful situation of Jefferson.— Brothers Glines.— Colonel Whipple.— His yearly visit to Portsmouth.— Story illustrating his care of his townsmen.— His capture by the Indians, and escape.— Mr. Gotham.— The importance of the discovery of the Notch.— Nash's discovery of the pass.— Gov. Wentworth.— Getting a horse through the defile.— Sawyer.— "Sawyer's Rock."— Mountain carriages.— Barrel of tobacco.— Barrel of rum.— Cutting the road through the Notch.— Hart's location, ... 58

CHAPTER V.

EARLY SETTLERS.

Early settlement of the locations. — Capt. Rosebrook. — Monadnuc. — Mrs. Rosebrook.— Scarcity of salt.— Great crops.— Removal from Monadnuc.- Settlement at Guildhall.— Mrs. Rosebrook's adventure with the Indians.— Removal to Nash and Sawyer's location.— Difficulty of finding his house in the drifts of snow.— Want of provisions.— His energy.— Cancer.— His death.— Ethan Allen Crawford, the giant of the mountains — His early youth.— Hardships.— The treacherous servant, ... 75

CHAPTER VI.

ETHAN A. CRAWFORD.

Mr. Crawford's impressive manner of story-telling.— The burning of his buildings.— His energy in repairing his losses.— His labors as a guide on to the mountains.— The difficulty formerly of reaching the mountains.— Story illustrating difficulty of travelling in those days.— Present modes of reaching mountains.— First ascent of the mountains.— Party of students from Fryburg.— Ease of ascending now.— First bridle-path.— Ethan's severe wound. — Granny Stalbard.— Carriage-road from Glen House.— Love of Hunting.— The gray cat.— Adventures with them.— Lassos and captures one with birch poles.— Wolves.— His annoyance and discomfiture by them.— Bear stories. — Catching the cub.— Capture of a full-grown bear, ... 83

CHAPTER VII.
THE CRAWFORD FAMILY.

Mr. Crawford's early death.— A remarkable man.— The Crawford family.— Abel Crawford.— Mrs. Crawford.— Her bravery during the night of the slides.— "Crawford House."— Death of Mr. Strickland on the mountains.— Danger of ascending mountains without guide.— Party of students lost on mountains.— Nancy's brook.— Story of Nancy.— Superstitions connected with the spot where she was found.— Owl story.— Beautiful auroral display at the Notch, ... 95

CHAPTER VIII.
THE SLIDES.

The effect of the turnpike upon travel through the Notch.— Coös teamsters.— Pleasure travel.— Want of public houses.— The first house built at the Notch.— Moving of Mr. Willey to the Notch.— The first winter after his removal.— The first slide in June.— The fears of Mr. Willey and his family. — The great storm.— The great drought previous to the storm.— Theory of slides.— The first signs of the storm.— The gathering of the clouds about the mountains, as seen from Conway.— Night of the disaster.— Very peculiar appearance of the mountains about midnight.— Rapid rise of the Saco in Conway.— First discovery of slides.— First news from the Notch.— The shrill voice in the darkness.— The confirmation of the first report.— The manner of communicating the news.— The trumpet at midnight.— Setting out for Notch.— Condition of the roads.— The appearance of the Saco valley.— Arrival at the "Willey House."— Search for the bodies.— Finding of some of the bodies.— Burial.— The prayer at the grave.— Finding of other bodies. — Oxen.— The first night spent in the house succeeding the storm, . . . 110

CHAPTER IX.
THE SLIDES, CONTINUED.

The family dog.— The first conjecture in regard to manner of destruction.— Second conjecture.— Third conjecture.— The dream.— Why all were destroyed.— The mutilation of the bodies.— David Allen.— The great rise of water.— Their terrible situation during the storm.— The effect of a storm upon a family in the same house a year after.— The storm, ... 129

CHAPTER X.

THE SLIDES, CONCLUDED.

The storm as witnessed by one at the mountains.— The view from Bethlehem. — Rapid rise of the Ammonoosuc.— Condition of Capt. Rosebrook's farm.— Slides as first seen.— Falls of the Ammonoosuc.— Difficulty of reaching Crawford's.— Attempt to ascend the mountains.— The camp.— Great destruction of trees, ... 141

CHAPTER XI.

BARTLETT.

General features.— Rocky branch.— Incident on its bank.— Incident of Ellis' river.— First settlement.— Loss of the horses.— Snow caverns.— Brothers Emery.— Humphrey's obstinacy.— Their perilous escape from freezing.— Hon. John Pendexter.— His removal from Portsmouth.— Children.— "Raising" scene.— Mrs. Pendexter.— The great distance of a market.— Difficulty of reaching market.— Traps for catching wild animals.— The common log trap.— Figure four.— Pequawket mountain.— Adventure with a rattlesnake. — The "Chapel of the Hills."— Mrs. Snow.— Its dedication, ... 147

CHAPTER XII.

JACKSON.

The valleys of the mountains.— The directions in which they run.— Moose pond. — Moose bathing.— Moose.— The Conway hunter.— The leap of a moose over a horse and sleigh.— Eagle ledge.— Mineral resources.— General features of Jackson.— Benjamin Copp.— His endurance.— Mr. Pinkham's account of his first entrance into Jackson — The hog.— The house.— Scarcity of salt.— Incident of Capt. Vere Royce.— Tornado.— Expedient to save children.— Bear story.— Freewill Baptist society.— Elder Daniel Elkins, . 163

CHAPTER XIII.

CONWAY.

Beautiful scenery of Conway.— Autumnal foliage.— Attractions of Conway to hunters and early settlers.— Elijah Dinsmore.— Expedient to keep from starving.— Story of Emery.— Great freshet.— Maple sugar.— Mr. Willey's encounter with a bear.— Stephen Allard's bear story.— Schools.— Boys and the hogs.— Congregational church.— Dr. Porter.— Baptist church.— Chataque. — North Conway.— Ledges.— Family burying-place.— Names of the family destroyed at the Notch, ... 174

CHAPTER XIV.

FRYBURG.

The importance of Fryburg in early times.— The grant of town to Gen. Frye. — Conditions of the grant. — First settlers. — Their hardships. — Oliver Peabody.— Indians.— Sabatis.— Encounter with a catamount.— Love of the water.— Indians' love for Mr. Fessenden.— Old Phillip.— Fryburg expedition to Shelburne.— Fryburg academy.— Buildings. — Preceptors. — Paul Langdon.— Daniel Webster.— Amos I. Cook.— Rev. William Fessenden.— Marion Lyle Hurd, ... 189

CHAPTER XV.

LOVEWELL'S FIGHT.

View from Pequawket mountain.— Lovewell's pond.— Sufferings of the early settlers in Dunstable.— Expedition to Winnipiseogee lake.— Expedition of Lovewell to Pequawket.— His company.— Encampment on the shore of the pond.— Situation of the Indian village.— " Carrying place."— Discovery of the first Indian.— Kill the Indian.— The battle.— Retreat of Lovewell's men.— Chamberlain and Paugus.— Council at night.— Retreat.— Ensign Wyman and companions.— Mr. Frye.— Jones.— Farwell and Davis.— Traces of the battle.— The old ballad, ... 204

CHAPTER XVI.

GILEAD.

Situation of Gilead.— Soil.— Wild river.— Early settlers.—Ministers.— First church.— Slide.— Bears.— Encounter of one Bean.— York's warm reception by a bear.— Oliver Peabody's loose ox.— Famine among bears.— Bear and hog story.— Horrible tragedy, ... 222

CHAPTER XVII.

SEGAR'S NARRATIVE.

Attack on Bethel.— Segar.— Indians.— Capture of Segar and companions.— Mrs. Clark.— The journey to Canada.— Pettengill's house.— Hope Austin.— Capt. Rindge.— Murder of Poor.— Clark's escape.— Encampments at night. — Umbagog lake.— Sufferings from hunger.— Arrival at St. Francis' river. — Indian dance.— British protection.— Return home, ... 234

CHAPTER XVIII.

SHELBURNE:

Situation of Shelburne.— Mountains.— Evening drive among the mountains.— Mount Moriah.— Moses' rock.— Granny Starbird's ledge.— Why so called.

— Mineral wealth of this town.— Early settlers.— Mr. Daniel Ingalls.— Moses Ingalls.— Killing the devil.— Robert Fletcher Ingalls.— Sufferings of the early settlers.— Indian massacre.— Terrible encounter with wolves.— The famished soldier, ... , 244

CHAPTER XIX.
GORHAM.

White Mountain Indians.— Col. Clark.— Molly Ockett.— Peol Susup.— Indian eloquence.— Gorham.— Influence of the railroad upon it.— Alpine House. Glen House.— Mount Washington road.— Carriages.— Building of the "Summit House."— Weather on the summit in May.— Origin of Peabody river.— Wonderful endurance of cold, ... 258

CHAPTER XX.
ALBANY, FRANCONIA, AND BETHLEHEM.

Drake's version of Chocorua's curse.— Popular legend connected with this curse.— Cause of the disease among cattle in Albany.— Remedy for the disease.— Beavers.— Military incident.— Franconia.— Iron mine.— Extent of the mine.— Knight's moose story.— Village of Bethlehem.— View of the mountains from Bethlehem.— Early settlement.— First road to the White Mountains from Bethlehem.— Expedient to keep from freezing.— First townmeeting.— Building bridge over Ammonoosuc.— Scarcity of provisions.— Extremity to which inhabitants were driven.— Bethlehem of the present day, ... 271

CHAPTER XXI.
GEOLOGY.

Indian theory of creation of world.— Indian idea of the creation of the White Mountains.— Dr. Jackson's theory.— Sir Charles Lyell's theory, ... 283

CHAPTER XXII.
TEMPERATURE OF THE MOUNTAINS.

Thermometrical table.— Synopsis of the weather.— Comparison of weather with Long Island weather.— Earthquakes.— Thunder-storms.— Wind.— Cold and frost.— Clearness of the atmosphere.— Length of days.— Springs — Combustion, ... 291

CHAPTER XXIII.

Conclusion, ... 300

CHAPTER I.

THE MOUNTAINS.

THE EXTENT AND LOCATION OF THE MOUNTAINS. — THEIR HEIGHT AND THE GREAT DISTANCE AT WHICH THEY ARE SEEN. — THE INDIAN NAMES. — THE ORIGIN OF THESE NAMES. — DR. BELKNAP'S DESCRIPTION. — THE EARLY VISITORS. — VINES' AND GORGE'S VISIT. — JOSSELYN'S ACCOUNT OF HIS VISIT. — THE CENTRAL GROUP OF MOUNTAINS. — HEIGHTS OF DIFFERENT SUMMITS. — GATE OF THE NOTCH. — NOTCH. — MOUNT WEBSTER. — GIANT'S GRAVE. — VIEW FROM GIANT'S GRAVE. — THE TOPS OF THE MOUNTAINS. — THE FOLIAGE ON THEIR SIDES. — THE VEGETATION ON THE HIGHER SUMMITS. — THE SHADOWS OF CLOUDS. — INSECTS ON THE MOUNTAINS. — BIRDS. — THE DEAD TREES. — THE MOUNTAINS DURING A STORM — AS SEEN BY MOONLIGHT — AS SEEN IN WINTER. — THE SLIDES. — VIEW FROM THE SUMMIT OF MOUNT WASHINGTON. — VIEW AT SUNRISE. — INDIAN TRADITION.

"Mount Washington, I have come a long distance, have toiled hard to arrive at your summit, and now you seem to give me a cold reception."
DANIEL WEBSTER.

THE White Mountains embrace the whole group of mountains in northern New Hampshire, extending forty miles from north to south, and about the same distance from east to west. The term has sometimes been applied exclusively to the central cluster, including the six or seven highest peaks, and very properly, though in its comprehensive sense we think it should embrace the extended group. Mount Blanc and Mount Jura constitute not the whole of the Alps; neither do Washington and Monroe, the White Mountains. Clustering around their central height, like children of one large family, no merely arbitrary division should ever separate them.

These mountains are the highest land east of the Mississippi river, "and, in clear weather, are descried before any other land by vessels approaching our eastern coast; but, by reason of their white appearance, are frequently mistaken for clouds. They are visible on the land at the distance of eighty miles, on the south and south-east sides. They appear higher when viewed from the north-east, and it is said they are seen from the neighborhood of Chamblee and Quebec."

The Indian name of these mountains, according to Belknap, is Agiocochook. President Alden states that they were known to some of the more eastern tribes of Indians by the name Waumbekketmethna; Waumbekket, signifying white, and methna, mountains. And still other tribes gave them the appellation Kan Ran Vugarty, the continued likeness of a Gull. All these names, we see, have the same general meaning, and refer to the white appearance of the mountains.

"During the period of nine or ten months the mountains exhibit more or less of that bright appearance, from which they are denominated white. In the spring, when the snow is partly dissolved, they appear of a pale blue, streaked with white; and after it is wholly gone, at the distance of sixty miles, they are altogether of the same pale blue, nearly approaching a sky color; while, at the same time, viewed at the distance of eight miles or less, they appear of the proper color of the rock. Light fleecy clouds, floating about their summits, give them the same whitish hue as snow.

"These vast and irregular heights, being copiously replenished with water, exhibit a great variety of beautiful cascades; some of which fall in a perpendicular sheet or spout; others are winding and sloping; others spread, and form a basin in the rock, and then gush in a cataract over its edge. A poetic fancy may find full gratification amidst these wild and rugged scenes, if its ardor be not checked by the fatigue of the approach. Almost everything in nature, which can be supposed capable of inspiring ideas of the sublime and beautiful, is here realized. Old mountains, stupendous elevations, rolling clouds, impending rocks, verdant woods, crystal streams, the gentle rill, and the roaring torrent, all conspire to amaze, to soothe, and to enrapture."

These mountains were first visited in 1632, by one Darby Field, whose glowing account of the riches he had discovered on his return, caused others immediately to make the same exploration. The visit of a Mr. Vines and Gorges is thus described by Winthrop: "The report brought by Darby Field, of shining stones, &c., caused divers others to travel thither; but they found nothing worth their pains. Mr. Gorges and Mr. Vines, two of the magistrates of Sir F. Gorges' province, went thither about the end of this month (August). They set out, probably, a few days after the return of Field, dazzled by visions of diamonds and other precious minerals, with which the fancy of this man had garnished his story.

"They went up Saco river in birch canoes, and that way they found it ninety miles to Pegwagget, an Indian town; but by land it is but sixty. Upon Saco river they found many thousand acres of rich meadow; but there are ten falls which hinder boats, &c. From the Indian town they went up hill (for the most part), about thirty miles, in woody lands. Then they went about seven or eight miles upon shattered rocks, without tree or grass, very steep all the way. At the top is a plain, about three or four miles over, all shattered stones; and upon that is another rock or spire, about a mile in height, and about an acre of ground at the top. At the top of the plain arise four great rivers; each of them so much water at the first issue as would drive a mill: Connecticut river from two heads at the N. W., and S. W., which join in one about sixty miles off; Saco river on the S. E.; Amascoggin, which runs into Casco bay, at the N. E.; and the Kennebec at the N. by E. The mountains run east and west, thirty or forty miles; but the peak is above all the rest. They went and returned in fifteen days."

Josselyn, who visited them still later, has thus curiously described them: "Four score miles (upon a direct line), to the N. W. of Scarborow, a ridge of mountains runs N. W. and N. E., an hundred leagues, known by the name of the White Mountains, upon which lieth snow all the year, and is a landmark twenty miles off at sea. It is a rising ground from the sea-shore to these hills; and they are inaccessible, but by the gullies which the dissolved snow hath made. In these gullies grow saven bushes, which, being taken hold of, are a good help to the climbing discoverer. Upon the top of the highest of these mountains is a large level, or plain, of a day's journey over, whereon nothing grows but moss. At the further end of this plain is another hill, called the sugarloaf — to outward appearance a rude heap of mossie stones, piled one upon another — and you may, as you ascend, step from one stone to another, as if you were going up a pair of stairs, but winding still about the hill, till you come to the top, which will require half a day's time; and yet it is not above a mile, where there is also a level of about an acre of ground, with a pond of clear water in the midst of it, which you may hear run down; but how it ascends is a mystery. From this rocky hill you may see the whole country round about. It is far above the lower clouds; and from hence we behold a vapor (like a great pillar), drawn up by the sunbeams out of a great lake, or pond, into the air, where it was formed into a cloud. The country beyond these hills, northward, is daunting terrible; being full of rocky hills, as thick as mole-hills in a meadow, and clothed with infinite thick woods."

The mountains which have more particularly attracted the attention of the tourists and writers, are near the northern boundary of the group, extending from the "Notch," a distance of fourteen miles in a north-easterly direction. The different peaks of this cluster gradually increase in height from the outside to the centre, where towers Mount Washington high above all. The lower and surrounding mountains are beautifully wooded to their very tops; while the bold Alpine summits of the central ones rise up far above the limits of vegetation, amid the clouds.

The heights of the different summits, as given by Professor Bond, of Cambridge, are, perhaps, the most accurate. Commencing at the "Notch," and giving the heights of each peak as it stands in the range, — Mount Webster is 4,000 feet above the level of the sea; Jackson, 4,100; Clinton, 4,200; Pleasant, 4,800; Franklin, 4,900; Monroe, 5,300; Washington, 6,500; Clay, 5,400; Adams, 5,700; Jefferson, 5,800; Madison, 5,400.

Approaching the central cluster from the south-east, the mountains gradually close upon you, until they come together at the gate of the "Notch." This gate, or chasm, is formed by two rocks standing perpendicular at the distance of twenty-two feet from each other. Here, by great labor, a road has been constructed on the side of a little brook, whose rugged bed was formerly the only opening in the mountains. The entrance on each side is guarded by high overhanging cliffs, and the walls adjoining the road rise up perpendicularly fifty feet. This defile was known to the Indians, who formerly led their captives through it to Canada; but it had been forgotten or neglected, till the year 1771, when two hunters (Nash and Sawyer) discovered and passed through it.

The Notch itself is a narrow pass, about three miles in length, running in a north-westerly direction, turning to the right a little at the northern extremity. The mountains here are abruptly torn apart, forming a very narrow valley, through which flows the Saco. "The sublime and awful grandeur of the Notch baffles all description. Geometry may settle the heights of the mountains, and numerical figures may record the measure; but no words can tell the emotions of the soul, as it looks upward and views the almost perpendicular precipices which line the narrow space between them; while the senses ache with terror and astonishment, as one sees himself hedged in from all the world beside. He may cast his eye forward or backward, or to either side — he can see only upward, and then the diminutive circle of his vision is cribbed and confined by the battlements of nature's cloud-capt towers, which seem as if they wanted only the breathing of a zephyr, or the wafting of a straw against them, to displace them, and crush the prisoner in their fall."

Facing the north, on either hand, rise up steep perpendicular walls, two thousand feet above the road at their base, regular and equal, for a great part of the way. On the left is Mount Willey, gloomy and grand; its sides torn and furrowed by the slides, and here and there abrupt ledges, over whose topmost edge the gathering mass of rocks and earth leaped into the depths below.

On the right is Mount Webster. "This vast and regular mass rises abruptly, from the plain below, to the height of about two thousand feet. Its shape is that of a high fort, with deep scarred sides; its immense front apparently wholly inaccessible. Its top, nearly horizontal and rough with precipitous crags, juts over with heavy and frowning brows; so mighty a mountain wall, so high, so wide, so vast, and so near the spectator, that all its gigantic proportions and parts are seen with the utmost distinctness. It fills at once the eye and the mind with awe, admiration, and delight. In a bright day, when its outline at the top is seen sharp and distinct against the blue sky, its gray granite cliffs and ledges colored with iron-brown or stained with darker shades, its sides seamed with long gullied slides of brown gravel, its wide beds of great loose rocks, black with lichens, contrasted with the summer greens, or varied autumnal colors of the trees, make it as beautiful and interesting in its varied hues and parts, as it is great and sublime in its total impression."

Passing through the gate of the Notch, we come to the valley of the Ammonoosuc; and after a distance of four miles, generally through a thick wood, which prevents all views of the surrounding mountains, we come out suddenly into a wide cleared opening, where the whole mountain cluster bursts upon our view. Standing upon an isolated eminence, about sixty feet in height, known as the Giant's grave, the whole range of mountains is in sight.

You stand in the centre of a broad amphitheatre of mountains; the lofty pyramid of Washington, with its basin-shaped top, resembling the crater of a volcano, and its bare gray rock sides marked by long gullies, and lower down by broad slides, directly before you, while, far away on the right and left, Mounts Webster and Madison stand at the extremities of the range.

The tops of the mountains are covered with snow from the last of October to the end of May. Occasionally, during the months of July and August, they are almost white with a new-fallen snow or sleet. As the snow melts away, on most of the rocks may be seen mosses and lichens of various hues; while here and there, in the spaces sheltered by high rocks, beautiful and brilliant flowers, tiny alpine plants, spring up, mixed with the coarse mountain grass.

"The base and sides of the mountains are clothed with a dense and luxurious forest of the trees of the country; and the ground beneath their shade is ornamented with the beautiful flowers of the northern woods, and deeply covered with a rich carpet of mosses. Below is the sugar-maple, with its broad angular leaves, changing early in autumn, when every leaf is a flower, scarlet or crimson, or variegated with green, yellow, and brown; the yellow birch, of great size, with its ragged bark, and wide-spreading arms; the beech, with its round trunk, its smooth bark, marbled, clouded, and embroidered with many-colored lichens; its stiff slender branches, and its glossy leaves; the white birch, with its smooth and white bark — most abundant in the districts formerly burnt — showing, after its changed yellow leaves have fallen, its slender, wand-like white trunks ranged closely and regularly on the hill sides. With these are mixed a frequent, but generally less abundant growth of black spruces and balsam firs, — the tall spruce, with its stiff and ragged outline, and horizontal branches, the fir, with its beautiful spires, regularly tapering from its base to its tip, and its dark rich foliage, often, as it grows old, hoary with the long, hanging, entangled tufts of the beard-moss, which here so abundantly covers its dying branches. Of the many other trees, smaller or less frequent, we will only mention the striped maple, the mountain ash, the aspen poplars, the hemlock, and the white pine. Higher up, the spruce and fir become the prevailing growth, with the yellow and white birch, gradually growing smaller as they ascend, until the dwarf firs, closely interwoven together, and only a few feet high, form a dense and almost impenetrable hedge, many rods wide, above which project, in fantastic forms, like the horns of a deer, the bare, bleached tops and branches of the dead trees. The dwarf trees are so closely crowded and interwoven together that it is as easy to walk on their tops as to struggle through them on the ground; and the road is made by removing them with their roots. Above this hedge of dwarf trees, which is about four thousand feet above the level of the sea, the scattered fir and spruce bushes, shrinking from the cold mountain wind, and clinging to the ground in sheltered hollows by the side of the rocks, with a few similar bushes of white and yellow birch, reach almost a thousand feet higher. Above are only alpine plants, mosses, and lichens."

Over the mountains are scattered a variety of berries, such as cranberries, whortleberries, and several other kinds. They grow high up the mountains, and some of them far above any other vegetable, except grass and moss. Their flower is, however, very different from those of the plain. Even the whortleberry, which grows on these hills, has, in its ripest state, considerable acidity.

The vicissitudes of sunshine and shade are here very frequent, not exactly like the shadows flying over the plains; for here the individual is actually enveloped in the cloud, while there it only passes over him. The cloud is discovered at a considerable distance, rolling along on the surface of the mountain; it approaches you rapidly; in an instant it encircles you, and as soon passes away, to be followed by others in endless succession. These phenomena are presented only when the clouds are light and scattered. When they are surcharged with rain, even at mid-day, all is darkness and gloom.

Although the waters of these hills apparently give life to no animal or insect, yet, in the heat of summer, the black fly, a little, tormenting insect, is very troublesome. At the same time, the grasshopper is here as gay as on the finely-cultivated field. The swallow, too, appears to hold his flight as high over these mountains as over the plain. It is, however, a place of extreme solitude. The eye often wanders in vain to catch something that has life and animation; yet a bear has been known to rise up, even in this solitude, to excite and to terrify the traveller.

Says a correspondent of the New York Express, writing from the top of Mount Washington: "I have seen but few birds here, and they do not tarry long after getting here; the ground-sparrow and plover are the only species I have noticed. Insects are quite plenty, and of various kinds. The honey-bee and humble-bee occasionally find the way up here, but are not plenty. There are scarcely any of the common house-fly here, but a large blue fly, and another of a bright gold color, are exceedingly plenty in warm days, but the first fog that arises scatters them, and they are not seen again for several days."

The dead trees, slightly referred to by Oakes, are deserving of more notice. From different persons these trees have received different names. Some call them buck's horns, and others bleached bones. The winds and weather have rendered them perfectly white; and, as neither the stem nor branches take any definite direction, they are of all the diversified forms which nature, in her freaks, can create. The cold seasons, which prevailed from 1812 to the end of 1816, probably occasioned the death of these trees; and their constant exposure to the fierce winds which prevail on the mountains has, aided by other causes, rendered them white. It can hardly be doubted that, during the whole of the year 1816, these trees continued frozen; and frost, like fire, is capable of extinguishing life, even in the vegetable kingdom. Fire could not have caused the death of these trees; for fire will not spread here, in consequence of the humidity of the whole region at this elevation.

The mountains, seen, with their well-defined outlines and shapes, in a clear day, present not the only aspect in which to behold them. Clouds sailing up their long ranges, now floating along their sides, severing their summits from their base, now settling down and capping their peaks; now drooping down still lower, till rock, and moss, and flower, and luxuriantly wooded base, are all hid in the dun, thick pall; then, bursting and fleeing with a wind-like speed, as the storm clears up, and the mountains come out, their wet sides glistening, in the returning rays of the sun, like huge piles of burnished silver, give to the rugged heights an aspect of beauty unsurpassed. The mountains are seldom seen free from clouds. Light, fleecy vapors are almost continually hovering about the different peaks.

By moonlight, in those clear, autumnal evenings, when the

full, round moon looks so calmly down, throwing the shadows of the mighty giants broadly over the valleys, peopling each hidden nook and lurking ravine with grotesque forms and superstitious fancies, gazing on those majestic heights, one almost involuntarily repeats the matchless lines of Coleridge : —

> ' Thou, most awful form,
> Risest from forth thy silent sea of pines,
> How silently ! Around thee and above
> Deep is the air, and dark, substantial black,
> An ebon mass ; methinks thou piercest it
> As with a wedge ! But when I look again,
> It is their own calm home, thy crystal shrine,
> Thy habitation from eternity !
> O, dread and silent mount ! I gaze upon thee,
> Till thou, still present to the bodily sense,
> Didst vanish from my thought ; entranced in prayer
> I worshipped the invisible alone.''

Nor in winter are they destitute of beauty. Their white summits standing out so distinctly from the deep blue depth of sky in the background, the trees around their sides and base loaded with ice, glistening in the dazzling rays of the sun like the enchanted diamond and jewelled halls of Eastern story, the reflecting and glittering of the moonbeams upon the frozen crust, all give to them a bewildering splendor indescribable.

The slides now seen at the White Mountains are mostly those which took place in the year 1826. At the Notch they present the appearance of deep gullies a few rods wide. On Mount Washington and the higher peaks many of the slides are a quarter or a half a mile in width. The amount of matter torn in that one night of dreadful storm from the mountains, and hurled into the valleys below, is incalculable. Thousands of acres of rocks, and earth, and trees, slipped from their fastening, and were thrown into the valleys. As seen from a distance of twenty or thirty miles, they look like long roads, winding up the mountains in all directions.

From the summit of Mount Washington the eye commands the circumference of the entire group of mountains. You stand in the centre, looking down upon a multitudinous sea of ridges and peaks, here extending out in long ranges, enclosing broad valleys, through which wind rivers, glittering amid the forest and settlement like polished metal, now towering up like insulated cones, now grouped together like loving friends.

"In the west, through the blue haze, are seen in the distance the ranges of the Green Mountains; the remarkable outlines of the summits of Camel's Hump and Mansfield Mountain being easily distinguished when the atmosphere is clear. To the north-west, under your feet, are the clearings and settlement of Jefferson, and the waters of Cherry Pond; and, further distant, the village of Lancaster, with the waters of Israel's river. The Connecticut is barely visible, and often its appearance for miles is counterfeited by the fog rising from its surface. To the north and north-east, only a few miles distant, rise up boldly the great north-eastern peaks of the White Mountain range, — Jefferson, Adams, and Madison, — with their ragged tops of loose, dark rocks. A little further to the east are seen the numerous and distant summits of the mountains of Maine. On the south-east, close at hand, are the dark and crowded ridges of the mountains of Jackson; and, beyond the conical summit of Kearsarge, standing by itself, on the outskirts of the mountains, and, further over the low country of Maine, Sebago Pond, near Portland. Still further, it is said, the ocean itself has sometimes been distinctly visible.

"The White Mountains are often seen from the sea, even at thirty miles distance from the shore; and nothing can prevent the sea from being seen from the mountains, but the difficulty of distinguishing its appearance from that of the sky near the horizon.

"Further to the south are the intervales of the Saco, and the settlements of Bartlett and Conway, the sister ponds of Lovell in Fryeburg, and, still further, the remarkable four-toothed summit of the Chocorua, the peak to the right being much the largest, and sharply pyramidical. Almost exactly south are the shining waters of the beautiful Winnipisogee, seen with the greatest distinctness in a favorable day. To the south-west, near at hand, are the peaks of the south-western range of the White Mountains; Monroe, with its two little alpine ponds sleeping under its rocky and pointed summit; the flat surface of Franklin, and the rounded top of Pleasant, with their ridges and spurs. Beyond these, the Willey Mountain, with its high, ridged summit; and, beyond that, several parallel ranges of high wooded mountains. Further west, and over all, is seen the high, bare summit of Mount Lafayette in Franconia."

The appearance of the mountains and the surrounding country at sunrise is worth the journey and toil from any part of the country to witness. In the language of the eloquent Brydone, "The whole eastern horizon is gradually lighted up. The sun's first golden ray, as he emerges from the ocean, strikes the eye, and sheds a glimmering but uncertain light; but soon his broad disc diffuses light and beauty, first on the hills, and soon on the region eastward. The sides of the mountains fronting him appear like a solid mass of gold dazzling by its brightness. While this process is going on to the eastward, the whole country to the westward is shrouded with darkness and gloom. The eye turns away from this comfortless scene, to the gay and varied one to the eastward. If this prospect is beheld immediately after a rain, the tops of a thousand hills rise above the fogs, appearing like so many islands in the midst of a mighty ocean. As these mists clear away, the houses, the villages, and the verdant fields within the circle of vision, arise to view. At the moment of the sun's rising, the noble vale of the Connecticut, which stretches along from the north till it is lost among the hills at the south-west, appears like an inland sea. This is occasioned by the vapors which had ascended from the river during the night. As the sun advances in his course, these vapors are chased away by his rays, and the farms in Jefferson, Bethlehem, and Lancaster, with its village, appear as if rising by magic from what but a little time before seemed nothing but water. The various hills, in the mean time, which surround the mountains, appear to be arranged in many concentric circles; and the circle the furthest removed seems the highest and most distinct, giving to the whole an air of order and grandeur beyond the power of description."

From this lofty summit the Indians had a tradition that Passaconaway, a powerful chief, famed to hold a conference with the spirits above, once passed to a council in heaven.

> " A wondrous wight! For o'er 'Siogee's ice,
> With brindled wolves, all harnessed three and three,
> High seated on a sledge, made in a trice,
> On Mount Ogiocochook, of hickory,
> He lashed and reeled, and sung right jollily ;
> And once upon a car of flaming fire,
> The dreadful Indian shook with fear to see
> The king of Penacook, his chief, his sire,
> Ride flaming up towards heaven, than any mountain higher."

CHAPTER II.

MOUNTAINS CONTINUED.

THE MANY OBJECTS OF INTEREST. — THE GREAT GULF. — OAKES' GULF. — TUCKERMAN'S RAVINE. — SNOW CAVERN. — SOURCE OF THE MANY SPRINGS ON THE MOUNTAINS. — SACO AND MERRIMAC RIVERS. — ELLIS AND PEABODY RIVERS. — CASCADES. — SILVER CASCADE. — THE FLUME. — THE DEVIL'S DEN. — CRYSTAL FALLS. — GLEN ELLIS FALLS. — AMMONOOSUC. — FALLS OF THE AMMONOOSUC. — FRANCONIA MOUNTAINS. — MOUNT LAFAYETTE. — EAGLE CLIFF. — CANNON MOUNT. — OLD MAN OF THE MOUNTAINS. — PROFILE LAKE. — OPTICAL ILLUSION FROM CANNON MOUNT. — ECHO LAKE. — THE BASIN. — THE FLUME. — THE POOL. — NARROW ESCAPE FROM A FALL INTO THE POOL.

"Ye crags and peaks, I'm with you once again."

IT would be vain to attempt a description of all the curious localities of interest connected with these mountains. Wander over them ever so much, and fresh wonders and beauties are continually being discovered. From no two points does the collected mountain-group present the same appearance to the beholder; while each separate mount will well repay the toil and labor of climbing its rugged sides.

Some of the most striking and peculiar scenery among the mountains are the deep ravines and hollows immediately surrounding Mount Washington. Leaving the old Fabyan road, the first path cut out by Ethan A. Crawford, from the old Rosebrook-place, not far from the summit of Mount Washington, and going a few rods northward, you come to the brink of an almost unfathomable abyss, known as the Great Gulf. It is a rocky, precipitous descent of two thousand feet. Rising up opposite you from the bottom of this Gulf, almost perpendicularly, is the great range of mountains, comprising Clay, Jefferson, Adams and Madison. This vast range may be seen from their roots to their summits by one standing on the brink. Deep down in the very bottom of the hollow are rough, confused piles of rocks, with narrow and deeply-worn ravines between them. Springing up occasionally, near the very base of the mountain range, are tall spruces, while further up on their sides are birches and small fir-bushes. Toward the east, the Gulf has an opening, surrounded on all its other sides by mountains.

Winding round the double-headed summit of Mount Monroe, far down on the right, is another seemingly bottomless abyss, known as Oakes' Gulf. It presents nearly the same general characteristics as the last — huge, rough boulders covering the lowest depths, while trees and bushes cover the steep and craggy sides, wherever the crevices contain soil enough to support vegetation. At times the wind drives the thick mist into these gulfs, filling them, like a "huge caldron, with dark-blue vapor, whirling and eddying round their sides."

Tuckerman's Ravine, on the eastern side of the mountains, for wildness and grandeur is unsurpassed. Ascending the mountains by the Davis road, from the Mount Crawford House, it lies to the right of the road, as it passes over the high spur immediately south-east of Mount Washington. Leaving the path, after arriving at the top of the spur, and turning to the right, you stand upon the edge of the ravine. Descending its rough, steep sides a great distance, you reach the bottom. It is a long, deep, narrow hollow; its craggy walls in many places almost perpendicular, and wholly inaccessible. A small stream runs through its whole length, forming beautiful cascades after a storm. In this valley, but above the ravine, is the great plain from which the ascent to the top of Mount Washington was formerly made. Early explorers always ascended from the eastern side of the mountains.

In winter all the snow which blows from Mount Washington lodges in this ravine, filling it to the depth of hundreds of feet.

"Huge recess,
That keeps till June December's snows."

As the warm weather approaches, the little brook thaws out upon the sides of the mountain, and gradually works its way through the vast mass covering its bed, forming a complete arch of pure snow. This arch continues to enlarge until the last of summer, when the intense heat and warm rains melt it away.

Last year the engineer of the White Mountain Carriage Road, measured the arch, and found it to be 180 feet long, 84 feet wide, and 40 feet high, on the inside; and 266 feet long, and 40 feet wide, on the outside. The snow forming the arch was twenty feet thick. The engineer went through this arch in the bed of the brook, to the foot of the cataract, which falls a thousand feet down the side of the mountain. This was done in July.

Nor for beauty and grandeur were those bold summits reared so far up among the clouds. New England owes to her granite peaks more than to her extensive commerce and flourishing trade. Her thousand mills, and the ripening harvest of her hardy husbandmen, are the offspring of these Alpine cliffs. Wealth and health flow from their sides; and liberty is always safe among their passes.

"The immense bed of moss," says Belknap, "which covers these mountains, serves as a sponge to retain the moisture brought by the clouds and vapors which are frequently rising and gathering round the mountains. The thick growth of wood prevents the rays of the sun from penetrating to exhale it; so that there is a constant supply of water deposited in the crevices of the rocks, and issuing in the form of springs from every part of the mountains."

From the springs originate some of the largest and finest rivers in New England. Barren themselves, these mountains send wealth and fertility to five different states. On the southern side, the Saco and the Merrimac, —

> "Two rills which from one fountain flow,
> But eastward one, the other westward hies;
> Both to a common goal their journey go, —
> But this one's path along green meadows lies,
> Through flowery banks, and under softest skies;
> That o'er its rocky bed, with turbid flow,
> Mid noise and tumult to the ocean flies."

On the eastern side, Ellis and Peabody rivers start their downward courses so near together that they may be stepped across at one stride. On the western side, far up on the mountains, at the "Lake of the Clouds," starts the Ammonoosuc, a tributary of the Connecticut. The streams on the eastern side run parallel with the ranges of mountains; while on the western side they run at right angles.

Cascades innumerable are formed by these brooks and rivulets as they come tumbling down the mountains. The glittering of these different falls in the moonbeams, Dr. Belknap thinks, gave rise to the idea of the huge carbuncles, the superstitious Indians saw suspended over the steep precipices and cliffs. These cascades are unrivalled in their romantic beauty.

About half a mile from the gate of the Notch, on the southern side, is seen the Silver Cascade, issuing from the mountain on the right, about eight hundred feet above the adjacent valley, and about two miles distant. It is said to be one of the most beautiful in the world. Ordinarily it is but a mere rill, falling over high perpendicular ledges, with sufficient current to make it perfectly white. The following, an excellent description, is from the pen of Mr. D. P. Pages: "Imagine yourself, gentle reader, standing upon a narrow bridge, under which one of these cascades finds its way to the Saco, now on your left. Away, for more than a mile to your right, and far up toward the summit of the mountains, you see the silver thread of falling water, now still, now tremulous, glittering in the sunbeams. Now it disappears behind a crag, and now it struggles on amid some broken rocks; anon it approaches an abrupt precipice, from which it gayly leaps off, scattering its pearls and gems in rich profusion, as it salutes the rock below. Now it flows on; for a moment slowly, through a little pool in the lofty hill-side; now again, in a dozen streamlets, it is seen gushing forth, among the fragments of rock, and thence seems to slide for a long distance down the unbroken surface of the smooth ledge. Thence it dashes among the rocks, throwing its whitened spray above them; again it falls over a projecting brink, and plunges murmuring into another basin. Once more it quickly issues from this enclosure, as if enraged at every obstruction. On it rushes, dashing, eagerly pressing its way, and becoming more noisy at every step. It is now within fifty yards, and has disappeared behind a thicket. You hear again a plunge and a rush, and the enraged current has burst forth, foaming and bounding along at your very feet. You almost feel the bridge tremble beneath you; and as you turn toward your left you see the mountain-torrent tumble noisily into the bosom of the Saco. You pass on a little, and what a moment ago was boisterous noise, occasioned by the angry rush of many waters, is now hushed and softened into a gentle murmur, and you would almost fall asleep, soothed by the richest strains of the music of the waters."

Further down from the Notch is a second cascade, called the Flume. It falls a distance of two hundred and fifty feet over three precipices. It falls in a single current over two precipices, when it divides and falls over a third steep in three currents, and unites them all again in a small basin formed in the rocks at the bottom.

Opposite to these cascades stands Mount Willard. Near its top is the mouth of a large cavern, called the "Devil's Den." Curiosity was formerly on tiptoe to know what was in it. Perhaps, proceeding inward a few steps, passages and steps led down into the very bowels of the mountain. Who knew but within these hollow shells, chambers and halls ample and brilliant were waiting to be explored? Perhaps, winding along the thousand passages, one might reach the hollow cavities of Mount Washington — might stand upon the edge of some almost boundless abyss, from whence issued forth the force which threw the mighty giant far aloft in air. A venturous young gentleman, some years since, thought to satisfy curiosity on this point. Ropes and tackling were carried to the top of the mountain, and stout companions lowered him down to the mouth. As he neared the dark opening, bones and skulls were seen. Perhaps it was a den; could he not see eyes?

> "Ere long they come, where that same wicked wight
> His dwelling has, low in a hollow cave,
> Far underneath a craggy cliff, ypight,
> Dark, doleful, dreary, like a greedy grave,
> That still for carrion carcasses doth crave ;
> On top whereof, aye dwelt the ghastly owl,
> Shrieking his baneful note, which ever drave
> Far from that haunt all other cheerful fowl ;
> And all about it wandering ghosts did wail and howl.
>   * * * * * *
>   * * * * Arrived there,
> That barehead knight, for dread and doleful teen,
> Would fain have fled ; he durst approachen near."

Having, however, sufficient strength to give the signal, he was soon with his friends on the summit.

On the eastern side of the mountain are two falls which should not be forgotten. Near Tuckerman's Ravine, before mentioned, Peabody's river and Ellis river descend from the mountain in parallel courses, until they reach the valley, when both turn at right angles; Peabody river, flowing northeast, a tributary of the Androscoggin; Ellis river, southeast, a tributary of the Saco river.

Some hundred rods from the angle Ellis river forms in changing its course, in a secluded ravine to the left of the present road, as you go from Jackson to the Glen House, the little stream comes foaming down over the rocks most romantically and noisily. From its high starting-point, winding round amid the rocks and low undergrowth, through hidden recesses and glens, it has scarcely seen the day until

CRYSTAL FALLS, PINKHAM NOTCH.

GLEN ELLIS FALLS PINKHAM NOTCH.

it reaches the chasm between the piled-up rocks, and comes tumbling over the steep ledges and projections.

The fall is eighty feet, though not in one unbroken descent. About half the distance up is a shelf, or stair, on which the water strikes, rebounding in copious showers of spray, and rushing over the projection with greatly expanded surface. This has been known as the Crystal Falls.

But a short distance from this, further down the Ellis river, on the right of the road, are other falls, more nearly resembling Silver Cascade, known as "Glen Ellis Falls." The water here falls seventy feet in a narrow bed between very steep and precipitous rocky cliffs on either hand. The basin below looks like a deep well amid the hills, open only on one side. It was known formerly as "Pitcher Falls."

The Ammonoosuc is the most rapid, violent, wildest river in New Hampshire. It falls six thousand feet from its source on the mountain, to where it enters the Connecticut. The whole distance of thirty miles is over rough, craggy rocks, and down steep perpendicular precipices. Cascades innumerable are formed along its whole course. There are several thirty or forty feet in height. One has attracted much attention.

About a mile from where stood the Mount Washington House, to the westward, on the way to Littleton, may be seen the falls of the Ammonoosuc from the road. Bursting forth from a forest of pines, the waters come tumbling over large broad granite shelves, laid with all the order and regularity of the most finished masonry. Through these successive layers, the stream has worn its bed; at places the edges of the layers looking like the stone abutments of large bridges; at other points the layers are pulled up and broken off, forming broad flat steps, over which the water comes foaming like boiling torrents, where rains have filled the channel. These layers are frequently many yards in extent, and from a few inches to a foot in thickness. The height of the fall is thirty feet, and, when the water is very high, it is tossed at the base into heaps as large as haycocks.

The Franconia Mountains, another group of the White Mountains, situated near their north-western boundary, are inferior only to the more central cluster. The Great Haystack, or Mount Lafayette, the highest peak in this range, is 5,200 feet high. The mountains are situated on each side of a narrow valley, through which flows the Pemmasawasset river. At one point they approach to within half a mile, and, rising up very steep and abrupt from their base, form a narrow pass, which has been called the Franconian Notch.

The mountains in their general features resemble those of the central range of which we have spoken; their bases thickly wooded and their summits bare rock, beaten and furrowed by time and storm. The view from Mount Lafayette is as extensive and varied as that from Mount Washington itself. Near Lafayette is Eagle Cliff, so called from a pair of eagles, a few years since, having built their nest on its inaccessible sides.

Cannon Mountain, nearly facing Lafayette, and forming the western side of the Notch, has on its southern side one of the greatest curiosities in the world. Huge rocks are so piled up on its steep, precipitous sides, as to form to the beholder the exact outline of the human face.

Said an eccentric speaker, at a celebration a few years since in Fryburg, "Men put out signs representing their different trades; jewellers hang out a monster watch; shoemakers, a huge boot; and, up in Franconia, God Almighty has hung out a sign that in New England he makes men."

The top of the mountain is about 2,000 feet above the level of the road, and 4,000 feet above the level of the sea. Near the summit, an oblong rock resembling a cannon has given a name to the mountain. The sides are covered with a thick growth of maple, beech, birch, and spruce.

The Profile Rock itself is more than 1,200 feet above the level of the road; it being situated far below the summit of the mountain. The profile is composed of three separate masses of rock, one of which forms the forehead, the second the nose and upper lip, and the third the chin. Only at one particular place are they brought into their proper position, which is on the road leading through the Notch, about a quarter of a mile south of the Lafayette House. The expression of the face, as it stands out in bold relief against the sky, is quite stern. The mouth alone betrays any signs of age and feebleness. But the "Old Man of the Mountains" has never been known to flinch. "He neither blinks at the near flashes of the lightning beneath his nose, nor flinches from the driving snow and sleet of the Franconia winter, which makes the mercury of the thermometer shrink into the bulb and congeal."

Passing down the road from the particular spot where it can be seen in perfection, the Old Man's countenance changes first into a "toothless old woman in a mob cap," and soon the profile is entirely lost. In passing up the road, the nose and face flatten until the forehead alone is seen.

The length of the profile, from the top of the forehead to the lowest point of the chin, is eighty feet. The face looks towards the south-east, and is perhaps half a mile distant from the observer in the road.

At the base of the mountain, directly beneath the Old Man's eye, is a quiet little pond about a quarter of a mile in length, and half as wide, called Profile Lake. Its waters are destitute of fish. It was never frequented by the Indians from fear of the stern image reflected in it.

Oakes speaks of a beautiful optical illusion to be seen from the summit of Cannon Mountain.

"In a bright day in October, a most delightful optical illusion may be seen over the summit of the mountain, which I first noticed in the autumn of 1845, while looking with a spy-glass, and which I have since often seen. Near the middle of the afternoon, when the sun has just sunk behind the top of the mountain, the spruce and fir trees seen against the sky near the sun, and a large space of the sky above them, are bathed in a pure golden light, bright and intense, in which the branches and trunks of the trees are distinctly visible; but of the same brightness as the surrounding space, as if they were transparent gold. Around this mountain pyre I saw hovering, floating and gliding, issuing and returning, with the most graceful motion, beautiful white birds, like the departed spirits of eastern fire-worshippers around the element they adore. I found, at last, that these phantom-birds were thistle down, wafted over the lake by the gentle south wind, in reality quite near the eye, but only visible in the light at the top of the mountain.

'I took it for a fairy vision
Of some gay creatures of the element,
That in the colors of the rainbow live.
And play in the plighted clouds.'"

North of the Cannon Mountain, beneath Eagle Cliff, is the small, but exceedingly deep pond, called Echo Lake. It is entirely surrounded by mountains. From the centre of this lake the voice in common conversation will echo two or

ECHO LAKE FRANCONIA NOTCH.

three times distinctly, while the firing of a gun is like the discharge of a park of artillery. No wonder the poor Indian thought the heard the war-whoop of the Gods sounding, during his wild carousals.

One pleasant morning, in the summer of 1850, a friend and myself pushed out into this little pond. Around us on all sides the clear water reflected back the high cliffs in all their beauty and wildness. As we gave a loud halloo, the mountains directly before us gave back the cry, like an army of men shouting from its summit. As that died away, the mountain behind us caught up the sound, and returned it like the shouting of an opposing army; and, as that died out, the hills upon our right and left tossed back and forth the lessening shout, until it could be heard far off taking its flight. The several echoes are very distinct, and each commences as the preceding closes.

Five miles south of Franconia Notch, in the town of Lincoln, are very interesting curiosities.

Near the road-side the Pemmasawasset river has worn, in the solid rock which forms its bed, a very curious cavity, known as the Basin. It is forty feet in diameter, and twenty-eight feet from the edge to the bottom of the water. The water, rushing in with great force at one side, whirled rocks round in its current, until it has worn the solid rock to its present shape and depth. It is almost perfectly circular, and the water rushes round it several times with great velocity before it goes out at the opposite side. It would take a strong swimmer to buffet its waters. The water itself is usually ten or twelve feet deep. The sides above the water are very smooth and regular, and the bottom is strewn with rocks bright and round. The water, as it falls over the brink into the cavity, forms a beautiful cascade, white with foam.

The lower margin of the basin where the water passes out, worn off by the current, has been formed into a very striking representation of a human leg and foot.

During a freshet, the whole basin is filled by a foaming, whirling torrent, of great quantity and force.

Leaving the road just below the basin, and turning to the left up among the hills, after nearly a mile's walk, you come upon a slightly-inclined granite ledge, more than one hundred feet in length, and thirty feet wide, bare, solid, and very smooth. Over this runs a small stream — now murmuring along in a narrow, shallow bed, and now spread out over the whole width.

Near the top of the ledge you enter what has been called "The Flume." Twenty feet apart rise up perpendicular walls of solid rock, fifty feet in height. The uplifted walls were evidently split apart far back in time by some convulsion in nature; in many places the projections on one side corresponding with like depressions on the opposite. Through this vast and regular fissure flows the little stream we have just mentioned; its bed so narrow as to afford sufficient room for dry footing through the entire extent. These walls are covered with a green moss, and, within, the air is very damp and cool. This recess is several hundred feet long, gradually narrowing to the upper extremity, where it is but ten or eleven feet wide.

About midway, a huge boulder, weighing several tons, has rolled down from the top of the cliff, and caught in its descent in a somewhat narrower space, and remains suspended half-way down between the perpendicular walls. Several years ago a pine-tree fell across the Flume, near its top, and its trunk forms a rude and dangerous bridge over the chasm.

Near the Flume is a deep natural well in the solid rock. A small stream flows over its northern brink, finding egress in a narrow opening opposite. It is more than one hundred and fifty feet from the brink of the well to the surface of the water below. The diameter of this "Pool" is about sixty feet. The water in the bottom is about forty feet deep, and greatly agitated.

Several years since, a gentleman from New Orleans made a misstep and fell into this pool. Though the water was icy cold, and he was encumbered with his clothes, he had presence of mind to swim to a crag of the rock on a level with the water. There were no means of ascent except by ropes, which were procured by friends who were with him at the time of the fall. He fastened a rope round his body, and was raised aloft, drenched and bruised; but the only human thing, we presume, that ever came from the pool alive after such a fall.

These are but a few, and imperfectly described, of the many interesting localities among the mountains. They should be seen to be appreciated — the mighty monarch with all the noble cliffs clustering around him.

Heaven bless him, with all his sun, moon and stars! Call him the noblest of "the mountain kings." "His subjects are princes, and gloriously they range around him, stretching high, wide, and far away; yet all owing visible allegiance to their sole and undisputed sovereign. The setting and rising sun do him homage. Peace loves to dwell within his shadows; but high among the precipices are the halls of the storms."

CHAPTER III.

THE INDIANS.

THE UNCERTAINTY OF THE MANY TRADITIONS. — THE SUPERSTITIONS OF THE INDIANS. — PROBABLE CAUSE OF THOSE SUPERSTITIONS. — TRADITION OF A FLOOD. — GREAT TREASURES OF GOLD AND GEMS. — SEARCH FOR TREASURES. — THE PARTICULAR TRIBES INHABITING THE MOUNTAINS. — INDIAN RELICS IN CONWAY — IN OSSIPEE — IN FRYBURG. — THE SOKOKIS. — THEIR DESTRUCTION BY THE PESTILENCE. — ACCOUNT OF VINES. — OF HIS VISIT TO THEM. — SQUANDO. — DEATH OF HIS CHILD. — ASSACUMBUIT. — VISIT TO FRANCE. — DESTRUCTION OF HAVERHILL. — POLAN. — WHITTIER'S VERSES ON HIS BURIAL. — CHOCORUA. — HIS CURSE. — ANASAGUNTICOOKS. — THEIR CHIEFS. — HON. ENOCH LINCOLN'S INTEREST IN INDIANS OF THIS REGION. — VISIT OF GOV. LINCOLN TO NATALLUCK. — INDIAN MYTH. — THE LITTLE INDIAN INFANT. — CURIOUS MARRIAGE CUSTOM

> "For many a tale
> Traditionary, round the mountain hung,
> And many a legend, peopling the dark woods."

THE Indian history of the White Mountains, as elsewhere, is involved in mystery. From the many myths and tales but few reliable facts can be obtained. That powerful tribes once lived beneath the shadow of their heights, once hunted these valleys, not only tradition, but their remains attest. But their ancient encampments, their favorite retreats, the hills they were accustomed to ascend, and the waters they dare fish, are unknown.

The highest peaks they never dared ascend. They peopled these mountains with beings of a superior rank, who were invisible to the human eye, but sometimes indicated their presence by tempests, which they were believed to control with absolute authority. The ascent they deemed not only perilous, but impossible.

And to one who has visited the mountains, and heard their singularly loud and almost deafening echo, the fears of the superstitious savages may not seem entirely without foundation. The terrific thunder-showers, which frequently occur among these cliffs, are enough to startle the boldest. To

> "The poor Indian, whose untutored mind
> Sees God in clouds and hears him in the wind,"

these storms were appalling beyond expression. Trembling with fright, he sees the evil spirits of his imagination, on their dark black clouds, gathering around these lofty summits, where

> "Unusual darkness broods. . . . A reddening gloom,
> . . . . . . A boding silence reigns
> Dread through the dun expanse : save the dull sound,
> That from the mountains, previous to the storm,
> Rolls o'er the muttering earth, disturbs the flood,
> And shakes the forest leaf, without a breath,
> 'T is listening fear, and dumb amazement all ;
> When to the startled eye the sudden glance
> Appears — eruptive through the cloud,
> And following shower in explosion vast,
> The thunder raises his tremendous voice,
> * * * * * * * *
> Amid Carnarvon's mountains rages loud
> The repercussive roar ; with mighty crush,
> Into the flashing deep, from the rude rocks
> Of Penmanmaur heaped hideous to the sky,

> Tumble the smitten cliffs ; and Snowden's peak,
> Dissolving, instant yields his wintry load."

Slides must have occurred before the ones in 1826, judging from appearances of the mountains, but where, or how extensive, we know not. Traditions of these existed, undoubtedly, among the Indians, tending greatly to increase their fear and veneration. The suddenness and violence of the storms they had themselves witnessed, and the exaggerated tradition of still more violent ones experienced by their fathers, had produced a fear they could never overcome. Darby Field, the first explorer of the mountains, not only could not persuade them to accompany him

> " To those mountains, white and cold,
> Of which the Indian trapper told,
> Upon whose summits never yet
> Was mortal foot in safety set ;"

but they were most earnest in their entreaties for him not to undertake the daring feat, and thus so stir up the wrath of the Gods.

A tradition, similar to what has been found to exist among most savage tribes, concerning a deluge having once overspread the land, prevailed among the Indians. Every human being was destroyed, and the world was drowned, save the White Mountains, where a single powow and his wife retreated and were saved. These mountains they climbed, found protection from the rising water, and thus preserved the race from extermination.

Suspended at immense heights over the precipices, and beyond the reach of human hands, the Indians saw huge carbuncles, which, in the darkness of night, shone with the most brilliant splendor.

And even among the early settlers, vast treasures, guarded

by evil spirits, were supposed to be hidden among the hills. Says Ethan A. Crawford: "I recollect a number of years ago, when quite a boy, some persons had been upon the hills, and said they had found a golden treasure, or carbuncle, which they said was under a large, shelving rock, and would be difficult to obtain, for they might fall and be dashed to pieces. Moreover, they thought it was guarded by an evil spirit, supposing that it had been placed there by the Indians, and that they had killed one of their number, and left him to guard the treasure; which some credulous, superstitious persons believed, and they got my father to engage to go and search for it. Providing themselves with everything necessary for the business, and a sufficient number of good men, and a minister well qualified to lay the evil spirit, they set out in good earnest and high spirits, anticipating with pleasure how rich they should be in coming home laden with gold; that is, if they should have the good luck to find it. They set out, and went up Dry river, and had hard work to find their way through the thickets and over the hills, where they made diligent search for a number of days, with some of the former men spoken of for guides; but they could not find the place again, nor anything that seemed to be like it, until, worn out with fatigue and disappointment, they returned; and never since, to my knowledge, has any one found that wonderful place again, or been troubled with the mountain spirit."

The Indians inhabiting more particularly the White Mountains, were the Sokokies, or Pequawkets, and Anasagunticooks, tribes of the Abenakis. Traces of their ancient encampments are frequently discovered on the banks of the rivers, and near the ponds. In Conway, near the homestead of my father, pipes, and pieces of kettles, of a soft substance, easily cut with a knife, and of a whitish color, have often been discovered. The pipes and kettles must have been quite large. On Crocker's point, in Conway, formed by one of the many turnings and bends of the Saco river, guns and hatchets were found, in former years, in considerable numbers.

Further down, on the same river, on what is known as Merrill's intervale, are indications of a large encampment. Fields, embracing acres, where the Indians formerly raised corn, are clearly marked out. Amid the growth of trees which have since sprung up, the corn-hills, such as are seen in any harvested corn-field, are quite distinctly seen. The older settlers say that, from appearances, the first growth of trees had been destroyed by "girdling" them; an operation consisting merely in peeling the bark off entirely round the trees, causing them to decay and fall.

Some years since, in Conway, while digging the cellar where at present stands the house of a Mr. Furber, the perfect skeleton of a human body was found in a sitting posture.

> "The Indian, when from life released,
> Again is seated with his friends,
> And shares again the joyous feast."

In Ossipee is a large mound of earth, forty-five or fifty feet in diameter, perfectly round, and about ten feet high. It is one hundred rods from the western shore of Ossipee Lake, in a large meadow. The trees, which covered this mound, were cut off not many years since, the stumps of some of them measuring a foot in diameter. Extensive excavations have never been made in this mound; and yet, there have been taken from it, by only digging from the top, three entire skeletons. One of these was full-grown, in a sitting posture, with a piece of birch-bark over his head. Tomahawks, and many pieces of coarse earthen-ware, have been found on the surrounding meadow. Corn-hills, in several directions, were distinctly discernible when the land was first cleared. This was undoubtedly, at one time, the residence of the Indians.

Not far from this mound are yet to be seen the remains of the fort, built by Lovewell, on his way to fight the Pequawkets, an account of which we have given in another place. This appears to have been only palisaded, or a stockade fort. Its eastern face fronted the lake, and was situated on the top of a small bank, near the river which here empties into the lake. At the north and south ends of the fort, considerable excavations of earth were made, resembling cellars in size and appearance. A ditch, in which the palisades were set, appears to have run round the whole tract which the fort contained, which was about an acre.

In Fryburg there are many mounds and other indications of their ancient encampments. At one place there the mounds are five in number, and situated near together. The principal one is sixty feet in circumference, and within this is a smaller, in which a tree of considerable size formerly stood. There are four others, extending out from the centre one, so as to form eight angles.

Here was one of the large villages of the Pequawkets. The side of the village is about one mile and a half west from Lovewell's pond, on the eastern bank of the Saco river, and nearly two miles west from Fryburg village and the academy. The peculiarly favorable situation of this spot for an Indian encampment we have spoken of in another place.

The Sokokies were originally a large people, but became much reduced by their many wars. The principal residence of their sagamores was upon Indian island, just above the Lower Falls, where now stands Saco village. There were two branches of the tribe, and two lodgments; one at Fryburg, which we have referred to, and the other at Ossipee pond. Here, before Philip's war, they employed English carpenters and built a strong fort of timbers, fourteen feet in height, with flankers, intending it as a fortification against the Mohawks.

Until their decided overthrow and almost annihilation by Lovewell, in the well-known battle of Saco pond, an account of which we have given in another place, the Sokokis were the most feared of all the northern Indians. The mere mention of the Pequawkets, more particularly, would have awakened fear in the heart of the boldest adventurer in the frontier settlements, and frozen the blood of the timid with horror. So sudden were their movements, so well sustained and so indescribably cruel their massacres, that the English never felt safe from their attacks; but the least sound heard through the still night was interpreted to be the stealthy footsteps of the Pequawkets; and quick came the breath, and big drops of sweat oozed out, as the listener lay expecting each moment to hear their shrill war-whoop.

This tribe appears to have suffered, in common with all the eastern Indians, by the terrible sickness which desolated New England immediately preceding its settlement by the English, so startlingly described by Morton, in his New English Canaan. "But contrary wise, in short time after, the hand of God fell heavily upon them, with such a mortall stroake, that they died in heaps, as they lay in their houses, and the living, that were to shift for themselves, would runne away and let them dy, and let their carkases ly above the ground without buriall. For, in a place where many inhabited, there hath been but one left alive to tell what became of the rest; the living being (as it seems) not able to bury the dead.

They were left for crowes, kites, and vermine, to prey upon. And the bones and skulls, upon the severall places of their habitations, in that forest nere the Massachusetts, it seemed to me a new-found Golgotha."

Mr. Vines and his companions, who partially explored this region in the year 1616, describe the natives as suffering greatly, not only from the ravages of the pestilence, but from the death of the Bashaba, or chief sachem, whom the Tarratines, a tribe living east of the Penobscot, had attacked by surprise, and destroyed with all his family. "Great dissensions had immediately followed among the different tribes, who were engaged in a destructive war with each other, when the pestilence made its appearance. In the midst of these evils, the Englishmen passed with safety among them, and slept in their cabins without suffering from the contagion."

Squando, the first chief of this tribe mentioned, was, in the language of Mather, "a strange, enthusiastical sagamore." He was very tall, and large of person, dignified in his deportment, impressive in his address, and possessed naturally of great strength of mind. With the wild superstitions of the savage had become mingled, in his mind, the truths of Christianity, which he had learned in his intercourse with the whites. He aspired to the character of a prophet, and made his followers believe that he held communion with the invisible spirits. God, he said, in the form of a tall man in dark clothes, had appeared to him, and commanded him to worship him more faithfully, to forbear hunting and laboring on the Sabbath, to abstain from drinking strong liquors, to pray, to attend the preaching of the gospel, and had made known to him the entire extinction of the English by the Indians in a few years. These commands he is said to have observed strictly for a long time.

But in 1675 came, as he said, the fulfilment of the latter part of his vision. And the solemn, earnest chief wrought up the eastern Indians, by revengeful eloquence, to the highest pitch of excitement. Josselyn had reported that young Indian children could "swim naturally, striking their paws under their throat like a dog, and not spreading their arms as we do;" some sailors, to prove the truth of the assertion, had overset the canoe in which was Squando's wife and child. The child sank rapidly, and was only saved by the mother, who, diving, brought it up alive. Not long after, the child died, and its death was imputed, by its parents, to the ill treatment received. "So highly did this exasperate Squando, that he resolved to use all his arts and influence to arouse and inflame the Indians against the settlers." And how successful he was, the annals of 1675 and 1676 but too faithfully depict.

Drake thus closes his account of this chief: "He was a great powow, and acted in concert with Madokawando. These two chiefs are said to be, by them that knew them, a strange kind of moralized savages; grave and serious in their speech and carriage, and not without some show of a kind of religion, which no doubt but they have learned from the prince of darkness. In another place, Mr. Hubbard calls him an 'enthusiastical or rather diabolical miscreant.' His abilities in war gained him this epithet."

Assacumbuit, of all the chiefs of the Sokokis, was the most famous. Unlike Squando, he possessed no good qualities. To brutal courage he added a turpitude and ferocity unparalleled. Mather tells the story of a beautiful little girl, Thomasin Rouse, this chief had kidnapped from her parents. The tears of the little captive provoked his wrath, and his daily practice was to whip the poor child till she could not stand. One day she had been beaten by him till he supposed her dead, when she was kicked into the water and left. The poor girl was rescued by a kinder Indian, and afterwards restored to her parents. Mather says, in conclusion: "This Assacumbuit hath killed and taken in this war (they tell me), one hundred and fifty men, women and children. A bloody devil."

He became, by his demoniac cruelties, not only the dread of the English, but incurred the intense hatred of the Indians by his arrogance and pride. He always carried a huge club, on which were notches denoting the number of English he had killed. He was particularly attached to the French, and under some of their leaders won great renown. And so highly did the French esteem their ally that in 1705 Vaudreuil sent him to France. Here he was an object of great curiosity. At Versailles he was introduced to Louis XIV., surrounded by his splendid court. The king presented him with a beautiful sword, the undaunted chieftain remarking, as he held out his hand to receive it, "This hand has slain one hundred and forty of your majesty's enemies in New England." This so pleased the king that he knighted him, and commanded a pension of eight livres a day to be allowed him for life. On his return to America, he wore upon his breast the insignia of his knighthood displayed in large letters.

He was so "exalted that he treated his countrymen in the most haughty and arrogant manner, murdering one and stabbing another, which so exasperated those of their relations, that they sought revenge, and would have instantly executed it, but that he fled" for protection to the French. Still faithful to his former masters, he accompanied Rouville in his attack upon Haverhill.

> "Quiet and calm, without a fear
> Of danger darkly lurking near,
> The weary laborer left his plough,
> The milk-maid carolled by her cow ;
> From cottage door and household hearth
> Rose songs of praise, or tones of mirth.
> At length the murmur died away,
> And silence on that village lay.
>
> A yell, the dead might wake to hear,
> Swelled on the night air, far and clear ;
> Then smote the Indian tomahawk
> On crashing door and shattering lock ;
> Then rang the rifle-shot — and then
> The shrill death-scream of stricken men ;
> Sunk the red axe in woman's brain,
> And childhood's cry arose in vain.
> Bursting through roof and window came
> Red, fast, and fierce, the kindled flame ;
> And blended fire and moonlight glared
> Over dead corse and weapons bared."

Assacumbuit, in this attack, fought by the side of Rouville, and performed prodigies of valor with the sword that had been presented him by the King of France. In the retreat he was wounded in the foot.

Whittier has so beautifully described the burial of one of the chiefs of the Sokokis, that we can but give it here. Polan was a chief that lingered around the hunting-grounds of his fathers after the majority of his tribe had removed to Canada. He was an inveterate enemy of the settlers, shrewd, subtle, and brave. He was killed in a skirmish at Windham, on Sebago lake, in the spring of 1756. After the white men had retired, the surviving Indians "swayed" or bent down a young tree, until its roots were turned up, placed the body of their chief beneath them, and then released the tree to spring back to its former position.

* * * * *

"Scarce have the death-shot echoes died
Along Sebago's wooded side;

And silent now the hunters stand,
Grouped darkly, where a swell of land
Slopes upward from the lake's white sand.

Fire and the axe have swept it bare,
Save one lone beech, unclosing there
Its light leaves in the April air.

With grave, cold looks, all sternly mute,
They break the damp turf at its foot,
And bare its coiled and twisted root.

They heave the stubborn trunk aside,
The firm roots from the earth divide-
The rent beneath yawns dark and wide.

And there the fallen chief is laid,
In tasselled garb of skins arrayed,
And girdled with his wampum braid.

The silver cross he loved is pressed
Beneath the heavy arms, which rest
Upon his scarred and naked breast.

'T is done; the roots are backward sent,
The beechen tree stands up unbent —
The Indian's fitting monument!"

Chocorua, another of the chiefs who remained after his tribe had left the country, has given his name to one of the peaks on the extreme boundary of the White Mountains. It is a singularly-shaped mountain, its top rising up like a tower crowned by turrets at its corners. To the south the ascent of the summit is perpendicular, rising up smooth rock some hundred feet.

To this, tradition says, Chocorua had retreated, pursued by a miserable white hunter. To the highest point he had climbed, and there he stood unarmed, while below, and within gunshot, stood his pursuer. Chocorua besought the hunter not to kill him. He plead his friendliness to the whites, and the harmless, scattered condition of his few followers. But the hardened hunter was unmoved; the price of his scalp was too tempting; gold plead stronger than the poor Indian. Seeing that he should avail nothing, the noble chieftain, raising himself up, stretched forth his arms, and called upon the Gods of his fathers to curse the land. Then, casting a defiant glance at his pursuer, he leaped from the brink of the precipice on the south side to the rocks below. And to this day, say the inhabitants, a malignant disease has carried off the cattle that they have attempted rearing around this mountain.

The Anasagunticooks, originally a numerous and powerful tribe, claimed dominion of the waters and territories of the river Androscoggin, or, as it was formerly called, Amariscoggan; meaning "banks of a river abounding in dried meat."

They were a warlike people. No tribe was less interrupted in their privileges of fishing and fowling; and yet none were more uniformly and bitterly hostile towards the colonists. Tarumkin, Warumbee and Hagkins, their sagamores, were brave men; but the tribes wasted away during the wars, and, in 1747, they were unable to muster more than one hundred and sixty warriors fit to march. With the Pequawkets they early retired to St. Francois, in Canada. A few, however, remained lingering around their ancient encampments. Till within a few years, small encampments of three or four lodges would be found occasionally where game was plenty, or they could obtain easily the material to construct their baskets and other trinkets. They were very harmless and inoffensive, and always bore about them an air of dejection and sadness. But within a few years they have almost entirely disappeared, and an Indian is now seldom seen.

The Hon. Enoch Lincoln took great interest in the few Indians remaining around the White Mountains and the lakes. When governor of the State of Maine, he visited one Natalluck, who had built a hut, and was residing with his daughter, on the shores of the Umbagog. The old chief had become blind, and depended almost entirely upon his young daughter for support. Warmly did he welcome the governor, however, and many were the excursions they made over the lake in the birch canoe of the Indian, paddled by the blind old chief. He remained a number of days, sharing with the chief all the rude accommodations of his wigwam.

In Governor Lincoln's younger days I well remember visiting with him an encampment of six or seven Indians, who were residing near Fryburg. Many were the myths and tales told us, one of which I distinctly recollect. An Indian had been drowned. The search for him had been long and close, but no traces of his body had yet been discovered. One bright starlight night, as they were setting out upon their last search, the moon rose, and said to them, " I will aid you. By my light you shall find your dead brother. My bright beams shall point out his hiding-place." Many other stories were related by the intelligent squaw.

After one of the bloody engagements, in which the Indians had taken part, an English officer was wandering over the field where the encounter had taken place. As he passed among the dead, he noticed, lying near the body of a stalwart savage, the dead body of a beautiful squaw. From appearance, the affectionate wife had sought her husband amid the heaps of slain, and had perished in his embrace. As he turned to leave the spot, he espied — what before had escaped his notice — two little black eyes, smilingly peeping at him from behind its mother. On examining, he found a little pappoose strapped to its mother's back. There it lay, a beautiful little infant, its sparkling eyes looking him directly in the face, all unconscious of its dreadful situation. As he stood watching the little creature, a brutal soldier rushed up, and, ere he could be prevented, struck the little Indian on the head with his gun, instantly killing it.

A curious marriage custom also prevailed among these Indians. The claims of rivals to the hand of the beautiful squaws was decided, not by the more modern practice of pistols and powder, but by hard fist-fights; the coveted beauty acting as umpire, and deciding on the merits of her lovers. At a time when some officers and soldiers were quartered in the region, it was noised abroad that a battle was to take place between two Indians, to see which of them should be entitled to the hand of a captivating young squaw, who had stolen the affections of both. As such a thing seldom took place, it was determined to make the most of it, and accordingly the officers persuaded the Indians to have their contest in the fort. The fort, by the way, was an inhabited log house.

The officers and soldiers arranged themselves around the room; the children of the family occupying the house fled to the chamber, to look down through the cracks in the floor upon the combatants, and the middle of the room was left clear for the scuffle. Like some ancient Goddess, the dark-skinned beauty was hoisted on a table, and seated on a box, to watch the contention of her lovers. All being ready, the young Indians entered. An older Indian stripped them of all weapons, that they might not take life in the heat of their passions. Being thus prepared, on a given signal they rush upon each other with all their strength. In Indian fashion, they seize, with an iron grasp, each other by the hair, and, according to our narrator, "pulled, twitched, and jerked one another about the room with all their might, till, at last, one being a little stronger than the other, smashed him violently against the cellar-door, so that both went through and struck upon the bottom, holding their grasp till the fall." On the return of the poor fellows from the cellar, the squaw chose for her husband the strongest.

CHAPTER IV.

COÖS COUNTY.

COÖS AS A FARMING COUNTY. — THE OPINION OF HON. ISAAC HILL. — DR. DWIGHT'S ACCOUNT OF THE CLIMATE. — THE MANY AND PECULIAR SHAPES OF TOWNS. — KILKENNY. — PILOT AND WILLARD MOUNTAINS. — STORY OF WILLARD AND HIS DOG. — RANDOLPH. — EXTENSIVE VIEWS FROM RANDOLPH. — ASCENT OF MOUNT JEFFERSON. — GREAT DANGER IN A STORM. — VIEW FROM JEFFERSON. — JEFFERSON. — BEAUTIFUL SITUATION OF JEFFERSON. — BROTHERS GLINES. — COLONEL WHIPPLE. — HIS YEARLY VISIT TO PORTSMOUTH. — STORY LLUSTRATING HIS CARE OF HIS TOWNSMEN. — HIS CAPTURE BY THE INDIANS, AND ESCAPE. — MR. GOTHAM. — THE IMPORTANCE OF THE DISCOVERY OF THE NOTCH. — NASH'S DISCOVERY OF THE PASS. — GOV. WENTWORTH. — GETTING A HORSE THROUGH THE DEFILE. — SAWYER. — "SAWYER'S ROCK." — MOUNTAIN CARRIAGES. —BARREL OF TOBACCO. — BARREL OF RUM. — CUTTING THE ROAD THROUGH THE NOTCH. — HART'S LOCATION.

Coos is a habitable county in the northern part of New Hampshire, meaning crooked; and Coos was the Indian name of the Connecticut river, near Lancaster. It is neither too mountainous to be cultivated, nor too sterile to be productive. It is not covered with perpetual snow; and, though its climate is somewhat cold in winter, its inhabitants are healthy and long-lived. We know that this is not the opinion which has been formed in the minds of most in respect to it. A shudder will almost involuntarily creep over one as he thinks of the barren, inhospitable regions north of the White Mountains. Along its rivers are beautiful intervals, and on its uplands are the finest wheat-farms in New England. Said the late Hon. Isaac Hill: "Prompted by an ardent curiosity to learn locations, and duly estimate the value of that part of the north which has been passed by as scarcely fit for settlement, I made my way through the northernly part of Vermont, into the Canada townships, to the Indian stream country, and down through New Hampshire, during the past summer. I was surprised at the extent and value of this whole country for farming purposes. I believe the tract of country for one hundred miles south of the forty-fifth degree eastward of Lake Champlain, over Vermont and New Hampshire, through the whole extent of Maine to the Bay of Fundy and the sea, to be the most valuable tract of land in New England. The Canada townships, of ten miles further north, are splendid; Stanstead may be taken as a sample. The best township of Vermont is said to be Derby, lying side by side of it. The cattle and the productions of these two towns are all on a larger scale than we find down south. Both in the Canada townships, and within our own limits, there are thousands on thousands of acres of beautiful lands, covered with the heaviest and most valuable timber, yet to be taken up. The climate here, most conducive to health and long life, should be regarded as no obstacle to the settler. The railroads are destined to make every standing tree valuable. The splendid growth need not to be cut down, girdled or wasted, upon these lands. Upon this region the snow, falling in November, sometimes covers the ground till May. Contrary to my previous expectations, I am led to consider this annual covering a benefit rather than an injury. It gives a time for active business to all who have a desire to stir about. There the winter is the gayest and most desirable season. Clothed with its white covering, the ground is generally preserved from deep frost, and the spring opens as a continued summer for the growth of vegetation."

Dr. Dwight, in his travels, has also remarked the beneficial effect of the snow upon the ground, preventing it from freezing deeply, and protecting it from much frost. The season of vegetation directly north of the mountains is consequently as long, and in some spots longer than in places much further south; and the climate of the towns lying under the mountains on the north, he says, is as mild and pleasant as many towns in the southern part of the state. The south-east winds are entirely checked, or so elevated by their passage over the mountains, as not to be felt by the towns skirting the northern side; while the north-west winds, rebounding upon themselves, produce an entire calm. This corresponds well with the facts; the climate of Lancaster and Jefferson is mild and warm compared with many towns on the southern side.

"But nothing could surprise me again," writes an eminent English traveller, "after having been told one day in New Hampshire, when seated on a rock in the midst of the wild woods, far from any dwelling, that I was in the exact centre of the town.

"'God made the country, and man made the town,' sang the poet Cowper; and I can well imagine how the village pupils must be puzzled until the meaning of this verse has been expounded to them by the schoolmaster." Most truly some very queer-shaped towns has man made among these mountains, and quite a learned schoolmaster we think it would take to find the centre of many of them. There is a Chinese puzzle, consisting of a box and seven or eight different-shaped pieces, triangles, squares, parallelograms, which can be put into hundreds of different and very odd shapes.

We think the first surveyors must have studied deeply this puzzle, and, with the many queer figures still floating in their brain, laid out these towns. How else to account for their shape we know not. We do not think they could be ascribed to political purposes, as many queer-shaped towns and districts have been; for Farmer, speaking of them even so lately as 1823, does not seem to think them worthy of much political anxiety. He says, speaking of the inhabitants, "They are poor, and, for aught that appears to the contrary, must always remain so, as they may be deemed actual trespassers on that part of creation, destined by its author for the residence of bears, wolves, moose, and other animals of the forest!" This description applies more particularly to Kilkenny, the most irregular of the many irregular townships. It is in the form of a triangle surmounted by a parallelogram many miles in length, but hardly a mile in width. Its northern boundary, the base of the triangle, lies amid the rich interval land of which we have been speaking in the beginning of this chapter, while the opposite extremity of the town is located upon the mountains, many miles south in the locations. Pilot and Willard Mountains cover a large part of the town, affording some fine farms along their base, and higher up excellent grazing land. They were so named from a hunter and his dog. A bold, hardy class of adventurers, similar to the first pioneers of the Western States, seem to have hunted and lived around these mountains many years previous to their first permanent settlement. Their particular history, who or what they were, beyond their name, and one or two isolated facts, it is impossible to learn. Hardly a town but contains some stream or mountain bearing their name. Sometimes we find two living together, but not often.

> "Alone, (how glorious to be free !)
> My good dog at my side,
> My rifle hanging on my arm,
> I range the forests wide.
> * * * *
> Now track the mountain stream, to find
> The beaver's lurking-place."

This Willard had pitched his tent on the eastern side of the most northerly mountains, and set his traps on the streams around. He was a stranger, entirely unacquainted with the region, and for a time must depend upon the game he already had in his camp for subsistence. In his explorations he one day became confused, and at last completely lost. He knew not whether to turn to the right or left. There was nothing to direct him, or give him any stand-point from which he might shape his course. If he climbed trees he could hardly see over the tops of the surrounding ones; or if he scaled the "mountain-top,

> "And (solitude profound !)
> Not even a woodman's smoke curls up
> Within the horizon's bound."

For two or three days he wandered thus until he was nearly famished. At last he bethought him of his dog, and he was gone; and he recollected that each day at such a time he had left him, and after being gone a short time would return. Impatiently he now waited his return, and, giving up the search, on the following day, guided by his dog, he reached his camp, not far from which he had been wandering.

Randolph, adjoining Kilkenny on the east, was granted to one John Durand, of London, in the year 1772. It bore the name of its proprietor till the year 1824, when it was changed to Randolph. Its southern boundary is far up on Mount Madison. The views of the whole mountain group are the best from this town that can be had. From Randolph Hill, Madison, Jefferson, and Adams, can be seen entire from base to summit. The hill is not many miles from the Glen House, and it is now a favorite resort of visitors, as in fact many eminences in this town are for their extensive prospects. Adams, as seen from its northern side, resembles an extinct volcano. But few ever ascend these peaks; the ambition of most travellers being satisfied with ascending Mount Washington. We accidentally have found, in the Portland Transcript, an account of a party who ascended several years since, which we copy at length.

"We had all the while determined on ascending the northern part of the range to Mount Jefferson, partly on account of its superior wildness and grandeur, and partly because of the exceedingly few visitants to this place, compared with those to Mount Washington—the facilities for reaching the latter being so much greater, and the curiosity of the traveller not sufficiently strong to induce him to take the necessary toil for the former. The difference in the height of the two is barely more than nominal. The view, too, is said to be better from Jefferson; and, in our scale of estimation, the great ones, whose names these summits bear, stand on the same parallel. One wielded the sword, the other the pen. One prepared the way, spread the ægis; the other laid the platform on which to rear a nation's independence.

"We were informed by our guide, when we commenced the toilsome ascent, that one third of the mountains was hidden in clouds; the truth of which was afterwards realized. The weather was warm and salubrious, with a gentle breeze from the north-west. We had advanced about half a mile, when the roar of the Moose and its tributaries, leaping down the mountain's declivity, broke upon our ear.

"In the vicinity of these streams the eye is greeted with many pleasing cascades. We had proceeded about a mile up the ascent, when we came into a mist, which, as we advanced, grew into a shower of rain, that continued the whole day. Twice we held council whether to proceed or abandon the pursuit; but, on being assured the wind was north-west, which we had been led to doubt in consequence of the reigning storm, we pushed on.

"We had now ascended to the colder regions, which very sharply reproved me for my imprudence in the morning; for, though I had taken thick clothing, the weather was so warm when we started, I concluded to travel thinly clad. Nor could we at the time define the sudden changes of weather from fair to foul, together with the duration of the storm; and, what was the most singular phenomenon of all, while we were enshrouded in fog, and drenched to the skin in rain, we could look back to the spot from which we had started, and, far around as the eye could see, behold beautiful sunshine as ever lighted up the face of the earth; houses dry; yellow fields of corn waving in the western breeze, and rivers sparkling in beams of light. This was at first a mystery; but solved by recurring to a few simple principles. We are informed by philosophers that certain great natural conductors of electricity disturb the clouds and tend to produce rain, as proof of which the Andes are cited, in some parts of which it rains almost constantly. It is a fact, too, that when two clouds of different temperature meet, the one colder than the other, rain is produced. It is further a fact, that vapor, passing from a warmer to a colder region, will be condensed and fall in drops. There is vapor in the atmosphere ordinarily, and at the time of which we are writing it must have been increased in consequence of the exceedingly warm weather and the heated state of the earth's surface. Borne rapidly forward by the breeze, in its ascent to pass the mount, it met the embrace of a colder atmosphere. This and the other causes cited, no doubt, had conspired to give us a thorough drenching.

"The majority of our number, to avoid cold and wind, had determined to go around a mile out of the way to ascend on the eastern side, against which we protested, till courtesy dictated we should yield, then making a minority report that they little understood the character of the mountains, the right of which experience proved too sadly; for a part of the way was so steep, we were obliged, by the aid of shrubs, to draw ourselves up by our hands. We then retraced and travelled on till we arrived above the growth, which begins heavy at the base, gradually declining in size and height to a shrub, from this to a moss, and all beyond is naked rock.

"We had thought to reach the summit that night, but the sun was now not more than half an hour high, and we were obliged to travel back to the growth, where we erected a kind of Indian camp, covered with boughs and moss, to serve us for shelter. We then prepared to make a fire, when to our astonishment our guide had but six matches, and those he had carried in the wet all day. By means of an old spike, he had already struck the fourth, which failed to ignite. I then warned him of his folly, of the misery he had brought upon us, and in desperation told him, outright, if he missed the others, I was resolved to kill him on the spot.

"A more deplorable situation cannot well be imagined. Night had almost approached. We could not find our way off the mount. If we attempted it we must be dashed to pieces over some tremendous crag. At an elevation of five thousand feet, cold and wet, with clouds above and below, in the midst of rain, and an atmosphere like the last days of December; if we went back we must die, if we staid where we were we must freeze to death.

"We then summoned all our prudence, succeeded in getting some dry wood, by divesting a dead tree of its wet outside, with a hatchet, and our guide ordering us, five in number, to sit down in a ring to break off the wind, taking off his hat and placing in it some birch which we had fortunately taken for buckets, struck his fifth match, which also failed. The sixth took, and firing the birch we added the wood, when he began to be alarmed for his hat, which we withheld from him till it was nearly burned to a scrap. We then cut some fir-trees, which kept us a good fire, and we got partially dry. A longer night I never experienced, and I never wish to again. Our guides by this time had become chagrined and almost inexorable, the one having lost his hat, and the other his tobacco, which threw him into such a fever, he openly said he would return in the morning, and never visit that mountain again. * * * One of our party complained in the night that a flea had bitten him, and asked how he supposed he came there. He tauntingly replied, 'Just such a fool as we were — came up to look off!' His sanguine temper was now irritated to the pitch which bordered on wilful absurdity. He pronounced a curse upon the little roof that had sheltered us through the inclement night, and carried it into execution next day by setting fire to it on our return.

"Not ten rods from our camp there was a mountain ravine, a steep of two or three hundred feet, and it was terrible to stand upon the brink, and see the clouds beneath you, pass through like winged messengers of the storm. Ere morning it cleared away; the stars shone out, the moon reflected on the hills, dawn threw forth his gray twilight from the east, 'shadow, nursed by night,' began to retire from the mountain's brow, we resumed our march, and reached the summit in time to see the sun rise.

"Strange majesty! You stand upon that flinty cap, with feelings that you are not of this earth. Exalted to the third heavens, you seem almost in the very presence of Deity. Looking down on the habitations of men, the soul reels with the giddy height of so vast an elevation. The brain grows wild at the awful prospect. Ten thousand columns, supporting as it were the very heavens, spring up and compose one great family. To the east the ocean stretches along two or three hundred miles, like a vast white wall, —

> 'The glorious mirror, where the Almighty's form
> Glasses itself in tempest.'

"Apollo's showery bed, out of which he appears to rise, encircled in rainbow, dawning upon that colossal statue, and fringing the hills with his golden rays.

> 'What grandeur, Jefferson! thy lofty head
> O'erlooking sea, and lake, and hill, and wilds;
> The day-god loves to drive from ocean bed
> His heavenward chariot to give thee his smiles.'

"The western view is bounded by the Green Mountain chain, traversing the whole length of Vermont.

"Within these limits the eye sweeps over every variety of natural scenery. Mountains dim in the distance; hills diminished to knolls; and houses but as bushels. All the creations of man are but as the works of the feeble insect. Lakes of sunniest waters, among which we noticed the Pequot, where, a hundred years ago, that fierce and warlike tribe, under the chieftain Paugus, was broken by the brave Captain Lovell and his Spartan band, when in full encounter the red man shrieked the defying death-shout, and where the crimson tide of life ebbed forth in sacrifice for our infant settlement. The story, the battle-ground, its horrors, the suffering, all come up before you, as you stand proudly overlooking it from that towering cliff. Beneath your feet start out the rivers Moose, Peabody, Ammonoosuc and Saco. To the north you trace the Androscoggin almost to its source; while to the south, Mount Washington, with all its incidents and features,— the Notch, the Slide, the fated Willey family,— springs up to crown these natural wonders. But this were a twice-told story; its history has been written, and the many visitants to the spot would make its repetition stale.

"It would seem that nature had chosen for this stupendous mass her poorest material, and reared it to heaven to astonish and edify mankind. We discovered a single piece of felspar, the rest being nothing but the coarsest gray rock.

"On its top is a pond of considerable extent, which, Caspian-like, has no visible outlet; with water cold as ice and clear as crystal. In it you behold no living thing. The eagle is the only bird of heaven that sees himself reflected in its bosom. We drank of it several times, and if it is not the Castalian spring, and we were not impelled by classic thirst, but the cravings of nature, to taste its waters, we venture to say it is as beautiful as satisfying to the thirsty.

"I have never 'looked on Ida with a Trojan's eye,' seen 'the eagles fly on Parnassus,' the eternal glaciers of 'the joyous Alps,' visited Athos, Olympus, Etna, or Atlas; but I believe we have mountains, for natural sublimity, as worthy of song, cascades as beautiful, cataracts as awful, and lakes as glorious, as any the Old World can boast. I have seen Mount Jefferson, than which no more wild or beautiful majesty exists in nature.

"The way to this eminence is toilsome and strange; huge recesses beneath, the fit abodes of spirits of hate and demons of despair. You stand upon the dizzy verge, and at the gaze the heart recoils with dread. Around are scattered rocks of a thousand tons, tumbled down by frosts or some great natural causes; high above project bold, ragged and impending cliffs, threatening your approach, as if ready to grind you to powder.

"Chiselling our names in the adamant of this everlasting monument, and taking a last survey of the sublime prospect, we left, silent, filled with reverence, at having 'looked on nature in her loftier mood.'"

Bounding Kilkenny on the west is the town of Jefferson, granted to one John Goffe, in the year 1765, under the name of Dartmouth. It is quite hilly; but the gently-rising slopes are cultivated to their tops, producing large crops of wheat, rye, barley and oats. The higher hills afford excellent grazing land, pasturing immense flocks of cattle and sheep. We know not a more beautiful pastoral scene than that which presents itself to one making the northern circuit of the mountains, as he ascends Cherry Mountain. Before him in all its loveliness is the town of Jefferson. Flourishing fields of grain are waving upon all the green slopes. Here and there, in the secluded valleys, or sheltered by overhanging cliffs, are snug farm-houses, amid the scores of out-houses; and scattered amid all, and giving life to the scene, are the "cattle upon a thousand hills." Mount Pliny, in the eastern part of this town, and Cherry Mountain, if further from the higher peaks of the White Mountains, would be considered quite high elevations. John's river and Israel's river water the town. Two brothers, John and Israel Glines, who hunted beaver and other animals on these rivers previous to the settlement of any part of the country, gave their names to these streams.

Colonel Joseph Whipple, one of the most widely-known men in New Hampshire in his day, was one of the earliest settlers. He was an extensive land-holder, owning most of the valuable land north of the mountains. More thoroughly versed in the ways of the world than his poorer neighbors, his influence became almost absolute in this region. He, however, never abused his position and power. The early inhabitants invariably speak of him as a father to them. He made a ready market for all the region, always purchasing whatever they had to sell. His annual visits to Portsmouth were regarded by the inhabitants with almost as much interest as the arrival of the yearly vessel by the first inhabitants of Greenland. "They have one bright epoch; for it is a happy time, when the ice is loosed from the rocky coast, and they can expect the arrival of the vessel which alone reaches their solitude. Often deceived by the floating iceberg, forming itself in mockery into the shape of their friendly visitant; at length they see the white sails, the towering masts, the blessed guest riding at anchor in the bay. By this vessel their wants are supplied. The active and pious housewife busies herself in arranging the stores of the ensuing twelvemonth. There are letters, too, from friends and from relations, and books, and newspapers; and, banished as they are, they live again in Denmark, in 'their father-land.'"

INCIDENTS IN WHITE MOUNTAIN HISTORY. 71

He was very exact in his dealings with his neighbors, paying and receiving pay to the smallest fraction. He always brought with him, on his return from Portsmouth, a large bag of half cents to make change with.

A good story is told illustrating his fatherly care and solicitude for his own townsmen. During a time of great scarcity of provision, he refused to sell grain to any save his own neighbors, fearful lest there should not be enough to supply even them. A party of men from Bartlett, driven to extremities, at last set out for Colonel Whipple's, a distance of thirty miles. It was in the depth of winter, and the journey at that season through the mountains was perilous in the extreme. Hunger nerved them on, and they at length arrived with their hand-sleds at the colonel's. Very unexpectedly he refused to sell them any grain. All their pleading could extort from him not a bushel. Determined not to return without it, they at last agreed upon a stratagem by which to obtain it. Apparently very much disappointed, they set out on their return. When out of sight, they stopped and waited for the night. Under cover of the darkness, they stole back to the corn-house, which they had previously examined, and, getting under the floor, bored a hole up through with an auger, and through it filled their sacks. The colonel afterwards learned the fact, but, sensible that he had been wrong in refusing them, never mentioned it to them.

During the war of the revolution, he was captured by the Indians in his own house. The party acted under the authority of the English, and the object was to get information in respect to the designs of the Americans in this region. Suspecting nothing, he admitted them as usual to his house, and was a prisoner before he imagined their intention. With his usual presence of mind he made no objection to accompany them; but said they must wait a short time for him to get ready. He immediately commenced active preparations, and contrived in the bustle to tell his housekeeper, Mrs. Hight, to take up the attention of the Indians with some articles of curious mechanism which he had, while he should escape from the window. So occupied were they in examining the curiosities, that they suffered him to go into his bedroom to change his clothes, as he told them, and through the window of this he fled. He went directly to a meadow, where he had men to work, and, ordering each man to seize a stake from the fence and shoulder it as he would a gun, soon presented himself again to the Indians, who were already in search of him. Seeing him in the distance, as they supposed at the head of a large company of armed men, they hastily seized what plunder they could lay hands on, and fled. A Mr. Gotham, residing in the family, chanced to be coming towards the house at the time the Indians arrested Colonel Whipple, but saw them in time to make good his escape. They fired upon him, as he was crossing the river upon a log, but did not hit him.

These lands were almost entirely valueless, at the time of their first settlement, for want of communication with the seaboard. A wide circuit must be made, either to the right or left, before one could get to the lower settlement. Hunters on foot did cross the huge barrier; but it was with much peril. It was for a long time a matter of much anxiety to the authorities of the state, how a way should be opened through this almost impassable chain, and many were the inducements held out to the fortunate discoverer of a pass. Nash, one of those solitary hunters of whom we have before spoken, climbing a tree one day on Cherry Mountain in search of a moose, discovered, as he thought, the long-sought pass. Steering with a hunter's cunning for the opening he had seen, he soon struck the Saco river, a mere brook, which he followed down until he was stopped at what is now known as the gate of the Notch. Here the huge rocks came so near together as to prevent his following further the stream. Perceiving, however, that, with a proper amount of labor and expense, a road could be opened at the point, he scaled the cliffs and continued on to Portsmouth, where he made known his discovery to Governor Wentworth. The wary governor, fearful lest there might be deception in the matter, told him if he would get a horse down through the gorge from Jefferson, and bring it to him, he would grant him the tract of land now known as Nash and Sawyer's Location. This was somewhat a difficult operation, and to accomplish it he admitted one Sawyer, a brother hunter, to a share in his trade. By means of ropes they succeeded in getting the horse over the projecting cliff, and carried him to the governor. Sawyer, as they lowered the old horse from the last projection upon the southern side, drank the last drop of rum from his junk bottle, and breaking it upon the rock, called it Sawyer's Rock, which name it has since borne.

It was many years before a carriage-road was cut through the gorge; but the inhabitants profited much by the discovery. A horse, with much labor, pulling him up and steadying him down with ropes, could be got over the obstructing rocks. Two long poles fastened together by two bars in the centre, somewhat similar to the modern trucks, without wheels, the smaller ends serving as thills in which to harness the horse, and the larger ends resting on the ground, was their only carriage. This could easily be carried over the rocks, and the delay of three or four hours thus caused by lifting over the horse and load was trifling, compared with the long journeys they were formerly compelled to make around the extremities of the long range. The first articles carried over the pass show the great articles of trade in those days. One Titus Brown carried down to Portsmouth a barrel of tobacco, which he had raised in Lancaster, and the rudely-finished road was so crooked at that time, that between the Pass and Bartlett, but a few miles, they crossed the Saco river thirty-two times. The first article carried up through the Notch was a barrel of rum. A company in Portland had offered it to any one who would get it up through. This, Captain Rosebrook succeeded in doing with some assistance, though it was nearly empty, "through the politeness of those who helped to manage the affair," says Mr. Crawford, when he got it home.

Some years after its discovery, a road was attempted through the pass. The magnitude of this undertaking can be estimated only by remembering that the committee, appointed to locate the road, deliberated for many days on which side of the river to attempt it. The cutting through this mountain of rock would be a gigantic operation, even at the present time, with all the improvements and inventions. How much more difficult fifty years ago!

Hart's Location, bounding Nash and Sawyer's on the south, was granted to one Thomas Chadbourne, by Governor Wentworth, for services rendered by him during the Indian wars. It was afterwards sold to Richard Hart for fifteen hundred dollars, and the present name affixed to it.

CHAPTER V.

EARLY SETTLERS.

EARLY SETTLEMENT OF THE LOCATIONS. — CAPT. ROSEBROOK. — MONADNUC. — MRS. ROSEBROOK. — SCARCITY OF SALT. — GREAT CROPS. — REMOVAL FROM MONADNUC. — SETTLEMENT AT GUILDHALL. — MRS. ROSEBROOK'S ADVENTURE WITH THE INDIANS. — REMOVAL TO NASH AND SAWYER'S LOCATION. — DIFFICULTY OF FINDING HIS HOUSE IN THE DRIFTS OF SNOW. — WANT OF PROVISIONS. — HIS ENERGY. — CANCER. — HIS DEATH. — ETHAN ALLEN CRAWFORD, THE GIANT OF THE MOUNTAINS. — HIS EARLY YOUTH. — HARDSHIPS. — THE TREACHEROUS SERVANT.

THE story of the early settlement of these locations, and the history of the few settlers, is very interesting. The hardships they endured, and the obstacles they overcame, in making themselves a home among these

—— " mountains reared aloft to mock
The storm's career, the lightning' shock,''

are almost incredible. These hills have truly been

" The nursery of giant men,
Whose deeds have linked with every glen,
And every hill, and every stream,
The romance of some warrior-dream ! "

The first permanent settler in Nash and Sawyer's Location — if not the first, the first deserving of particular notice — was Capt. Eleazer Rosebrook. He was a native of Massachusetts, born, in the year 1747, in the town of Grafton. He married, when twenty-five, a Miss Hannah Hanes, and soon after left his native state for the wilds of New Hampshire. He first stopped at Lancaster, making, however, but a short stop, and then settled more permanently in Monadnuc, which is now Colebrook, full thirty miles from any inhabitant, and with no path or road to their cabin but "spotted trees." Here life in the woods commenced in earnest. Frequently, when Mr. Rosebrook had been absent to some of his "neighbors," Mrs. Rosebrook would fasten her eldest child, a little girl, in their cabin, and, with an infant in her arms, set out in search of their cow, which roamed at large through the thick woods. Over logs and sticks, through bushes and brakes, now in some secluded glen, and now stumbling over rocks and wading rivers, she would wander, listening attentively for the "bell," until at last, as the moon came up over the trees, the "old cow" would be discovered. Getting her home as best she could through the darkness, she would milk with the infant still in her arms, and, after securing the cow for the night, retire to rest.

The forest so closely surrounding them abounded in wild game, easily taken, and easily prepared for food. This, indeed, furnished them with a great part of their living, fresh in summer, but dried and smoked in winter. Salt was very scarce. At one time Capt. Rosebrook was compelled to go on foot to Haverhill, a distance of eighty miles, the whole distance through the trackless wilderness, following down the Connecticut river as his guide, in order to procure this article. One bushel he there obtained, and, shouldering it, trudged back over the same rude path to his home. So much did some families suffer for want of salt, that their children's necks swelled badly, and brought on disease in the neck, cured only by visiting the salt water, and applying the skin of salt fish to the affected part.

Small patches of land were cultivated, as the land could be cleared and seed procured wherewith to plant it. The first experiment in raising potatoes equalled, almost, the extravagant western stories of "great crops," so rife a few years since. One Major Whitcomb, after travelling fifty miles, procured one bushel of potatoes, which, by cutting, he made to plant four hundred hills. These he watched with all the interest of Crusoe over his grains of barley, and so well did they do, that he harvested, from his small sowing, one hundred bushels of good potatoes.

Capt. Rosebrook did not remain long, however, at Monadnuc. Like a true pioneer, he was restless and ever on the move. He did not remain long enough here to build his "two-story wooden palace," but was soon on the look-out for some new home. Guildhall, Vermont, less distant from the settlements, and containing more inhabitants, he chose as his new place of residence, and thither removed his family. He had joined the Revolutionary army as a volunteer, shortly before leaving Monadnuc, and was, consequently, absent from his family most of the time. Hardy, fearless, and wary, he was of great value to the American forces in the irregular warfare which they were compelled to carry on with the Indians, under English officers, on the Canadian frontier. Many are the "hair-breadth" escapes he made by his superior cunning.

Guildhall was quite a rendezvous for the Indians, and his own cabin, some distance from any other, was their favorite place of resort when he himself was gone, and no one at home but his wife and little daughters. She, however, had no fear of them, and freely admitted all that came to her house.

Generally they were very quiet, and, after spending the night, would leave peaceably. Their excursions to the settlements were for the purpose of exchanging their furs for trinkets and "uncupy," or spirit, which they carried in bladders taken from the moose and dried. At one time, however, near the close of the war, and shortly before the return of Capt. Rosebrook to his family, many Indians, loaded heavily with uncupy, came suddenly to his cabin, near night. Mrs. Rosebrook, as usual, kindly received them, and gave them permission to remain all night. Soon after entering, however, she perceived that they had drank too freely, and feared they might become noisy and unmanageable. Determined to be mistress of her own house, and knowing a bold bearing was her only safety, in case they became unruly, when, late in the evening, they became boisterous and rude, she ordered the whole tribe out of doors. At first they thought to resist, but, intimidated by her boldness, they left her as she commanded them. One squaw, only, sought to test the courage and strength of Mrs. Rosebrook, and she was soon dragged by the hair to the door, and pitched out among her companions. As the brave woman was fastening the door, after expelling her savage intruders, a tomahawk, thrown by the same squaw, came so near her as to cut off the wooden latch on which rested her hand. The same squaw, however, be it said to her credit, returned the next day, and asked Mrs. Rosebrook's forgiveness, and promised better for the future.

Capt. Rosebrook remained long enough at Guildhall to become the possessor of a fine farm. The broad, beautiful interval lands of the Connecticut, so easy to cultivate, and yielding so abundantly, it would have been hard for any other man to have abandoned for the wilderness. Still restless, and fond of the excitement attendant upon the life of a pioneer, in the year 1792 he sold his farm in Guildhall, and moved into Nash and Sawyer's Location. Excepting the Crawfords, twelve miles further down among the mountains, in the Notch Valley, he had no neighbors nearer than twenty miles. A log house had been erected here a few years previous, but had been abandoned, and into this he moved his family. It was in the depth of winter; the snow was piled up in huge drifts, and the entrance to his little hut could with difficulty be found, even after the monster pile had been discovered, beneath which his cabin lay buried. After much shovelling he succeeded in finding the door and making an entrance for his shivering family. They had brought but little provision with them, and were dependent, almost entirely, upon the game he could capture, and what could be obtained from their neighbors. Often were the children sent, through the snow, to the Crawfords', a distance, as we have said, of twelve miles, to obtain such articles as were absolutely necessary to the sustenance of the family. From these long errands, through the snow and cold, frequently they would be unable to reach home until a late hour of the night. But Capt. Rosebrook, by his energy and industry, soon put an entirely different aspect upon this secluded spot. On what is called the Giant Grave, he built a large two-story house, very convenient. He also built, within a few years, large barns, stable, sheds, and a saw-mill and grist-mill. His farm was very productive, to which he added, yearly, many broad acres redeemed from the surrounding forest. His saw-mill, he says, was of great profit to him; but his grist-mill was so far from his house, and "the mice injured the bolt so much, that it was difficult to keep it in repair."

Hardly, however, had Capt. Rosebrook become comfortably situated, when a cancer broke out upon his lip, which, after a few years of intense suffering, caused his death. Patiently he bore his suffering, and though unused, heretofore, to the confinement of a sick-room, murmured not, and at length died, peacefully, September 27th, 1817. In all respects Mr. Rosebrook was a remarkable man, large in stature, athletic, and very strong. His whole life was one of daring adventure. He loved the rugged scenes of pioneer life, and was never more in his element than while scaling the mountain or trapping the wolf or bear. There are men enough who prefer the city, and cling fondly around their native village; but he could never endure the restraints connected with our larger settlements — the restraints of artificial life; but freely, his arms and broad chest all bare, must breathe the strong, pure air, as it came rushing along through those mountain gorges.

Ethan Allen Crawford, the "Giant of the hills," was the heir to Capt. Rosebrook's property, and continued, after his death, to reside on the same place, to which he had removed, a few years before, to take care of Capt. Rosebrook and his wife. The Crawfords have been so intimately connected with the mountains, that to omit them would be to pass over entirely the history of these valleys. Ethan Crawford was nearly as well known to all the earlier visitors, and of almost as much interest, as Mount Washington itself. Many a lady, we presume, will recollect, distinctly, the kind assistance he lent them in descending those rugged heights — nay, even at times taking them, when very weary, on his broad shoulders, and carrying them down those precipitous paths, as tenderly as a father carries his infant child. We think now of one who said he carried her more than half way down Mount Washington on his shoulder. Ethan Crawford was born at Guildhall, Vermont, but his parents early removed to the mountains, and located themselves in Hart's Location, on the very spot where now stands the Old Crawford House. Here he spent his youth until he was nineteen years old. Many stories of his early life, which he was accustomed to relate, show the hardships which the early settlers of that region were compelled to endure. "Until I was nearly thirteen years old I never had a hat, a mitten, or a pair of shoes of my own. Many times I have chopped wood through the day, and at night my hands, which had been bare, would swell and pain me so badly, that my mother would have to get up and poultice them, before I could sleep. But so accustomed did I become to the cold, that I could harness and unharness horses, in the coldest winter weather, with my head, hands and feet, nearly bare." Tough, hearty and courageous were all these mountaineers. Their training was one long process of toughening and daring. Says Mr. Crawford, "Shortly after my parents came into this place, they went, one Sabbath day, to Bartlett, expecting to return the next day, and left myself and next older brother in the care of a hired man, with provisions enough prepared to last until their return. Soon after they had gone, the hired man picked up whatever was valuable, that he could carry, and, taking all the victuals cooked in the house, left us for the woods. The day wore away without our thinking much about it; but, as night came on, we grew very hungry and a little frightened. We had a cow, but neither of us were large enough to milk her. Compelled, however, to satisfy our hunger in some way, we, at last, got some potatoes and roasted them in the ashes. On these we made our supper. After eating, as it grew darker and darker, and we got tired of talking and wishing our parents would return, we went to bed, and, hugging ourselves up together as close as possible, went to sleep." On the return of the parents on Monday, the father immediately set out in pursuit of the man, and, just as he was leaving the woods at Franconia, caught him, and after taking the stolen goods, severely flogged him and let him go. What men brought up under such circumstances would not have courage?

CHAPTER VI.

ETHAN A. CRAWFORD.

MR. CRAWFORD'S IMPRESSIVE MANNER OF STORY-TELLING. — THE BURNING OF HIS BUILDINGS. — HIS ENERGY IN REPAIRING HIS LOSSES. — HIS LABORS AS A GUIDE ON TO THE MOUNTAINS. — THE DIFFICULTY FORMERLY OF REACHING THE MOUNTAINS. — STORY ILLUSTRATING DIFFICULTY OF TRAVELLING IN THOSE DAYS. — PRESENT MODES OF REACHING MOUNTAINS. — FIRST ASCENT OF THE MOUNTAINS. — PARTY OF STUDENTS FROM FRYBURG. — EASE OF ASCENDING NOW. — FIRST BRIDLE-PATH. — ETHAN'S SEVERE WOUND. — GRANNY STALBARD. — CARRIAGE-ROAD FROM GLEN HOUSE. — LOVE OF HUNTING. — THE GRAY CAT. — ADVENTURES WITH THEM. — LASSOS AND CAPTURES ONE WITH BIRCH POLES. — WOLVES. — HIS ANNOYANCE AND DISCOMFITURE BY THEM. — BEAR STORIES. — CATCHING THE CUB. — CAPTURE OF A FULL-GROWN BEAR.

MR. CRAWFORD'S many adventures among these mountains should be heard from his own lips to be fully appreciated. As told by another they lose the advantage of his own giant figure, emphatic gesticulations, and the quaint original style in which his ideas were expressed. Says his wife, "It was always a rule with him to make short stories, and not go a great way round to effect a small thing."

Very soon after the death of Mr. Rosebrook, the ample buildings which he had reared, and in which Mr. Crawford was residing at the time, were burned to the ground. It was a severe loss to Mr. Crawford, and one from which he never fully recovered. He was already in debt, and the loss of so much property seemed almost to shut out the hope of his ever extricating himself. But his courage did not forsake him, and, with his characteristic energy, he commenced to repair his losses. His family was immediately moved into a small log house, with but one door, one common apartment, no windows, and a chimney raised only to the chamber floor. This he repaired by degrees, as he had leisure, and by the next winter had a comfortable house.

His time was much occupied with travellers, many of whom had already begun to visit the mountains. His services were almost constantly in demand by those wishing to ascend to the summit of the mountains. At present it is hardly possible to realize the difficulties, not only of ascending, but even of reaching, the mountains themselves. When cumbersome, unwieldy "stages" only lumbered out of Concord and Dover, and Portland, giving aches and pains and bruisings innumerable to the weary occupant, a journey to the White Mountains was no trivial affair; and these could but carry him to Fryburg or Conway, some thirty miles from his destination, while the journey must be finished on horseback. Slow, slow was the rate of travel in those days, and fortunate was the traveller if he reached the Crawfords in four or six days.

A curious incident, illustrating this point, as well as some of the other earlier New England customs, is related by Mrs. Crawford. On a time, "when they were to have a training, an officer went fifty miles to Lower Coös, as it was called, or Haverhill now, for two quarts of spirit to treat his company with. As they had no carriages in those days, neither had they a road suitable for one, he took his horse, put on a saddle, and then a pair of large saddle-bags, filled with provisions for the journey, and a jug for the spirit, and provender for his horse, and, as they travelled at that time, it took him three or four days to perform this journey. When on his way home, by some unknown accident, the cork got loose, and the bottle was emptied of its contents into the saddle-bags. The liquor would have been saved had not the oats soaked up a part of it; he, however, saved enough to treat his company with."

At present the traveller has but to take his seat in a "spacious and well-ventilated railroad-car, elegant in its appointments as a parlor," enjoy all the pleasures ascribed by the poet to "Riding on a rail," —

> "Singing through the forests,
> Rattling over ridges,
> Shooting under arches,
> Rumbling over bridges;
> Whizzing through the mountains,
> Buzzing o'er the vale,"—

and presently he is set down at the very base of the mountains themselves on the eastern side. If he prefer to approach them from the south and west, the best modern coaches will bear him over good roads to the very centre of the wide cluster of mountains. Having reached the base of the mountains, the ascent, though now difficult and fatiguing, is not to be compared to the wearisome and perilous undertakings of the first visitors. Mr. Crawford gives the account of two young men, who undertook the ascent so late as 1818, with his father, the elder Crawford, as their guide. "They rode to the top of the Notch, then sent back their carriage, and proceeded to the woods. They had much difficulty in managing to get through; they, however, proceeded slowly, sometimes crawling under a thicket of trees, sometimes over logs and windfalls, until they arrived to where they could walk on the top of trees. This may seem strange, but it is nevertheless true. They never reached the summit, but managed to get along on some of the hills.

"As the day was drawing to a close, they returned to the woods, in order to pass the night, and erected a shelter for their protection. A dense fog arose, and during the night it rained. In the morning, owing to the darkness, they could not tell the best way to proceed; but took the surest way by following the Ammonoosuc river, and came to my house. These men wore fine and costly garments into the woods; but when they returned their clothes were torn and much injured by the bushes; and their hats looked as if they had been through a beggar's press. They were much exposed all night, without food or fire."

And often have I heard my father and eldest brother relate the perils of their first ascent, made in company with a party of students from Fryburg Academy. They went up from the east side of the mountain, as, in fact, most travellers did in those days. Many of the party, entirely overcome by the fatigue and difficulty of proceeding, fainted, and were obliged to return. Such, however, as did succeed, will probably never forget the undertaking. For the first few miles the difficulties were no more than one would encounter in any forest. But, as they ascended, the trees, changed from the maple and beech to the spruce and hemlock, became much smaller in size, at the same time thicker, while their way was much more broken and rough. At length, from forcing their way through the thick growth, they were compelled to stoop and go under the scraggy tops of the rough, stiff, hemlocks, and spruces, sending out their long limbs and interlacing them so firmly as to form an impassable barrier. At each ascending step they were forced to stoop still lower, until from right angles they almost touched the ground with their faces. When they could proceed no further in this way, they forced their way up through the matted tops of the trees and walked on the low, stunted vegetation as upon moss. In this manner they passed the limits of vegetation and reached the summit. From their account I should judge a sorrier-looking set of men never descended Mount Washington. Their clothes were not only almost torn from their backs, but their bodies were lacerated sorely, by their perilous march through the dwarfish growth.

At present the ascent, though rough, is much easier. Visitors can start from any of the houses around the mountains, and ascend with nothing in the shape of stumps or trees to obstruct their way. Bridle-paths have been cut from all these points to the top of the mountains, so that even now females can ascend them on horseback. The first bridle-path was made by Ethan Crawford in 1821. He says of it: "In March I hired Esquire Stuart to come with his compass, and go into the woods, and see if there could not be a better and more practicable way found to ascend the mountains. He spent three days in making search, and returned well satisfied that he had found the best way; for the road which we had heretofore travelled is an uneven one, going up a hill and then down again, and this in so many successions, that it made it tiresome to those who were not accustomed to this kind of journeying; and the way which we had now found is over a comparative level surface for nearly seven miles, following the source of the Ammonoosuc, or Ompomponoosuc, until we arrived at the foot of Mount Washington, and then taking a ridge or spur of the hill.

"In the summer, just before haying, I hired men and went with them to cut this path, and while in the woods, at the distance of three miles from home, as I was standing on an old log chopping, with my axe raised, the log broke, and I came down with such force that it struck my right ankle, and glanced, nearly cutting my heel-cord off; I bled freely, and so much so that I was unable to stand or go. The men that were with me took the cloths we had our dinner wrapped in, and tied up my wound as well as they could, and then began to contrive means to get me out of the woods. They cut a round pole, and with their frocks which they wore tied me in underneath it, and thought they could carry me in like manner as we bring dead bears through the woods; but in this way I could not ride. They then let me down, and took turns in carrying me on their backs, until we got out of the woods. There happened to be at my house, then, Mrs. Stalbard, who is known in our country, and bore the name of Granny Stalbard, whose head was whitened with more than eighty years. She was an old doctress woman; one of the first female settlers in Jefferson, and she had learned from the Indians the virtues of roots and herbs, and the various ways in which they could be made useful. Now the old lady said it was best to examine this wound, and have it properly dressed up; but, as it had stopped bleeding, I told her I thought it was better to let it remain as it then was; but she, thinking she was the elder and knew better, unwrapped it, and it soon set bleeding afresh, and it was with difficulty she now stopped it. She, however, went into the field, plucked some young clover-leaves, pounded them in a mortar, and placed them on my wounds: this stopped the blood so suddenly that it caused me to faint." This is the history of the first bridle-path.

But these bridle-paths are but "notched trees" compared with what energy, enterprise and capital, have already commenced. At an expense of one hundred thousand dollars, a carriage-road is being constructed to the very summit of the mountain. "The length of the road from the Glen House to the top will be eight miles. It is to be fifteen feet wide, clear of all obstructions, McAdamized in the best manner, and the average grade will be a rise of one foot to eight and a half, with level spots at various points of interest, where travellers may rest and examine the scenery. Wherever the road is on the side of declivities, strong walls will be erected, the road itself inclining inwards. The carriages are to be peculiarly constructed. They will be broad and low, and so arranged with screws that, whether going up or down, the body of the coach will be on a perfect level. A fine hotel is to be erected on the summit by the company, with an extensive carriage-road around it, so that visitors may at their ease see every aspect of nature below."

But to return to Mr. Crawford. Almost constantly occupied as he was in summer with his visitors and farm, he yet found much time for hunting, which was his favorite recreation. His winters were almost entirely devoted to this, and generally quite profitably. The mountains were then teeming with wild animals; very valuable for their meat and skin. By his great strength, cunning, and courage, no animal could escape him.

> "His rifle flashed,
> The grim bear hushed his savage growl;
> In blood and foam the panther gnashed
> His fangs, with dying howl;
> The fleet deer ceased its flying bound,
> Its snarling wolf-foe bit the ground,
> And, with its moaning cry,
> The beaver sank beneath the wound
> Its pond-built Venice by."

Alone and unarmed he would attack the fiercest animal of the forest; — the gray cat, or Siberian lynx, such a terror to the hunter, even when in company and armed with his rifle. This animal differs considerably from the wild-cat, with which it is often confounded; resembling more in its appearance and disposition the caracal of Asia. It is perfectly untamable, and lives entirely upon the smaller animals of the forest. "At one time," Mr. Crawford says, "these animals became very bold, making great havoc among our sheep and geese, and causing us many fears for the safety of our children. I set many traps for them, baiting them with a variety of meats, from hens cooked, to chickens alive with feathers on; but nothing would tempt them, until I chanced to try pickled fish. The night after I had baited with this, one got into the trap. He was quite large, and moved the trap some distance into a clump of bushes, so that in the morning, when I came to look for him, it was some time before I could find him. He was lying partly concealed by the bushes, and I did not see him before I had my foot raised to step on him. He sprang and I sprang, fortunately far enough to get a large stick before he could attack me. With this I entered into an engagement, and it was some time before I was able to quiet him. I conquered, however, at last, and in triumph carried him home. He measured more than six feet in length. In this way I caught six of them."

At another time, as he was passing down through the Notch with his team, his dog discovered one, but a short distance from the road, in the top of a tree thirty feet high. Taking a small hatchet which he had with him, he cut two birch sticks, which he twisted together, so as to form one long pole. On one extremity of this he made with another stick a ring with a slip-noose to it. This he worked up through the limbs of the tree, and threw over the animal's head, somewhat as the Indian lassos the wild horse with his lariat. Jerking suddenly, as he threw the noose over his head, he brought the creature down ten feet, when the noose broke. He fixed another before the lynx could recover from the shock of the first jerk, and this time brought him to the ground. The dog instantly sprang upon him, but was soon glad to cry for quarters, and retreat with his skin nearly torn from his body. The fellow now became furious; but, unable to reach his captor, sprang into the top of a small spruce, four feet high, and here seemed determined to remain. The battle now commenced in earnest. By means of the halter, Mr. Crawford held him firmly in his place, and, with such sticks as he could readily lay his hand on, commenced beating him to death. It was a long and exciting struggle, requiring all his strength to keep him from springing into his face; but he delighted in such contests, and by his well-directed blows at length killed him.

On Cherry Mountain, he chased one into the tops of the thick trees, and, unwilling to lose it, climbed up, and for a long time continued the chase amid the branches; running round upon them almost as easily as the animal itself.

For hours he would amuse the traveller with his adventures in hunting, apparently as unconscious of anything remarkable as the boy who relates his exploits at a squirrel hunt. Wolves he dealt with as others do with a cat and kittens. Accidentally one day he came across a hollow log containing a nest full of young wolves. Two of them he carried home and domesticated, and in time so tamed them that they were delivered over to his little son to take care of them. He taught them all the tricks that boys teach dogs, even making them speak for their food before receiving it.

But once only they offered violence, and that was occasioned by attempting to remove some bones which one of them had buried.

With all his skill and courage, they would sometimes, he was compelled to acknowledge, annoy him exceedingly. His sheep he even had to sell, to prevent their being all destroyed by them. One cold December night a whole pack came suddenly upon his fold. The frightened sheep took refuge under the shed, and hid themselves among his cattle and horses. Wolves seldom attack these, unless driven to great extremity by hunger, and did not meddle with them, but satisfied themselves by digging up the carcases of some bears, which had been buried behind the barn. Their repast finished, they sat down upon their haunches directly in front of the house, and, as if in defiance of the master, commenced a most dismal howling. The very mountains echoed with their "lonesome music." The dog was first let out, hoping he might frighten them off; but the reception they gave him was soon manifest from his loud cries. They had nearly torn him in pieces when Mr. Crawford came to his rescue. Springing out of bed, he went out with nothing on but his night-dress. The cunning fellows, perceiving their advantage, dropped the dog, and sat "bolt upright" to receive him. He was fairly beaten; nothing could move them. Talk as loud as he could, they would not stir. They waggishly wagged their heads as he threatened, until at length the chill night-wind compelled him to retreat, and leave them masters of the field.

His fund of "bear stories" was almost inexhaustible. Hardly a week had passed, since he had lived among the mountains, that he had not had an encounter with one. Young cubs he would capture and carry home as one would a young pig. Driving one as large as a good-sized dog into a tree one day, he persuaded a young man with him to climb the tree, and drive him out, while he stood below to keep the old bear off. The cub, to escape his pursuer, ran out from the tree into a smaller one close by, where Mr. Crawford was standing. Keeping the old bear off as best he might, he shook the tree so hard that down came the young bruin pounce upon him. He simply remarked that he took good hold of him, and, tying his handkerchief about his mouth, carried him home. Such hand-to-hand encounters he frequently had with them, never fearing to match his own unaided strength with theirs. A very amusing account of such an engagement we give in his own words:

"Once, going to a celebrated place for bears, I found a good-sized yearling bear caught in a steel trap by one of his fore-feet, and he appeared not to have been long there. He had fastened the grapple to a bunch of roots, and there was a chain between the grapple and the trap. Here he was sitting in an humble and ashamed-looking position. I looked him over, and at length concluded to contrive means to lead him home. I cut a round stick, ten feet in length, sufficiently large and stout to lead him with; then, taking the throat-latch from the bridle, the stirrup-leather and the mail-straps from the saddle, I set the horse at liberty, and managed to get hold of the bear's hind feet; these I straightened and tied to a tree. I then went up to his head and secured his mouth, but not so tight but what he could lap water. While thus engaged, in spite of all my care, he put out his fore-paw — the one that was at liberty — and placed it so hard against one of my legs, that I really think, had it not been for a good strong boot, he would have torn the skin; but the boot prevented him from tearing my leg. He, however, took a piece of my pantaloons with him; still, I would not give up the idea of bringing him home alive. I then fastened a strap around him, before and behind, and the stick upon his neck, loosened his feet, and then began to try to lead him. Here we had a great struggle to see which was the stronger, and which should be master; and he played his part so well I could do nothing with him. He would turn upon me and fight me all he possibly could. I now thought I must kill him; but as I had never been beaten by a wild animal, I was unwilling to give up now. He would come to a tree, and hold on, so that I found I could not lead him. I again contrived a way to confine him, but with more difficulty than before, as his feet were entirely free, and, being quick and active with them, I had hard work to get them again; but, after a while, I made out to. I then tied his hind and fore feet together, in such a manner that he could not scratch me; then placing him on my shoulder, with one hand hold of his ear, to keep his head from coming too near mine, in case he wished to make a little closer friendship, I trudged on; but he was so heavy and ugly to manage, that it made me sweat; and I was obliged to lay him down often and rest, and whenever I came to water, I would let him lap it. I made out to get two miles, he all the while growing worse and worse; at last he actually turned upon me, and entered into an engagement with me, by scratching and trying to bite, and, after tearing my vest, I concluded I would once more lay him down — and the way was not easy. Lifting him up as high as I could, I let him fall, and, the ground being hard, the breath left his body. Here I left him, and went home, and sent a man after him."

CHAPTER VII.

THE CRAWFORD FAMILY.

MR. CRAWFORD'S EARLY DEATH. — A REMARKABLE MAN. — THE CRAWFORD FAMILY. — ABEL CRAWFORD. — MRS. CRAWFORD. — HER BRAVERY DURING THE NIGHT OF THE SLIDES. — CRAWFORD HOUSE. — DEATH OF MR. STRICKLAND ON THE MOUNTAINS. — DANGER OF ASCENDING MOUNTAINS WITHOUT GUIDE. — PARTY OF STUDENTS LOST ON MOUNTAINS. — NANCY'S BROOK. — STORY OF NANCY. — SUPERSTITIONS CONNECTED WITH THE SPOT WHERE SHE WAS FOUND. — OWL STORY. — BEAUTIFUL AURORAL DISPLAY AT THE NOTCH.

MR. CRAWFORD died young. The exposures and hardships of his early life had completely shattered his naturally strong constitution, and he broke down long ere he had reached the maturity of manhood. He suffered much in his last days through his bodily ailments and pecuniary embarrassments. The giant of nearly seven feet, whose feats of strength had been the wonder and astonishment for many miles around him, was at length compelled to yield to a foe that he could not withstand. His great strength was no aid to him in enduring the intense pain which he suffered, so acute at times, that he says, "I have put my hand to the top of my head, and felt the hair, to know if it did not stand straight on end, as I could feel it rise, and sometimes would think it would throw off my hat." Relieved, for brief periods, of this intense pain, he would forget all past suffering, and so great was his love for hunting and the mountains, that, gun in hand, he would totter after his game when scarcely able to stand. We always had a high estimate of Mr. Crawford, as one of nature's noblemen; but never more so than since we commenced to write the brief story of his adventurous life. Beneath his rough exterior lay concealed some of the noblest qualities in the human character. We cannot convey our idea of him more exactly than in the words of the poet:

> "He was one
> Who would become a throne, or overthrow one.
> *   *   *   *   *   noble
> In nature,   *   *   gentle, yet wary;
> Yet for all this, so full of certain passions,
> That if once stirred or baffled, as he has been,
> *   *   *   *   there is no fury
> In Grecian story like to that which wrings
> His vitals with her burning hands."

The whole Crawford family have been remarkable for their size and strength. Abel Crawford, the father, often styled the "patriarch of the mountains," at eighty was a stout, athletic man. A walk of five miles to his son Thomas J. Crawford, before breakfasting, at this advanced age, he performed with the greatest ease. At seventy-five he rode the first horse on to the top of Mount Washington that ever ascended. He represented, in the state legislature, the eight voters in his own location, and the few in Nash and Sawyer's Location and Carroll, with much ability, the five or six last years of his life. We can never forget his appearance not long before his death. So long had he been accustomed to travellers during the summer months, that he felt he could not die without seeing them arrive once more. His venerable locks, as white as the drifted snow, falling to his very shoulders, his tall, massive form, as erect as in the prime of his manhood, he sat supported by his affectionate daughter, as eagerly waiting for the coming of his visitors, as the dying sailor for the sight of his native shores. "Full of years," he died on their first arrival.

He was a good-humored man through all his life, and mingled as much of the playful with the sober as any you will ever see. After his days of toil in the field and on the mountain were over, and he was confined to his house through age, he spent much time in rehearsing amusing and interesting anecdotes to all who were disposed to listen to him, and from his visitors there were many such. Thus he greatly endeared himself to his guests, and through succeeding time not a few of them will rise up and say,

> "I remember well a man, a white-haired man,
> Pithy of speech, and merry when he would,
> A genial optimist, who daily drew,
> From what he saw, his quaint moralities.
> Kindly he held communion, though so old,
> With me, a dreaming boy, and taught me much
> That books tell not, and I shall ne'er forget."

Mrs. Crawford was the fitting companion of so hardy a man. She was the mother of nine children, eight sons and one daughter. Erastus, the eldest son, was six feet and six inches in height, strong, and very compactly made. Ethan Allen, as we have before remarked, was near seven feet in height; and no son, we believe, was less than six feet tall.

During the night of the dreadful storm, when my brother's family was destroyed, Mrs. Crawford was alone with her smaller children, in their house. The water rose at a fearful rate, bearing along on its current sheep and cattle, and hay and grain which were stacked in the fields. Before she could get her children to the upper story of the house, the water was twenty-two inches deep on the lower floor, putting out her fire, and washing the ashes about the room. After securing her children, finding that the immense mass of stuff, brought down by the water, was collecting against the house, and thus endangering it, she took her clothes-pole, and, during the continuation of that violent tempest, stood and pushed away the logs and timbers as they came rushing against the dwelling.

For years the Crawfords were the only ones to entertain travellers to the mountains. The house at the head of the Notch, formerly known as the "Crawford House," was built by Ethan and his father, and was kept, for many years, by one of the sons. All the bridle-paths, on the western side of the mountains, were cut by them, and for many years they were the only guides who dared conduct visitors to the summit. A melancholy incident is connected with the "Crawford House" bridle-paths, showing the folly of attempting to ascend those rugged and broken heights without a guide.

An Englishman, by the name of Frederick Strickland, came to the Crawford House, then kept by T. J. Crawford, Oct. 18th, 1840. The next day he left the house, in company with another Englishman and a guide, to ascend the mountains. When they reached Mount Pleasant, the guide and the other Englishman, on account of the cold, and snow on the mountain, proposed to return, and strongly advised Mr. Strickland to do the same. In defiance of all this, however, he persisted, and would go on. He delivered up his horse to the guide, and proceeded, on foot, toward the summit of Mount Washington, intending to come down Mr. Fabyan's bridle-path.

The guide and the other gentleman returned to Mr. Crawford's. In the mean time Mr. Crawford sent the baggage of Mr. Strickland to Mr. Fabyan's, with word that its owner might be expected to come down from the mountain and stay with him that night. But, as he did not come that night, Fabyan thought he had returned to Mr. Crawford's. The next morning, however, Mr. Crawford chancing to pass, inquired for him. This excited alarm, and they both started in pursuit of him. They found his track on the mountains, and followed that until night, making no discovery of anything but some of his clothes.

The next day they started, with others added, and found him dead. He had precipitated himself over some rough descent in his path, and lay at its base a lifeless corpse. He was the eldest son of Sir George Strickland, an eminent English baronet, recently member of Parliament for the county of York. He was about thirty-five years of age, and heir to large estates.

At the time of his death, he had been in this country but a few months. He was a graduate of Cambridge University, in England, and was a cultivated scholar.

The frightful condition of those lost on these mountains, during one of those sudden storms, which so frequently come upon them, cannot be better described than in the words of one who experienced all its horrors. A party of young men had rashly undertaken the ascent alone, quite early in the season. After wandering all day amid the precipices and defiles, night and a misty, foggy storm at last came on, completely bewildering them.

"The slanting remains of sunlight faded into deep shadow. The light troops of a vast army of dense mists, sweeping low over our heads, came shutting off the last light, and, even as we looked in wonder, the wonder faded into fear as the massive body of the cloudy host charged upon us. It was a cold, thick fog — the coldest and solidest I ever felt; apparently filled, indeed, with little particles of snow, which smote upon our summer clothing and chilled us through and through in an instant. Thicker and thicker it poured past, in interminable volumes, taking our remaining strength away with the warmth of our bodies, and our courage with our strength. We thought, in this perplexity, to follow the ridge on one of whose summits we were, downwards, and to grope our way out to the valley of the Saco, by following the fall of the ravines. We could not see twenty feet. The darkness, as the sun fell, momently increased. Our little local recollections having been frightened away by the mist, — thoroughly befogged in a double sense, — we had quite forgotten which way the ridge sloped downwards. Having followed it some distance in one direction, and coming to an ascent, we concluded we were going wrong, and went the other way. Undertaking, this time, to be persevering, we kept on until we got fairly away from the neighborhood of our resting-place, followed one or two cross ridges, which offered a fallacious prospect of leading us somewhither, and, just as night fell, were thoroughly lost; colder, wearier, hungrier, and more scared than ever. We could not now see a step; and, moreover, had been, for an hour, stumbling and even falling from the weakness of excessive fatigue. But we dared not sit or lie down, lest the numbing sleep of the frost-cloud should take our lives away on its white, cold wings. So we even betook ourselves to quadrupedal progression. We crawled cautiously along, lowering each hand and knee with a separate care, to avoid cuts and scratches, and feeling out forward into the gloom, which seemed to press close upon our eyelids, so dense and palpable was it. We spoke to each other continually, lest we should become separated. Over and over again I put forth my hand for the next step, and, upon quietly dropping it, found nothing under it. That was a sign that I was within six inches of some precipice. Then I called a halt, and cautiously advanced one foot over the brink. If I could reach a footing below, we crawled down; if not, we coasted along the edge, or tried another course. Over how many hundred feet of sheer descent I may have hung by the slippery hold of one hand and one knee,— over what dark and empty depths, floored with edged and pitiless ledges, teeth of primeval stone, I put out helpless hand or foot into the ghostly gloom,— I know not, nor do I care to know; but the helplessness of the unseen gesture yet burdens my memory. It has often haunted my rest. For years, if any slight disorder superinduced a dreaming condition, I was in dreams at intervals driven by cold mists or viewless winds through interminable chasms walking up to heaven, where I saw that seeking gesture repeated to infinity. Over every ledge would then be put forth a helpless hand, pointing to me, clutching at the thick mist, holding wide-spread fingers stretched stiffly out, sweeping slowly hither and thither, vibrating up and down in frantic indecision; indicating dreadful variations upon the solitary theme of utter and desperate loss and helplessness.

"So we wandered, until it became evident, as, indeed, it would have been before, if we had reasoned deliberately, that we should shortly become absolutely unable even to crawl, and should then, of necessity, fall over a crag, or stiffen and die. We, therefore, felt about for a soft rock; and having found one which, if not actually soft, was, at least, rather smoother than most, and, moreover, a little sheltered from the wind-driven frost-fog, we slept and watched alternately, in miserable five or ten minute snatches, until some time in the latter part of the night, spending the time allotted to watching in thrashing the arms about, kicking, stamping, and the other doleful manœuvres which are useful in fighting against severe cold and overpowering drowsiness. At last after an indefinite quantity — it might, so far as any perception of the passage of time was concerned, have been a week — of wretched dozing and waking, the last detachment of the dreadful fog scudded over us. The moon and stars shone out, most glorious and welcome to behold. We drained the remainder of our brandy, summoned the remainder of our strength, and resumed our last plan of getting out of the mountains, by following the fall of the water-courses. We climbed, with many falls and much danger, all stiff and chilled as we were, hardly retaining any sensation beyond our elbows and knees, and articulating only with difficulty, down into a ravine, along whose lowest rift we stumbled, sometimes in shadow and sometimes in the uncertain gleam of the moonlight, but free, at least, from the deadly cold and impenetrable darkness of the frost-fog."

Nancy's Brook and Nancy's Bridge are so familiar to all who have ever visited the mountains, or know anything of their history, that we could not, if we would, omit the incident which gave them this name.

The stream itself is about half a mile below the Mt. Crawford House, and comes rushing down from unknown heights in the dark forest above. "And any one, who has the least capability of appreciating scenes of wildness and desolation, will be amply repaid for following, for a mile, the course of the stream, among the crags, as it comes leaping in indescribable clearness and beauty down the mountain. During the lapse of ages, this stream has cut a channel, in some places thirty feet deep, through the rock, and rushes, foaming on its way, with perpendicular walls on each side. The rocks around are worn into most grotesque forms, and the eye is never weary in gazing upon the cascades and deep transparent basins. In one of its wildest portions the stream is spanned by a rustic structure called Nancy's Bridge."

Nancy was a servant-girl in the family of Col. Whipple, of whom we have before spoken in our account of Jefferson. A man, also in the employ of the colonel, had won the heart of the poor girl, and between them there was an engagement of marriage.

It was the intention of the two, or at least of Nancy, and she supposed of the man from what he had promised her, to accompany Col. Whipple on his usual fall visit to Portsmouth, and there be married. But a few days previous to the time she supposed they were to start, she gave her money, which the colonel had paid her for her services, to her lover for safe-keeping until their arrival at Portsmouth, and had gone to Lancaster, a distance of nine miles, to make some purchases necessary for the journey.

While she was away at Lancaster, suspecting no evil, the colonel and her lover set out upon their journey. Whether Col. Whipple was aware of her intention of accompanying him we cannot say. If he was not, no blame, of course, can be attached to him, but, if he was, he was equally guilty with his treacherous companion. But leaving the guilt, it is impossible to describe the grief and disappointment of the poor girl when she learned their departure without her. She had not left Lancaster when it was made known to her, but she determined at once to follow them. She immediately left Lancaster for Jefferson. At Jefferson the men in Col. Whipple's family endeavored to dissuade her from so perilous an undertaking, urging the many difficulties she would have to encounter, and that the colonel had been gone since early in the morning; but nothing could detain her. She tied up a small bundle of clothing, and set out, already wet and fatigued by her long walk from Lancaster. The snow was deep, no path but spotted trees, and night had already set in, when she again started. Since sunset, the snow had commenced falling, and a bitter north-west wind drove it in blinding masses against the almost frozen wanderer. Her object was to reach the Notch, a distance of thirty miles, where Col. Whipple had a camp, and would undoubtedly stop the night. Could she reach there before they had started in the morning her object would be accomplished. This hope buoying her up, she travelled on through the live-long night, and arrived at the camp not long after the colonel and his man had left, for the fire they had kindled had not yet gone out.

Completely exhausted and worn out, as she must have been, by fatigue and hunger, not having eaten anything since she left Jefferson, she still determined to persevere and overtake them if possible. Accordingly, after warming herself, she again set out. But it was too much; her already overtaxed strength gave out but a short distance after she had left the camp. In crossing the little stream, since called Nancy's brook, her clothes had become wet, and near the top of the opposite bank, she sat down at the foot of an aged tree to rest. Here she was found, not many hours after, her head resting upon her staff, frozen to death.

> "Cold's the snow at my head,
>   And cold's the snow at my feet;
> And the finger of death's at my eyes,
>   Closing them to sleep.
>
> Let none tell my father,
>   Or my mother so dear;
> I'll meet them both in heaven,
>   At the spring-time of the year."

When Nancy left Col. Whipple's, in Jefferson, the men who had tried to dissuade her from starting, thinking she would not go far in so blustering a night, but would soon return, did not think of following her. As the evening wore away, and she did not return, they grew anxious lest she should perish in the snow, and set out in pursuit of her. After expecting, during the whole night, their next step would bring them upon her, they at last reached the camp, where the fire she had just left was yet burning. Resting here but a few moments, they hurried on, and found her just across the brook as we have described.

The treacherous lover survived her not long, but died in a few years, a raging maniac, in a mad-house. A writer of fiction has made the moans and wailings of the poor lover to be heard even now at times around the death-place of the deceived Nancy. In the still night the mountains surrounding echo the bitter lamentations. A most amusing anecdote may illustrate all the noises of this description usually heard around the Notch. The above writer may have passed through a similar scene, and if so, he may readily be pardoned for his ghostly proclivities.

A peculiar, superstitious man, some years ago, passing up through the Notch to Lancaster from his residence in Bartlett, camped out in the woods, not far from his path. He was unused to camping in the woods, and in the outset felt some beatings of heart. He made the best of it, however, and laid down. He gained courage, and thought he should pass the night like a hero. He verged towards sleeping. It almost came to him. He was in a transition state, half-sleeping and half-waking. But, ah! what was that? A dismal sound was in his ears. What was it? Where was it? He rose up on his elbow, looked and listened. Now it comes again, right from over his head, a peal or a screech that pierced him through and through. Ah! indeed, thought he, for he dare not speak, what can that be? Now he trembled, he sweat, his head swam, his teeth chattered. He tried to think of something he should do or say. But, O! there it is again. Screech, screech, screech! It seemed as if the very hemlocks would shake off their leaves over his head. Now he was whist as the night-dew, still as he could possibly be, just breathing out from under his blanket, hoping the spirit would go; but no, there it is again. O, dear, what a screech! It comes again and again. It seems as if all the wizards in the universe were there. Now he rises up, shuddering though he did from his crown down to his very toes. For a moment he sat hesitating, one shudder following another, till he spake out, "You wizard, begone! I tell you, begone! Disperse yourself! I charge you, begone! Leave me!" He kept on in this way till finally he succeeded. The owl left, and after a while he lay down quietly under his blanket and slept.

A singular auroral display occurred a few years since at the mountains, causing almost as much wonder and astonishment to the beholders as the first appearance of the Aurora Borealis to the people of New England in 1719. A correspondent of one of the Boston papers, who witnessed the whole scene, has finely described it.

"WHITE MOUNTAIN NOTCH, *September*, 1851.

"Meteoric phenomena of such a wonderful kind were witnessed here last Saturday evening, that they seemed to those travelling in that region, who were fortunate enough to behold them, to demand some public notice, and I trust you will concur with us in our opinion, although no description, much less my own, can do justice to this singularly brilliant, and even appalling, display of celestial fire-works. During the whole of the evening we observed the ordinary tranquil aurora, illuminating a portion of the northern hemisphere, and shining with a mild, steady, white light, but remarked no variation of color or form ; and it was not till about half-past eleven that the avant courier of the coming exhibition appeared in the shape of a luminous band, stretching suddenly across the sky, oscillating with a tremulous motion. A gentleman from Philadelphia had proposed walking down into the Notch to view it by moonlight; and as we drew near it, the twin Titans guarding the entrance stood boldly forth against a sky of unusual clearness, while the mist collected in the valley, lit up by the moon and stars, resembled a sleeping lake.

"Having advanced quite a distance into the Notch, we reclined upon an elevated rock to contemplate the rugged grandeur of the cliffs as they rose in the clear, soft light, when our eyes were greeted by the above-mentioned phenomenon. As we lay flat on our backs, on a sudden, from the upper edge of the shining segment in the north, while the lower part grew dark, shot forth innumerable rays, like jets of liquid light, which preserved their form a moment, appearing like a resplendent diadem of solid diamond on the Egyptian brow of night. Oblong spots of a brilliant light now sprang into view in various quarters, which, becoming gradually elongated, burst at the top, scattering masses of light in all directions. Soon broad, shining columns emerged from different points in the horizon, moving slowly at first, then darting up with incredible swiftness, suddenly vanishing and reäppearing of increased brilliancy, eclipsing the light of the planets and moon — now chasing each other in lightning race around the sky, and finally enlarging, after infinite changes of form, so as to occupy the whole heavens. A universal, undulating motion, similar to the swell of the sea, or the motion of a wind-swept field of grain, but more rapid than the dart of the frightened serpent, now proved the precursor of increased beauty, and of the most truly amazing phenomena. A small pitchy cloud, of irregular form, appears at the zenith, which, as it were, kindles and emits tongues of flame of the most variegated and brilliant hues — green, purple, pink, golden and violet, and streams of fire, shooting in a sinuous course, as when

> 'Hell's standard-bearer,
> —— from the glittering staff unfurled
> The imperial ensign, which, full-nigh advanced
> Shone like a meteor, streaming to the wind,
> With gems and golden lustre rich emblazed;'

while, all over the heavens, cloud-like masses, flushed with the richest tints, like the glancing light on the polished steel, evolve in the twinkling of an eye countless forms of beauty, as, following the chieftain's ensign,

> 'All in a moment through the gloom were seen
> Ten thousand banners rising in the air,
> With orient colors waving.'

And sulphurous flames, seeming to issue from the mountain, darted from behind, resembling the bursting forth of volcanic fires. Such a scene, calculated to excite the noblest emotions, I never expect to behold again; it was worth a voyage across the Atlantic. It might be compared to a vast canopy, or tent, suspended from the zenith, inwrought with gold and silver, rubies and emeralds, and shaken by a mighty wind. And it would not require a vivid imagination, for one, shut in as we were by eternal rocks, with the sky kindling over our heads, to see above him the fretted roof of Pandemonium set with 'crests, fed with naphtha and asphaltus,' and around, gigantic forms reposing on their couches; or to think 'her stores were opened, and this firmament,' spouting cataracts of fire; 'impendent horrors threatening insidious fall.'

"Nearly all the colors of the spectrum were exhibited in dazzling succession, green being especially prominent, which our landlord told us, has never been seen here before, though red is quite common. Nothing was wanting except the hissing and crackling noises sometimes heard here, and frequent in high northern latitudes: the solemn stillness, however, added, I thought, to the sublimity of the scene.

"After the lapse of about half an hour, the varied colors gradually faded, and a dim, white light alone remained in the northern sky. The Aurora Borealis of Lapland, as described by Maupertuis and others, are very similar to this display. The weather at the mountains for two or three days has been the warmest of the season; the thermometer ranging ninety to ninety-eight degrees."

CHAPTER VIII.

THE SLIDES.

THE EFFECT OF THE TURNPIKE UPON TRAVEL THROUGH THE NOTCH. — COÖS TEAMSTERS. — PLEASURE TRAVEL. — WANT OF PUBLIC HOUSES. — THE FIRST HOUSE BUILT AT THE NOTCH. — MOVING OF MR. WILLEY TO THE NOTCH. — THE FIRST WINTER AFTER HIS REMOVAL. — THE FIRST SLIDE IN JUNE. — THE FEARS OF MR. WILLEY AND HIS FAMILY. — THE GREAT STORM. — THE GREAT DROUGHT PREVIOUS TO THE STORM. — THEORY OF SLIDES. — THE FIRST SIGNS OF THE STORM. — THE GATHERING OF THE CLOUDS ABOUT THE MOUNTAINS AS SEEN FROM CONWAY. — NIGHT OF THE DISASTER. — VERY PECULIAR APPEARANCE OF THE MOUNTAINS ABOUT MIDNIGHT. — RAPID RISE OF THE SACO IN CONWAY. — FIRST DISCOVERY OF SLIDES. — FIRST NEWS FROM THE NOTCH. — THE SHRILL VOICE IN THE DARKNESS. — THE CONFIRMATION OF THE FIRST REPORT. — THE MANNER OF COMMUNICATING THE NEWS. — THE TRUMPET AT MIDNIGHT. — SETTING OUT FOR THE NOTCH. — CONDITION OF THE ROADS. — THE APPEARANCE OF THE SACO VALLEY. — ARRIVAL AT THE "WILLEY HOUSE." — SEARCH FOR THE BODIES. — FINDING OF SOME OF THE BODIES. — BURIAL. — THE PRAYER AT THE GRAVE. — FINDING OF OTHER BODIES. — OXEN. — THE FIRST NIGHT SPENT IN THE HOUSE SUCCEEDING THE STORM.

"O loneliest, wildest, most forsaken spot !
  Here in the valley's lowest depth embowered,
  Reposed in humblest guise one poor, rude cot,
  Beneath its eaves the wild geranium flowered ;
On the few sharers of its lowly lot
  Plenty and Peace and Love their blessings showered.
But Danger came and rattled at its door ;
  Silence and Safety, the old warders fled,

INCIDENTS IN WHITE MOUNTAIN HISTORY. 111

> And one returned to that lone place no more ;
> A midnight darkness o'er the sky was spread,
> Lightning and storm, with flash and gusty roar,
> Loosened, and on its fearful errand sped
> The rocky avalanche, crashing, strong and blind,
> While Terror stalked before, and Death was close behind."

THE Tenth Turnpike in New Hampshire, says an old Gazetteer, was incorporated in the year 1803, December 27th, to extend from the west line of Bartlett through the Notch of the White Hills, a distance of twenty miles. It occupied the site of a laid-out but never well-finished county road, which had been projected years before. The effects of the labors of the incorporated company were soon seen in the increasing travel. In a short time from its opening it became one of the best paying turnpikes in northern New Hampshire. The only outlet to the large portion of country north of the White Mountains, beginning then to be settled, its numerous advantages were not long in being appreciated. Prior to the extension of the northern railroads, and the opening of the numerous markets along their lines, its demand, as an outlet to the Coös, was much more strongly felt than at present. The original cost of the road was forty thousand dollars, its repairs were many and expensive, and yet its dividends were large, and its stock always good.

Portland, the nearest and most accessible of the seaboard towns, was, in those days, the great market for all this part of New Hampshire. Well can we remember the long train of Coös teams which used to formerly pass through Conway. In winter, more particularly, we have seen lines of teams half a mile in length ; the tough, scrubby, Canadian horses harnessed to "pungs," well loaded down with pork, cheese, butter and lard, the drivers rivalling almost the modern locomotive and its more elegant train of carriages in noise and bluster. Hardy, resolute men were those early settlers of the Coös;

"—— Rough,
But generous and brave and kind.'

Besides this Coös travel, compelled, as it were, to pass through this gateway of the mountains, the mountains themselves had already begun to attract much attention. Visitors to them, though few in comparison with the large numbers which now resort thither, journeyed mostly in private carriages, and thus gave to their travel an importance far beyond what at the present time the same number would command.

The want of public houses on the road, especially through the mountains, to accommodate the increasing travel, was sorely felt. From the elder Crawford's to the old Rosebrook place, where recently stood the Mount Washington House, a distance of thirteen miles, there was no public house, indeed no occupied house. To appreciate fully the necessity there was for these places of shelter, one should pass north through the Notch in the depth of winter. The roads are then buried beneath the snow, piled up in drifts to a great depth. This is continually blown about by the wind so as to render impossible a well-beaten path. The traveller has, frequently, shovel in hand, to work his way through the mountains, the cold northern winds, concentrated by their passage through the Notch, blowing directly in his face, almost instantly penetrating and benumbing him.

To open, then, a public house somewhere on this distance, it was seen, would be not only a work of profit, but of kindness. For this purpose a house had been erected, some years previous to the time of which we write, by a Mr. Henry Hill,

INCIDENTS IN WHITE MOUNTAIN HISTORY. 113

and is yet standing, being familiarly known as the "Willey House." It was kept by Mr. Hill and others as a public house for several years, but was at length abandoned, and, at the time of my brother's moving into it, had been untenanted for several months. It was in the fall of the year 1825 that he first moved his family into this house. It had been roughly used by the mountain storms and winds, and needed much repairing. The fall was accordingly spent in making it comfortable for the winter. He enlarged the stable, and made such other improvements as time would allow, to make it a comfortable shelter for man and beast. But, with all his most earnest labors, he was but imperfectly prepared for the intense cold and storms of those mountain winters. Still he was hailed as a benefactor, and often were he and his shelter greeted with as much warmth by the traveller in those mountain passes, as the monks of St. Bernard by the wanderers upon the Alps.

The winter passed, nothing unusual occurring, beyond the arrival and departure of his various company. In the spring further improvements were projected and commenced in his buildings, with the design of making them worthy of the increasing patronage. Travellers, who had been his guests, often gave us flattering accounts of his success, and not the least apprehension was felt for his safety. The first thing that particularly diversified his history and awakened his fears, was the slide which took place in June following the spring just referred to.

In the afternoon of one dull, misty day during this month, he and his wife were sitting by a window, that looked out to the north and west. Before them rose in all its grandeur the mountain which is called by their name, "Willey Mountain." The clouds and mists almost entirely covered the mountain; but, as they cleared up and the surface came out to view, they saw distinctly a large mass of earth beginning to move. It passed slowly on, increasing in volume and extent, stopping occasionally, as it were to take breath, and at last rushed into the valley beneath. This was quickly followed by another, less in magnitude and extent. These slides took place near the house, and did no injury beyond greatly exciting their fears.

They were startled by them, and took counsel from their fears at first to leave the place. It is said, and is probably correct, that my brother, under the first panic, was even about getting ready his carriage to carry his family to some place of greater safety. He felt for the moment that he must leave.

But still it is certain he did not leave the place. He grew more calm in a short time, and, not long after the period referred to, became almost entirely unapprehensive of danger. I never saw him after this event, but was told repeatedly that he apprehended no danger to himself or family from what had passed. In conversation with a person on the subject, in reply to a query as to his feelings in relation to the recent slides, he said, "Such an event, we know, has not happened here for a very long time past, and another of the kind is not likely to occur for an equally long time to come. Taking things past in this view, then," said he, " I am not afraid." This was certainly fair reasoning on the matter, and such as we might all well make under like circumstances, though now we can see, in the light of all that is past, how little it availed in respect to the calamity that awaited him so soon. His unsuspicious calmness did not protect him from danger. It rather presaged evil than good. It was the dreadful felt stillness that often, perhaps always, precedes the earthquake.

Now we perceive that the events we have written above had a dreadful significance in them.

In August, succeeding the June we have just referred to, a storm took place in the region of the White Mountains, raging in and about the Notch with peculiar violence. It was memorable for its strength and for its disastrous effects. It can never be forgotten while a single individual shall exist that lived anywhere near the place in which it transpired, or any care be taken to transmit the account of it to succeeding times. I lived at North Conway at the time of it, and can, therefore, best present what I have to say from that point.

Previous to the time in which this storm took place, there had been a long and heavy drought. The earth, under a fervid sun, had dried to an unusual depth. This prepared the way for the surface of it to be operated on more powerfully by any quick and copious rain. The soil, dried deep and powdered somewhat, would slide easier under the pressure of any accumulating waters, especially if the roots of plants that traversed it had been made tender by the long-continued heat that had been upon them. In this, perhaps, we have as good a theory of slides as any that can be made.

As the month verged towards its closing, signs of rain began to appear. Clouds gathered on the sky, and though they would disperse in a short time, quickly they would gather again. They continued to do this a number of days in succession, every day assuming more permanence than they did the preceding one. At length they became so condensed, that they gave rain, small in quantity to be sure, but some — a signal of what was to follow. In this way, things went on till the storm came on in its strength.

The great disaster, in the destruction of my brother and

his whole family, consisting of his wife and five children, together with two hired men, took place on the night of the twenty-eighth of this month, August. That day came on Monday, and the disaster took place some time during the night of that day. I was away from home on an exchange the Sabbath previous, and remember well all the circumstances and events of the gathering storm. On Monday, as I came home, I recollect I was hindered by the rain, occasionally falling in showers; so that, though I had but comparatively a few miles to come, I did not reach home till near sunset.

On my way, as I came up from the south toward my residence, I had the most favorable opportunity to note the gathering clouds. Their movements were all before me, and I had only to look and see them. I had often seen storms gather in the regions of those compacted and elevated mountains, but never before with such grandeur and awfulness. The clouds were not so rapid in motion as I had seen before, but their volume and blackness made up, and more than made up, for the want of speed. Their comparative slow movement, indeed, added greatly to the sublimity of their appearance. They reminded one of some heavy armed legions moving slowly and steadily to battle. As they sailed up the giant outline of mountain range extending from Chicorua peak northward for miles, till you come to the White Mountains, and then, pressing upon them, covering them fold after fold with their dark solemn drapery, I could but think of the march of Napoleon, and the measured tread of his infantry, loaded heavily with armor, moving on to some warlike encounter.

They were, in all truth, the very significant portents of a most affecting scene of destruction. As we anticipated, things in the sequel transpired. At the close of that day, when the darkness was just coming on, it began to rain; and such a rain I never knew before. The way for it had been prepared, and now it came on in its fury. I was not conscious of all of it, especially the latter part. Being somewhat fatigued, I retired early and slept soundly. As it appeared afterwards, I slept calmly while others, not very far off, my kindred, even, were suffering and dying. Not long after midnight, I was waked suddenly by the slamming of a large door, on the barn, that was ajar and playing in the wind. I arose quickly and went out. As I passed round the corner of the house to go to the barn, which stood north, in the direction of the White Mountains, my eyes fell directly upon them. I saw something about them unusual. It was all clear overhead, not a cloud on the sky, and the moon shone brightly. The storm had passed off. On the White Mountains there lay, close down upon them, a large, dark covering of clouds. It appeared like a pall thrown over sugarloaves of unequal heights. Save this, all above and about them was clear and cloudless.

Out of them were seen, at short intervals, vivid lightnings. I heard no thunder; I saw only the lightnings. They continued till I had done my work, and returned to the house. These were unusual as we have said; but whatever there might be in them, peculiar in character, we may consider them now the after scene of the storm, just passed, and as impending the spot where death had just ceased its revel.

I had remained in the house but a short time when word came to my door that the intervales were being entirely covered with water, and that they must immediately be cleared of the cattle and horses that were upon them. As we came up from the intervales, having accomplished the object, we could but take notice of the marked effects of the storm on the White Mountains. There was plainly visible to the eye the terrible devastations it had produced. All the portions of them facing the south indicated clearly the desolating influences of the rains that had fallen so copiously on their summits and sides. I never saw such in all my life; and I had looked on those mountains, upon an average, scores of times every week for years. It was judged that more destruction of trees, and more displacing of rocks and earth, were made on the declivities of the mountain facing our post of observation, on that terrible night, than had been made since the country was settled. And this was but a part of the destruction produced. On other sides of the mountains, quite round the whole circumference, were gorges and grooves, made deep even on the hard mountain surface, to show that the destroyer had been there.

We were so occupied on Tuesday, the day succeeding the storm, with what was directly before us,— the heavy flood sweeping over the fields so near at hand, and the sight of wasting on the mountains looming up before us, — that we could hardly think of anything else.

On Wednesday early, perhaps on Tuesday, suggestions were made a few times in my hearing respecting things about the Notch; starting the inquiry how the storm might possibly affect my brother and his family. They were but suggestions, however, indicating no particular anxiety in relation to their safety, as there was certainly none with myself or any of his kindred near me. As yet we had heard nothing from him up nearly to the close of Wednesday.

Near the close of that day our suspicions were, for the first time, really aroused as to the safety of my brother's family. Dr. Chadbourne, our physician, on his return from

Bartlett, whither he had been on a visit to his patients, informed us that he had heard the whole family were destroyed. He had seen at Bartlett a man, who had just come down through the Notch, who had given him the information. So entirely unsuspicious had we been of any danger to them, and so unprepared for the reception of such tidings, that for the moment we were overcome.

Recovering somewhat from the stunning effects of such sad tidings, we went immediately to a sister's, who lived near. She had heard the same reports; but both of us, arguing rather from our hopes than the facts, were inclined to disbelieve the story. To satisfy ourselves, however, further on the subject, it was thought best to go at once to my father's, who lived two miles north of us, near Bartlett. Mr. Thompson, my sister's husband, and myself, accordingly set out.

We found him having received the news as we had, from the same source, and about the same in amount of information. He was entirely unimpressed with the correctness of the report, and immediately calmed our fears. He said he knew the Notch well, which was the fact, all its bearings and relations, and though he had heard what he had, still he did not think, from the best judgment he could make, that the family were destroyed. Though they were not in their late place of residence, he thought they were alive in some retreat, whither they had fled from the ruins of the storm. The idea that the family were all destroyed was too much for him to entertain. He thought that, notwithstanding all which had been reported, and all the danger that must have surrounded them that dreadful night, still they were among the living.

The calmness and reasoning of my father almost entirely reässured and convinced us that the rumors must be entirely incorrect. We sat some time conversing, and the evening was considerably advanced before we left for home.

It was quite dark, and very still. Our minds still occupied with the recent storm, and its terrible ravages, we were suddenly startled by a sharp, shrill voice, coming apparently from the river below us on the right, and saying, as we thought, "They are there." Breaking so suddenly upon the still night, it was like the shrill cry of some bird of prey piercing the darkness. It was many minutes ere we could collect ourselves to come to any satisfactory conclusion concerning the voice. Being nearly opposite Mrs. Lovejoy's, the mother of my brother's wife, we at length concluded that the family had had additional tidings from the Notch, and that one of the sisters was informing some one on our side of the river of the safety of the family at the Notch, and that they were all in their late home.

As we learned afterwards, we were correct in the conclusion at which we arrived; but not in the words of the speaker. It was "They are not there," instead of "They are there."

Much relieved by the contradictions of the first report by later news, as we supposed, we hastened home. Though we had seen on every hand the terrible ravages of the storm, — the mountains scathed and torn by the torrents, and the waters running in floods at our feet, before and behind us on all sides wasting destruction, — yet, so anxious were we that it should not be true, and so strangely forgetful of the awful danger which must have threatened our brother, that we retired to our beds almost entirely relieved of our anxiety.

But that delusive impression did not remain long. It did not continue through the night. The dawn of another day had scarcely come, when renewed tidings from the Notch made it quite certain that my brother and his family were destroyed. The manner in which these tidings were transmitted to us, at a certain point of their progress, it may not be uninteresting here to present. It shows how in all respects the whole scene of the Notch disaster was filled up with the most thrilling and soul-stirring incidents.

As I have said, my father was comparatively little moved under the first heavy tidings that came from the Notch. He reasoned them all down with his usual tact and calmness, and made them the occasion of little serious alarm to himself and others. But he must be corrected. He had come to a wrong conclusion, and a messenger was already on his way that would correct him. This messenger arrived in the adjoining neighborhood of my father about midnight, to which we have already referred, when that shrill female voice was heard in the darkness. He was there stopped by the Saco, swollen still with the effects of the recent storm. But he carried important tidings which must be communicated. He was sent for this very purpose. So, to get ears to hear them, he stood on the river's brink, the nearest possible point to my father's, and sounded a trumpet. It was a shrill blast, and startled all my father's neighborhood from their repose.

The startled sleepers, soon gathered on the river's bank, learned the sad tidings, but too truly confirming the reports of the previous evening; and then started most of them on their way to the Notch.

I did not hear that blast of the trumpet, — or those blasts, for the first was often repeated, — but those that did, say they never heard anything so impressive and solemn. At any time they would have been startling, pealing as they did through the darkness of midnight. But, under the circumstances before us, they were peculiarly impressive. The sad tidings of the evening before, though not generally credited, had yet left a deep impression and sadness on the minds of all in my father's neighborhood. With these feelings they had retired. Whether sleeping or waking, dim images must have been floating through their minds, from the evening's conversation, when suddenly they were roused by repeated trumpet-blasts, raising echoes from mountains in almost every direction.

> "Bursting suddenly, it calls and flies,
> At breathless intervals, along the skies,
> As if some viewless sentinel were there,
> Whose challenge peals at midnight through the air."

My brother, who heard these trumpet-calls, has often said he never heard anything to be compared with them for what was awe-inspiring and even dreadful in its character.

The confirmed reports soon reached all the relatives of the destroyed family. By daylight the news was spreading in all directions, and people were starting for the Notch. We went generally on foot, there being a few horses in the train until they were intercepted by the swollen river. We passed this river in boats and on trees fallen across it, the bridges being mostly carried away. With little of interest to diversify our way, save some additional reports that my brother's family were destroyed, we approached the scene of destruction, entering the opening a hundred rods perhaps below the Notch House, which was still hidden from our sight by an intervening ascent. We met the first great slide, which had crossed our path on level ground, and even ascending some, so great was the force which propelled it from the base of the mountains. After passing this, which consisted of large rocks, and trees, and sand, and which was impassable, except by footmen, and reaching the elevation,

WILLEY SLIDE.

we came in full view of the Notch House, and all the ruins that surrounded it. On our right stood in lengthened prospect the precipitous mountain, which had been riven by the fires and tempests of many succeeding years. On our left and in front, the mountains, though once covered with a wood of pleasant green, now presented their sides lacerated and torn by the convulsions of the recent storm. The plain before us appeared one continuous bed of sand and rocks, with here and there the branches of green trees and their peeled and shivered trunks, and old logs, which, from their appearance, must have long been buried beneath the mountain soil. With these the meadow which stretches along before the Notch House was covered, and so deep, that none of the long grass, nor alders that grew there, were to be seen. Moving on from this site, we came upon the next large slide, which continued till it met that of another, which came down below the Notch House, and within a rod of it. Thus far it was one continued heap of ruins, and, beyond the house, the slides continued many rods. The one back of the house started in a direction, in which it must have torn it away, had it not been arrested by a ridge of land extending back of the house to a more precipitous part of the mountain. Descending to this point, the slide divided, and sought the valleys, which lie at the base.; one part carrying away in its course the stable above the house, and the other passing immediately below it, leaving the house itself unimpaired.

Over this crude and extended mass of ruin we reached the house about noon. Many persons had already arrived there from both above and below the Notch. Some search had already been made for the bodies in that part of the slide, just described, which came down below the house. That not availing anything, there was a pause in this direction about the time our party arrived. The slide which we have referred to above as dividing back of the house, again united directly in front of it, and flowed on in the bed of the Saco, down the valley. Following down this slide, the accidental moving of a twig disclosed some flies which prey usually upon infected animal matter. Search was immediately commenced about this spot. This search soon disclosed one of the bodies. Immediately the news came to us, and we were soon crowding to the spot. It was no long time before the body first discovered was fully uncovered, and another not far off. These were the bodies of my brother's wife, and one of the hired men, David Allen. They were dreadfully mangled, especially my brother's wife. Scarcely a look of her, as seen in life, could be perceived about the remains. The body of my brother was soon found, near where those of his wife and hired man had been discovered. This was injured less than those of the two preceding. It could be recognized easily in any place by an intimate acquaintance.

All these bodies, after suitable time to make coffins from materials such as could be obtained there, were made ready for burial. It was decided to bury them near the house of their recent habitation, and let them remain there till they could be more conveniently moved to Conway the succeeding winter. One common wide grave was dug for them, and they were placed in its margin, to remain till the befitting and accustomed prayer at burial was performed. That prayer was made by a personal friend of my brother, and one who often ministered in holy things. The prayer was suited to the occasion, coming from a kind, sympathizing, pious heart. It was impressive as it came from the good man's lips; and then its impressiveness was greatly increased from the circumstances under which it was made. In the echoes that were awakened by his voice, the very mountains around us seemed to join with him in describing the majesty of God, and imploring his mercy on our stricken hearts. When, with slow and distinct utterance, the minister, at the commencement of his prayer, referred to the magnificence of the Deity, as described by the Prophet Isaiah, saying, "Who hath measured the waters in the hollow of his hand, and meted out heaven with a span, and comprehended the dust of the earth in a measure, and weighed the mountains in scales, and the hills in a balance," the echo gave back every word of this sublime description in a tone equally clear and solemn with that in which they were first uttered. The effect of all this was soul-stirring beyond description. I shall never forget the tears and sorrows that marked the faces of many that stood around that open grave, on that solemn occasion. The minister who made that prayer was Elder Samuel Hasaltine, then of Bartlett, now living in Bethel. After the prayer we buried the bodies, —

> "And then, one summer evening's close,
> We left them to their last repose."

It was dark before the burial was completed, and we were compelled to spend the night in the house so lately left by the buried family.

The next day the most of us left for our homes. Some remained to make further search for the bodies yet undiscovered. In the course of the day, the body of the youngest child, about three years old, was found, and buried near those of its parents, without any special religious service. Search was continued still the succeeding day, and the body of the eldest child, a girl of twelve years of age, and the other hired man, David Nickerson, were found and buried in the same manner. The bodies of the remaining children, two sons and a daughter, have never been found. They were covered so deep beneath the piles of rubbish, that no search has ever come at them. From the magnitude of the slide, and the amount of matter thrown into the valley, it is more remarkable that so many of the bodies were found, than that these were not found.

The destruction was complete; no living creature about the premises escaped it, except my brother's dog, and his two oxen. He had two horses, which were crushed beneath the falling timbers of the stable. These had been dragged out and exposed to view when the party I was in first arrived on the fatal spot. The oxen were imperiled by the disaster, but escaped without any material injury. One of them was crushed to the floor by falling timbers, but not killed. The other, standing by his side, being more sturdy, resisted them, so that they broke over his back, and, when found, he stood upright amid the ruins about him. In this condition, one crushed to the floor, and the other standing, they remained from Monday night until the next Wednesday morning.

They were then released by a Mr. Barker, the man who first visited the scene of ruins after it transpired. Coming down through the Notch, from the north, he reached the spot about sunset on Tuesday, and took up his lodgings in the vacated house for the night. When the hush of stillness and desertion, he first found about this house, became more settled, as he lay in his bed trying to compose himself to sleep, being weary, he heard a low moaning, as from some living creature. Under circumstances to interpret this most darkly, as being perhaps the suppressed wail of one of the family still living, — and, yet, not able to accomplish anything by rising, on account of the deep darkness in the house and about the premises, and unable to get any light to reliev eit, — he lay terror-stricken and sleepless till the dawn of day. With the first ray of light he arose, and, after a little search, found the cause of his excitement. It was the crushed ox we have referred to, moaning under the pain and uneasiness of his situation. He immediately released him from his confinement, and soon proceeded on his way down toward Bartlett and Conway. This was the man that brought to us the first tidings respecting the great disaster.

So far we have sought to bring out somewhat minutely the points in the great destruction of my brother and his family, so richly deserving a record and the lasting remembrance of all who survive them. Here we might cease, perhaps; still there may be lingering inquiries, with some, demanding attention. How were the family destroyed? What were the main circumstances pertaining to the great event of their destruction? In what manner did the great slide from the mountain, directly back of the house, which was certainly the agent of their destruction, come to bear upon them so as to produce their deaths?

In attempting a reply to these queries there is obviously nothing to aid but conjecture. There is no definite knowledge within our reach to bring to such a work.

> "Sire, mother, offspring — all were there;
> Not one had 'scaped the conqueror's snare,
> Not one was left to weep alone;
> The 'dwellers of the hill' were gone!
> Say, whither are those dwellers gone?
> Bird of the mountain, thou alone
> Saw by the lightning from on high
> The mountain-torrent rushing by;
> Beheld, upon its wild wave borne,

The tall pine from the hill-top torn.
Amid its roar, thine ear alone
Heard the wild shriek — the dying groan —
The prayer that struggled to be free,
Breathed forth in life's last agony !
In vain — no angel form was there ;
The wild wave drowned the sufferers' prayer ;
As down the rocky glen they sped,
The mountain-spirits shrieked and fled ! "

CHAPTER IX.

THE SLIDES, CONTINUED.

THE FAMILY DOG. — THE FIRST CONJECTURE IN REGARD TO MANNER OF DESTRUCTION. — SECOND CONJECTURE. — THIRD CONJECTURE. — THE DREAM. — WHY ALL WERE DESTROYED. — THE MUTILATION OF THE BODIES. — DAVID ALLEN. — THE GREAT RISE OF WATER. — THEIR TERRIBLE SITUATION DURING THE STORM. — THE EFFECT OF A STORM UPON A FAMILY IN THE SAME HOUSE A YEAR AFTER. — THE STORM.

THEY all perished together, and this was rather remarkable. Some one or more of the children, since the moving of their parents to the Notch House, had generally been with their relatives in Conway. That they should all have been at home, then, at the time of the disaster, and all have perished together, may be deemed as giving a peculiar aspect to the whole matter. Friends might have wished it otherwise, on some accounts, and yet, we must say, it was best as it was. No one survived to endure the deep anguish that must have come from the destruction of all his nearest kindred.

We have said if one of the family had survived we might have had some information about it. If even the family dog could have spoken, he would have told us more about the sad event than we now know. He would have described one of the most heart-rending scenes ever witnessed. He probably accompanied the family, as they commenced their march to death from their dwelling, but escaped by his superior sight and agility. We infer this from some contusions on his body discoverable when first seen after the disaster. This dog, to the best of his power, did try to inform some friends of the destroyed family of what had happened. Soon after this disaster, and before any news of it had come to Conway, this faithful dog came down to Mr. Lovejoy's, and, by moanings and other expressions of deep inward anguish around the persons of the family, tried to make them understand what had taken place; but, not succeeding, he left, and after being seen frequently on the road between the Notch House and the residence of the family just referred to, sometimes heading north, and then south, running almost at the top of his speed, as though bent on some most absorbing errand, he soon disappeared from the region, and has never since been seen. He probably perished through grief and loneliness combined with exhaustion of body.

In the absence of any exact information, then, from any quarter, respecting the manner of the destruction of the family, we are shut up entirely to the force of conjecture, as we have said. That most commonly indulged is this:

The family, at first, designed to keep the house, and did actually remain in it till after the descent of most of the slides. From the commencement of the storm in its greatest fury they were, probably, on the alert, though previously to this some of them might have retired to rest. That the children had, was pretty evident from appearances in the house when first entered after the disaster. My brother, it is pretty certain, had not undressed; he stood watching the movements and vicissitudes of the awfully anxious season. When the storm had increased to such violence as to threaten their safety, and descending avalanches seemed to be sounding "the world's last knell," he roused his family and prepared them, as he could, for a speedy flight, trembling every moment lest they should be buried under the ruins of their falling habitation.

At this hurried, agitating moment of awful suspense, the slide, which parted back of the house, is supposed to have come down, a part of which struck and carried away the stable. Hearing the crash, they instantly and precipitately rushed from their dwelling, and attempted to flee in the opposite direction. But the thick darkness covering all objects from their sight, they were almost instantly engulfed in the desolating torrent which passed below the house, and which precipitated them, together with rocks and trees, into the swollen and frantic tide below, and cut off at once all hope of escape. Amidst the rage and foam of so much water, filled, as it was, with so many instruments of death, they had no alternative but the doom which was before them.

Others have supposed that, as the storm increased during the night, thinking the stable a safer place than the house, being constructed of stronger materials, they went into the stable before the destructive slide came down which carried them away; and there they met death by the part of it which fell, and the mingled current of sand and timber which produced the fall, and were borne along on its course to where they were afterwards found. This conjecture arose, probably, from the fact that the remains of such of the family as were discovered were found very near the timbers of that portion of the stable which was carried away.

There is still another conjecture respecting the manner of the great disaster, suggested by a dream of my eldest brother, James Willey. In his dream he thought he saw the brother that was destroyed, and asked him why he and his family left the house, as they did, and thus exposed themselves to dangers abroad, when they might have been more safe at home. This has often been asked. In reply to this, my brother remarked that they did not leave the house until the waters rose so high in front, and came up so near, that they found they would carry away the house; so, to avoid being drowned, they took some coverings for shelter against the storm, and went out to the foot of the mountain back of the house, and from thence, soon after, were carried away by the great slide that came down in that direction.

This is an explanation of the manner of the disaster of which we might never have conceived but for the dream. But, when taken up from this source, it adjusts itself better to the great facts in the case than either of the theories we have heretofore considered. It explains why a bed was found on the ruins near the body of the eldest daughter. That bed was needed as a shelter from the storm, in the retreat the family made to the base of the mountain.

The theory of the dream, too, explains why the family were all destroyed, and some did not escape. On the supposition of the first theory, that the family fled precipitately from the house when they heard the crash of the stable, and were soon engulfed in the part of the great slide that ran below the house, it has always seemed strange to me, at least, that such as were in the rear of the fleeing party did not pause, or recede, even, when they found those in the advance carried off by the moving mass, and, perhaps, giving a sudden outcry that there was danger in the way. But, on the supposition before us, the family, just previous to the slide, were grouped together at the foot of the mountain. In this situation they would be an easy prey to the massive slide, coming upon them in its force, and be carried away before it in a body.

So, too, in regard to another point in the history of the great event; the great mutilation of all the bodies that were found after the disaster. The theory before us explains that better than either of those previously named. Under the idea that these bodies started from the base of the mountain on their way to death, we can better understand why they were so mangled, than if we conceive them just starting from the house on such a destiny. In this case, they would have a longer course over which to pass, and that course full of instruments suited well to disfigure and mar their bodies. We refer now particularly to the stable and its falling timbers, as furnishing those instruments. This stood in the path the bodies would naturally travel in passing from the base of the mountain to the place of their discovery after the disaster. It may be clearly seen, then, how the facts in the case sustain, so far, the theory of the dream, since, by means of that, we can much better conceive why the bodies were so mutilated, than why they should be so on the supposition that they started from the house, less distant from their deposit in death, and that less distance not so pregnant with instruments of mutilation.

In speaking of the disfigured condition of the bodies, we may properly refer to that of Allen, the hired man, first found.

This man, in life, was distinguished as one physically peculiar among all his race; earnest-looking, full and muscular in body, quick and strong in motion. In death he exhibited just the appearance those charactèristic features would naturally give him. He was found near the top of a pile of mingled earth and broken timbers, with head rather elevated, and hands clenched hard, and full of broken sticks and small limbs of trees.

> "The fragment in whose clenched hand told
> How firm on life had been his hold."

In these hands, and the position of his body, he gave clear evidence that before his death he had had a fierce struggle with the elements of ruin about him, and that at last he was overcome, and perished only in circumstances of peril, where no amount of bodily strength or agility could avail him, and from which no mortal could escape.

How long, it might be queried, now, was the conflict which this man had with the elements of ruin about him, before he finally perished? Was it commensurate with the signal marks of energy and firmness in the conflict itself, such as were stamped on every part of him in death? A solution of this query is certainly desirable. If, as suggested by the first conjecture, his course of contention with the elements of death were considered as extending only from the house to where he was found, such a course might be deemed too short for displaying such fierce encounter with the elements as he did, or exhibiting such marks of injury upon his person as were presented at the time he was found. But, if we consider his course to be from the base of the mountain to the bed of death on which he was found, then he had ample space to display all the energies of his strong physical nature. Commencing the struggle at the very onset of the slide, battling with the rocks and trees as they came upon him, trying to retain his hold on the ground at the foot of the mountain by grasping the small twigs and plants there, and then being torn away from them or with them in his hands, and carried down to the falling stable, and then again, if still alive, grasping its timbers, for relief, but finding some rather heavy beatings and bruisings on various parts of his body when he passed down to the end of his course he would be thoroughly beaten in the conflict, and exhibit just the marks of violence he did on his person.

There is another thing in this conjecture, accounting for the manner of the disaster, that is worthy of observation. This makes the rapid and elevated rise of the water about the house as the great reason why the family went back to the foot of the mountain, and there perished. Aside from this theory we might never have thought of such a state of things; and yet, when once presented, we see that it harmonizes perfectly with all the great facts in the case. We need the disclosure of this, indeed, to explain what has always been known in relation to the great disaster. Everything above and below the Notch House seems to point to a high and rapid rise of water there. In Conway, where I lived, twenty-five miles below this house, the water, on the night of the disaster, rose twenty-four feet in about seven hours. The Saco was forded about nine o'clock on the evening of that night, and, by daylight the next morning, its waters, as far down in their course as Bartlett and Conway, had risen, by exact admeasurement, twenty-four feet, as we have said, covering all the intervals, in those towns, on both sides of its usual channel. It is reasonable, then, to infer that there must have been a high and rapid rise of water at its source near the Notch House. And, besides this, all the mountains in the region of the Notch and Notch House indicated the pouring out of such torrents of rain from the clouds on their peaks and sides, as must have produced a great flood of water in those places. Slides on a mountain, produced by a common rain, generally begin slightly, at their summits, and increase as they go down; but here, from the very summits, the earth and rocks were driven down, as if some immense cistern had been emptied at once upon them. The great idea in reference to this seems to be, that before, the great storm came on in its strength and force, ample preparations had been made for it. We have already referred to this fact.

All the day previous to its commencement at nightfall, and even before that, for days, lighter clouds had been collecting; but all that day, especially, heavy, dark clouds, surcharged with water, were seen sailing up from the south, in close succession, and resting on the White Mountains.

With all this resource of clouds thus collected and embodied on such a spot, it was only necessary to compress them, and then would come a tempest in its strength. The magazine was ready — touch it, and it would pour out water enough to deluge all the region beneath it. This, from observation, seemed to be just the effect of the storm through all the great ravines from the Notch down below the Notch House. Pass down or up through all the length of that great ravine, and, under your feet and on either side of you, all that distance, you would see the very effect on mountain and plain, such as would come if great bodies of water were poured on them at once. Excavations in the hard earth were made so deep, large rocks were moved so far, stone and wooden bridges were so upturned, as to convince you, beyond a doubt, a deluge of water, far beyond what was ordinary, had been in their midst.

The above theories are undoubtedly the only ones that can be presented to point out the manner by which the family perished. Beyond these we cannot possibly conceive of another by which the great event could transpire; and which of these was the one expressing the real mode of it, we do not wish, even, to give our opinion. With the main facts before the eye of the reader, such as we have drawn out at some length, we had much rather he should decide for himself which is most probable. In the absence of certain knowledge, it is most likely that different persons may come to different conclusions respecting it. Where there is nothing but conjecture to guide any one in making up an opinion, certainly no one will be holden precisely to that of another. Every one for himself will make up the judgment he may think the great facts in the case shall best warrant. But, after all, the mere manner in which the family were destroyed is not the great thing. There are things enough known respecting it to give it a strong claim on our attention. We know the family perished; and we know the circumstances of their death must have been distressing beyond description. Bring them, for a moment, before your imagination. The avalanche, which only two months before had nearly caused their instantaneous death, if it had not induced timidity, must have greatly increased their sensibility to danger, and filled them with ominous forebodings when this new war of elements began. Add to this the horror of thick darkness that surrounded their dwelling; the tempest raging with unbridled violence; the bursting thunder, peal answering to peal, and echoing from mountain to mountain with solemn reverberation; the piercing lightning, whose momentary flashes only rendered the darkness and their danger the more painfully visible; huge masses of the mountain tumbling from their awful height, with accumulating and crashing ruins into the abyss below; their habitation shaken to its foundation by these concussions of nature; — with all these circumstances of terror conspiring, what consternation must have filled the soul! And then, the critical instant when the crashing of the stable, by the resistless mass, warned them to flee, if we adopt the first theory respecting the manner of the disaster; or, if we adopt the last, when, amidst the very enginery of death all about them, as they went back to the foot of the mountain, every moment expecting to perish by lightning, or moving rocks and timbers that swept the face of both mountain and plain like a destroying besom; who can enter into their feelings at such a crisis of the wildest uproar and confusion? It is impossible for any one now living, or any one who lived at the time of this destruction, to sympathize at all with the agonies of spirit that filled them to the surfeit. We may task our imagination to the highest point possible within our power, and we could not do it. We may strain our conception of mental horror and impressions of soul that might come upon us under the most startling forms of impending death, and, after all, we should fail entirely of coming to the dreadful reality. We may combine our deepest conceptions of what is dreadful in a moment of imminent death, with the most vivid descriptions, from books or friends, of what others have felt as they stood trembling on the verge of ruin, and still we could not comprehend what was felt by the family of my brother, when they went out from their dwelling on the terrible night of their destruction, and not only trembled under apprehension of death, but met it and realized it under one of its severest forms.

The best conception which any one could have of what was suffered by the family, on the eve of their destruction, was realized by a family which, for a time, occupied the same house from which they perished.

For the same reason that my brother and his family moved into the house, another man, named Pendexter, with his family, moved into the same house, more than a year after the terrible disaster. His object was mainly to afford entertainment for travellers during the winter; as, during that season, it was more needed in that spot than during the other seasons of the year. Some time after his removal, a heavy storm took place. It was not so severe as the one that destroyed my brother's family, but still it was severe enough to give one some pretty clear conception of the force of that. The same general movements, probably, transpired in the latter storm, that did in the first, though not so great in degree. During the progress of this, there were successive events of a most awe-inspiring character. At one time would be seen the sharpest lightning followed by the heaviest thunder; then would be seen streams, arising from the concussion of rocks on the face of the mountain opposite the Notch House, ascending from the base to the very summit, lighting all the valley about with a brilliant light. At the same time, the noise from the concussions would reverberate strong enough to drown the heaviest thunder. All the time, too, these lights were shining, and the peals of heavy thunder were alternating with concussions of rocks on the mountain sides such as to make the very earth tremble under your feet, the rain was pouring in deafening torrents. These impressive circumstances of the storm, together with reflections of what passed in the same house months before, so affected the then resident family, that not a word was spoken for near half an hour. They stood and looked at each other, almost petrified with fear. And yet, this storm, as we have intimated, was very much inferior in power to the one we have been considering, and which brought on the great disaster that has occupied so much of our attention.

In closing this whole account of one of the most terrible storms ever transpiring, we cannot do it better, perhaps, than in the words of Byron:

"The sky is changed! and such a change! O night,
And storm, and darkness, ye are wondrous strong!

                    Far along,
From peak to peak, the rattling crags among,
Leaps the live thunder ! Not from one lone cloud,
But every mountain now hath found a tongue,
And Jura answers, through her misty shroud,
Back to the joyous Alps, who call to her aloud.

Now, where the quick Rhone thus has cleft his way,
The mightiest of the storms hath ta'en his stand ;
For here, not one, but many, make their play,
And fling their thunderbolts from hand to hand,
Flashing and cast around ; of all the band,
The brightest through these parted hills hath forked
His lightnings, — as if he did understand,
That, in such gaps as desolation worked,
There the hot shaft should blast whatever therein lurked."

CHAPTER X.

THE SLIDES, CONCLUDED.

THE STORM AS WITNESSED BY ONE AT THE MOUNTAINS. — THE VIEW FROM BETHLEHEM. — RAPID RISE OF THE AMMONOOSUC. — CONDITION OF CAPTAIN ROSEBROOK'S FARM. — SLIDES AS FIRST SEEN. — FALLS OF THE AMMONOOSUC. — DIFFICULTY OF REACHING CRAWFORD'S. — ATTEMPT TO ASCEND THE MOUNTAINS. — THE CAMP. — GREAT DESTRUCTION OF TREES.

OUR account of this remarkable storm and its effects would be very imperfect were we to omit the following, written by a gentleman who was on the spot directly after the storm had passed:

"The rains had been falling nearly three weeks, over the southern parts of New England, before they reached the neighborhood of the White Mountains. At the close of a stormy day the clouds all seemed to come together, as to a resting-place, on these lofty summits; and, having retained their chief treasure till now, at midnight discharged them in one terrible burst of rain, the effects of which were awful and disastrous. The storm continued most of the night; but the next morning was clear and serene. The view from the hill of Bethlehem was extensive and delightful. In the eastern horizon Mount Washington, with the neighboring peaks on the north and on the south, formed a grand outline far up in the blue sky. Two or three small fleecy clouds rested on its side, a little below its summit; while, from behind this highest point of land in the United States, east of the Mississippi, the sun rolled up rejoicing in his strength and glory. We started off towards the object of our journey, with spirits greatly exhilarated by the beauty and grandeur of our prospect. As we hastened forward with our eyes fixed on the tops of the mountains before us, little did we think of the scene of destruction around their base, on which the sun was now for the first time beginning to shine. In about half an hour we entered a wilderness, in which we were struck with its universal stillness. From every leaf in its immense masses of foliage the rain hung in large glittering drops; and the silver note of a single unseen and unknown bird was the only sound that we could hear. After we had proceeded a mile or two, the roaring of the Ammonoosuc began to break upon the stillness, and now grew so loud as to excite our surprise. In consequence of coming to the river almost at right angles, and by a very narrow road, through trees and bushes very thick, we had no view of the water, till with a quick trot we had advanced upon the bridge too far to retreat, when the sight that opened at once to the right hand and to the left drew from all of us similar exclamations of astonishment and terror; and we hurried over the trembling fabric as fast as possible. After finding ourselves safe on the other side, we walked down to the brink; and, though familiar with mountain scenery, we all confessed we had never seen a mountain torrent before. The water was as thick with earth as it could be without being changed into mud. A man living near in a log hut showed us how high it was at daybreak. Though it had fallen six feet, he assured us it was ten feet above its ordinary level. To this add its ordinary depth of three or four feet, and here at daybreak was a body of water, twenty feet deep and sixty feet wide, moving with the rapidity of a gale of wind between steep banks covered with hemlocks and pines, and over a bed of large rocks, breaking its surface into billows like those of the ocean. After gazing a few moments on this sublime sight, we proceeded on our way, for the most part at some distance from the river, till we came to the farm of Rosebrook, lying on its banks. We found his fields covered with water, and sand, and flood-wood. His fences and bridges were all swept away, and the road was so blocked up with logs that we had to wait for the labor of men and oxen before we could get to his house. Here we were told that the river was never before known to bring down any considerable quantity of earth; and were pointed to bare spots, on the sides of the White Mountains, never seen till that morning. As our road, for the remaining six miles, lay quite near the river, and crossed many small tributary streams, we employed a man to accompany us with an axe We were frequently obliged to remove trees from the road, to fill excavations, to mend and make bridges, or contrive to get our horses and wagon along separately. After toiling in this manner half a day, we reached the end of our journey; not, however, without being obliged to leave our wagon half a mile behind. In many places, in those six miles, the road and the whole adjacent woods, as it appeared from the marks on the trees, had been overflowed to the depth of ten feet. In one place, the river, in consequence of some obstruction at a remarkable fall, had been twenty feet higher than it was when we passed. We stopped to view the fall, which Dr. Dwight calls 'beautiful.' He says of it, ' The descent is from fifty to sixty feet, cut through a mass of stratified granite; the sides of which appear as if they had been laid by a mason in a variety of fantastical forms; betraying, however, by their rude and wild aspect, the masterly hand of nature.' This description is sufficiently correct; but the beauty of the fall was now lost in its sublimity. You have only to imagine the whole body of the Ammonoosuc, as it appeared at the bridge which we crossed, now compressed to half of its width, and sent downward, at an angle of twenty or twenty-five degrees, between perpendicular walls of stone. On our arrival at Crawford's, the appearance of his farm was like that of Rosebrook's, only much worse. Some of his sheep and cattle were lost, and eight hundred bushels of oats were destroyed. Here we found five gentlemen, who gave us an interesting account of their unsuccessful attempt to ascend Mount Washington the preceding day. They went to the 'Camp' at the foot of the mountain on Sabbath evening, and lodged there with the intention of climbing the summit the next morning. But in the morning the mountains were enveloped in thick clouds; the rain began to fall, and increased till afternoon, when it came down in torrents. At five o'clock they proposed to spend another night at the camp, and let their guide return home for a fresh supply of provisions for the next day. But the impossibility of keeping a fire where everything was so wet, and, at length, the advice of their guide, made them all conclude to return, though with great reluctance. No time was now to be lost, for they had several miles to travel on foot, and six of them by a rugged path through a gloomy forest. They ran as fast as their circumstances would permit; but the dark evergreens around them, and the black clouds above, made it night before they had gone half of the way. The rain poured down faster every moment; and the little streams, which they had stepped across the evening before, must now be crossed by wading, or by cutting down trees for bridges, to which they were obliged to cling for life. In this way they reached the bridge over the Ammonoosuc, near Crawford's, just in time to pass it before it was carried down the current. On Wednesday, the weather being clear and beautiful, and the waters having subsided, six gentlemen, with a guide, went to Mount Washington, and one accompanied Mr. Crawford to the 'Notch,' from which nothing had yet been heard. We met again at evening, and related to each other what we had seen. The party who went to the mountain were five hours in reaching the site of the camp, instead of three, the usual time. The path for nearly one third of the distance was so much excavated, or covered with miry sand, or blocked up with flood-wood, that they were obliged to grope their way through thickets almost impenetrable, where one generation of trees after another had risen and fallen, and were now lying across each other in every direction, and in various stages of decay. The camp itself had been wholly swept away; and the bed of the rivulet by which it had stood was now more than ten rods wide, and with banks from ten to fifteen feet high. Four or five other brooks were passed, whose beds were enlarged, some of them to twice the extent of this. In several the water was now only three or four feet wide, while the bed, of ten, fifteen, or twenty rods in width, was covered for miles with stones, from two to five feet in diameter, that had been rolled down the mountain and through the forests by thousands, bearing everything before them. Not a tree, nor the root of a tree, remained in their path. Immense piles of hemlocks and other trees, with their limbs and bark entirely bruised off, were lodged all the way on both sides, as they had been driven in among the standing and half-standing trees on the banks. While the party were climbing the mountain, thirty 'slides' were counted, some of which began where the soil and vegetation terminate; and, growing wider as they descended, were estimated to contain more than a hundred acres. These were all on the western side of the mountains. They were composed of the whole surface of the earth, with all its growth of woods, and its loose rocks, to the depth of fifteen, twenty, and thirty feet; and wherever the slides of the projecting mountains met, and formed a vast ravine, the depth was still greater."

CHAPTER XI.

BARTLETT.

GENERAL FEATURES. — ROCKY BRANCH. — INCIDENT ON ITS BANK. — INCIDENTS OF ELLIS' RIVER. — FIRST SETTLEMENT. — LOSS OF THE HORSES. — SNOW CAVERNS. — BROTHERS EMERY. — HUMPHREY'S OBSTINACY. — THEIR PERILOUS ESCAPE FROM FREEZING.— HON. JOHN PENDEXTER. — HIS REMOVAL FROM PORTSMOUTH. — CHILDREN. —" RAISING " SCENE. — MRS. PENDEXTER. — THE GREAT DISTANCE OF A MARKET. — DIFFICULTY OF REACHING MARKET. — TRAPS FOR CATCHING WILD ANIMALS. — THE COMMON LOG TRAP. — FIGURE FOUR. — PEQUAWKET MOUNTAIN. — ADVENTURE WITH A RATTLESNAKE. — THE " CHAPEL OF THE HILLS." — MRS. SNOW. — ITS DEDICATION.

> " Go, call thy sons ; instruct them what a debt
> They owe their ancestors ; and make them swear
> To pay it, by transmitting down entire
> Those sacred rights to which themselves were born."

BARTLETT is a small, irregular-shaped town, lying near the White Mountains, having Jackson on the north and Conway on the south. Saco river runs through it, in a circling course, making almost a semicircle within its limits. On both sides of this river, through all its course in the town, is good land, to some extent from its banks ; and that is about all the good land the town affords. You soon come to the mountains, after you leave this stretch of land, which generally correspond with the course of the river in the direction of their ranges. None of these mountains are so large as to claim any particular notice.

Rocky Branch, a stream tributary to the Saco, empties into it near the centre of the town. It runs with a rapid current, most of the way from its starting, over a rocky bed, as its name indicates, till it mingles with its confluent stream. It rises very rapidly in times of great rains, as do most other streams in the region. At the time of the great disaster near the Notch, when my brother's family were destroyed, it was the scene of a most thrilling incident.

Previous to this time, near down to where it flows into the Saco, on a spot of level, smooth land, familiarly called Jericho, a man by the name of Emery had built a small log cabin, and moved his family into it. In the night, the same on which the great disaster occurred on the Saco, this stream, in the vehemence of its rapid, high-swollen current, brought down so many trees, and rocks, and logs, from the land along its banks, that it formed a sort of dam just below the spot on which the cabin stood. This made a pond of water, which started the cabin from its foundation, and buoyed it up on its surface like a boat. Here the family were, in the depth of a dark stormy night, with the water roaring in their ears, at the mercy of an angry flood. Their feelings in this situation can much better be imagined than expressed. They did the best they could, went into the highest part of the cabin, and there awaited the fearful issue. They expected every instant to be engulfed in the waters. For long hours, with little to be seen, but almost everything dreadful to be heard, they held death steadily before them. Their prospect of escape, under the circumstances, was the frailest imaginable. But they survived the peril. The waters at last subsided, their little ark rested on a miniature Ararat, and the family escaped to the mountains. For deep tragic interest this holds a place next in order to the great Notch disaster itself.

A little to the east of Rocky Branch river is another, called Ellis river, running about in the same direction from the White Mountains and emptying likewise into the Saco. This, in its general character, is very much like the preceding, rapid in its current, and very much affected in its rising by heavy rains. On the same night in which the incident occurred we have just recited, another took place on this river, showing the sudden and high rise of water on all the streams among the mountains at that time. Near its course up in Jackson, through which it flows on its way to Bartlett from its origin in the mountains, a man had a yard, into which he had collected some colts, to keep through the night. During that night, the river, rising near the yard, rose so high, that, flowing over its banks, it swept all the colts out of it, and carried some of them a longer distance down its current, and some a shorter one. They were all destroyed, however; some of their bodies, mangled by the rocks and roots lying along in the rough bed of the stream, went down as far as Bartlett, a distance of miles.

Bartlett was originally granted to William Stark, Vere Royce, and others, in consideration of services rendered by them during the French and Indian war in Canada. Capt. Stark immediately divided up his grant into lots, offering large tracts to any one who would settle on them. Two brothers Emery, and one Harriman, were among the first who located themselves permanently in the town. Settlements had been commenced at this time in most of the towns surrounding the mountains. In 1777, but a few years succeeding the Emerys, Daniel Fox, Paul Jilly and Capt. Samuel Willey, from Lee, made a settlement in Upper Bartlett, north of those already located. They commenced their settlement with misfortunes as well as hardships. Their horses, which they had brought with them, dissatisfied with the rich grazing land on the Saco, started for their former home in Lee. As it afterwards appeared, instead of following the Saco in all its turnings and windings, as the settlers did, the horses struck directly across the mountains to the south. On the first mountain they separated, some going further to the east and others to the west. This was all learned long after the loss. Diligent search was made at the time, but to no purpose. In the spring following the disappearance of the horses, some dogs brought into the settlement the legs and other parts of a horse. Suspecting that they might be parts of those they had lost, they followed the track of the dogs, and only about sixty rods from the settlement came upon the carcass of one. The horse had evidently been dead but a few weeks. He had sustained himself, it appeared, during the winter on browse, being protected from the cold by those immense snow-caverns which are frequently formed on the mountains. The snow had formed an entire roof over the tops of the thickly-matted trees, leaving the space beneath completely free and hollow. In one of these snow-houses the horse had lived all the winter. Flocks of sheep have been known to be protected so from the cold, coming out healthy and in good condition in the spring.

Most amusing stories are told of these brothers Emery. Enoch and Humphrey were their names, the mention of which, to this day, will provoke a smile. In their general characteristics they differed almost as much as it is possible for two individuals to differ. Enoch was frank, open, generous and manly in his nature, while Humphrey was sullen, obstinate and contrary. Humphrey had been haying. He was returning at the close of the day to his house with a large load, which he was drawing with a small yoke of oxen. On his way was a sharp, steep hill, which he was much afraid his oxen would be unable to surmount with the load. He was much worried, and it was with considerable anxiety that he reached the foot of the hill. Here he accidentally was met by one of his neighbors. He had not time to tell him his fears before his neighbor had already said, "Mr. Emery, your cattle will hardly be able to haul that load up this hill, will they?" This instantly roused Humphrey's opposition. Always differing, he could do no less than differ now. Not raising his head, he replied, in his sullen, dogged tone, " They shall do it;" and, plunging the brad into his poor oxen, made good his word.

Though differing so much from each other in their dispositions, these brothers were uniformly kind and attached to each other. They accommodated themselves to their several peculiarities, agreeing in all things to agree and disagree. The expedients of Enoch to manage Humphrey were many and ingenious.

In the depth of winter, once, both these brothers, living near each other, went into the woods to get out some timber. The cold was very intense, and, before they could get fairly to work, so as to warm themselves, Humphrey became very much chilled. Enoch felt the cold, but not so severely. He realized, however, that he needed a fire, and perceived that Humphrey needed it more than himself. The first thing for them, therefore, was a fire. Having fire-works with him, and being most active at the time, Enoch set himself to kindle one. But his fire-works did not work well. He failed to get from them, as soon as he expected, what he sought; and seeing Humphrey sinking under the cold, and fearing to consume any more time in trials upon them, lest Humphrey should perish before he succeeded, he resolved on some other expedient to warm him. He made appliance to his temper, which he knew to be generally quick and irritable. But this failed for some time, owing to Humphrey's being so benumbed with the cold. At length, however, he succeeded. He was roused. Then all that concerned Enoch was to keep out of his way. They ran over bushes and stumps and logs till they both dripped with perspiration.

Hon. John Pendexter came into this town, from Portsmouth, at an early period of its history, and planted himself down on the southern part of it bordering Conway. Here he spent the rest of his life, living to the advanced age of eighty-three years.

He, together with his wife, made their way to this spot through many hardships, and endured many after they arrived at it. They came a distance of eighty miles in winter, she riding on an old, feeble horse, with a feather-bed under her, a child in her arms, and he by her side, hauling his household furniture on a hand-sled. Nor was it a well-prepared home to which they came in this way,— a warm, neat house and cultivated lands,— but a forest mainly, and a rude cabin. These were all they had to cheer them on the way, besides some warm hearts already living near the place of their destination; such as they knew would greet their coming. And these were enough. Cheered on by them, at length they attained the end of their course, husband and father, wife and child. And here it may be remarked, that this child was cradled in a sap-trough, and ultimately became the mother to a class of sons and a daughter, all of whom do honor to their parentage; but one, especially, is a man very distinguished for talent and enterprise.

INCIDENTS IN WHITE MOUNTAIN HISTORY.   153

Under the labor of these hardy pioneers, the wilderness around them soon gave place to fruitful fields; and the rude cabin was exchanged for a nice, well-proportioned dwelling-house.

Mr. Pendextēr was a plain, earnest man, and for years was especially useful, in the region where he lived, as a carpenter. We have often seen him, with crews of men around him, in different places, engaged in preparing frames for the rearing; he, with dividers and rule in hand, marking the work for them, and they executing it with mallet and chisel and auger.

We have seen him often, too, when this preparatory work was done, and the frame was ready for raising, acting as master in the enterprise. There he stood, in his cherished element of life. "Men," said he, at the proper time, "are you ready, all ready?" "Yes," the response would be, "all ready." "Well, then, take her up, take her up, I say — bravely, bravely! There she goes, there she goes! Now man those spy-shoves well! Stand to your pick-poles firm! There she goes! there she goes! It's well done! well done! Look out for the feet of those posts there — see that they are entered in their places. There she goes again! Steady, now, steady, boys — steady! She is most up. Don't throw her over! Steady, boys, steady! steady! steady! there she is. All done. Now fasten her there, and make her sure."

Mrs. Pendexter, as we have seen, was the worthy helpmeet of such a man as he, braving the hardships of an emigrating life, and doing all in her power to make the home of his selection a retreat of quietude and plenty. She lived to a very advanced age — ninety-two years. Having known her well in our youth, but not having seen her for some twenty years or more, we made a friendly call upon her at a certain

time. She was then near her end, as it proved, confined to
her bed. As we approached her, in company with her
youngest son, who stood at my side, he, perceiving that she
did not know me, as he suspected from the beginning she
would not, said: "This is Mr. Willey, mother, who has come
to see you." "Mr. Willey!" she replied, "I don't know
who that is." "It is Mr. Willey," said he again, "the
minister. Don't you know him?" "Why, no," she replied once more, leisurely, "I don't know him," keeping her
eye on me all the while. "You know his father well," said
he again, "Esq. Samuel Willey. This is his son, that is a
minister." Still she did n't know me, she said. Then, taking the right conception, he said: "Mother, this is Ben
Willey, come to see you. You knew him once, when he and
his sister Hannah used to come and play with Patty and me.
This broke the spell. Inclining her head to me, and pressing
my hand still in hers, where it had been from the beginning
of the interview, she said, with an expression of face we shall
never forget: "O, yes, now I know him! How glad I am to
see you once more!" Her age, for a moment, seemed to be
renewed. That appellation, "Ben Willey," by which we
were often spoken of familiarly in our youth, was a ray of
light, playing with thrilling effect across her mind, and
carrying it along back, over the scenes of her long, eventful
existence, to earlier times.

Dover was the nearest market at this time; and thither the
settlers were obliged to go for all provisions and necessaries
not raised on their farms. In winter the journey was more
easily accomplished than in summer. With snow-shoes and
a hand-sled it was not esteemed a very hard task. In summer, however, it was exceedingly difficult and tiresome.
Rude boats were usually dug out from trees, large enough to

hold several hundred weight, and then substituted, at this season of the year, for sleds. The many falls and rapids of the Saco made this anything but easy. The heavy boat, heavily ladened, had to be carried around each rapid and fall; and, in the stillest water, managed with much skill, to keep from the many rocks and snags.

Frequently, during their absence, the river would rise to such a height as to be entirely impassable for days. The poor wives and children were once obliged to live on seven potatoes a day, for many days, until the river fell, and their husbands could cross.

Most of the living of the early settlers was the game which they captured. Deers and bears, and other smaller animals, were almost as common in those times as squirrels now. But little powder was used, it being too costly, and difficultly obtained. Traps and snares, of many devices and shapes, were used in its stead. A description of some of the more common may not be uninteresting, as illustrating the ingenuity of our fathers. Large steel traps were used by those who could afford them; but a majority of the settlers were too poor. The most common was a trap constructed of logs, on the principle of the common box-trap for catching mice and squirrels. A small log-house is first constructed, complete, with the exception of one end. A log door is then fashioned exactly to this end, and made to play up and down in grooves cut in the logs. Through the opposite end to the door is placed a long pole, having the bait on its inner end, and holding by its outer end the long pole which runs over the house, and raises the door. All baited, it is left for its prey. The hungry bear, suspecting evil, advances and retreats many times ere he ventures to enter. At length, after due amount of smelling and growling, his appetite overcomes his prudence;

and cautiously, at first very cautiously, he puts his head inside the door. He is not perfectly certain, yet, that there is no danger, and would like to get the bait without exposing more of his body; but he cannot do it; and, after reaching and stretching till out of patience, he determines to substitute speed for caution, and dashes at the bait with all his might. The fierceness with which he seizes the meat shakes the two poles from their fastenings; and down comes the door, leaving old bruin to lament his folly.

Another contrivance is to build a house in the same manner as the preceding, with like walls and covering. But, instead of such a door as there used, take timbers so small that they will bend, especially at one end; or, if large timbers are deemed best, hew them down so that they will yield to pressure at one end; place these in the ends of the house, in such a way that the elastic ends will approach each other somewhat, giving them, when all put up, a tunnel shape; the end of those outside farthest apart, and those within the house nearer together. Thus constructed, with bait put far into the house, the bear will press into the tunnel, the elastic ends of it yielding to the pressure of his body, and obtain the bait and the inside of the house. But now he has gone too far to retreat; the elastic ends of the timbers coming to their natural position, after the pressure of his body is taken from them, he is forbidden to return.

Another mode still for catching him was by means of a trap called the figure four. Put together large timbers, by passing over them other smaller transverse timbers, and fasten them together so as to make a large door, heavy enough to crush a bear. Put under the door, one side of it, a piece of timber answering to the diagonal in the Arabic figure four. Then add another, adjusted to this diagonal by a groove, and an edge on one of them, that answers to the horizontal part of such figure; then another, adjusted to both the diagonal and horizontal timbers, by a groove, an edge, and what are called gains, answering to the perpendicular line in such figure. Now put all these together, and you have a prop for the door we have named. When the door is placed on such a prop for use, put on the end of the horizontal timber that goes under the door the bait for the bear. Thus arranged, when the bear shall take hold of the bait to eat it, he must stand under the door, and, in devouring the bait, he must necessarily disarrange the figure, and bring the covering over him down upon his back.

In the south-east of this town, lying partly within its bounds and partly in Chatham, rises up one of those huge mountain piles, standing upon the outskirts of the White Mountains, and guarding, as it were, the approach to the central cluster. Pequawket Mountain is a wonder of itself; and, separated from all its companions, is worthy of a journey of many hundred miles. It rises up, in the form of a pyramid, or perhaps more cone-like, over three thousand feet, its southern sides, from base to summit, all visible to the beholder. The many surrounding mountains stand out from it on its lower sides, leaving it an isolated cone, towering up in all its majesty, and revealing its huge bulk in all its gigantic proportions. From the south it is seen nearly as soon as Mount Washington, and the view from its summit is quite as extensive, and much more satisfactory. A large hotel is built upon its highest point, and the cupola, covered with tin, is distinctly seen a distance of thirty or forty miles, glistening in the rays of the sun.

Game was very plenty in former days around the base of this mountain, and even to this day can be found here if anywhere. If one has the courage to explore the almost impenetrable swamps around its base, he cannot fail to find fine shooting and fishing. The many little hidden ponds are the favorite resort of multitudes of wild fowl in their season, and every secluded brook is overflowing with trout. Bears are occasionally seen upon its sides, or in its ravines and valleys, but are very timid and shy.

Berries are very plenty, of all kinds, upon its sides, and, in their season, it is the resort of the inhabitants for many miles around. A most exciting scene occurred once, to our own knowledge, during one of these berrying excursions. It was in the season of blueberries, and a large party had gone out, and among them a young lady, a member of my own family. The party had wandered far up on the mountain, where the growth was scantier and smaller. In the crevices amidst the rocks, and in the little, secluded nooks, lying under the vast piles of rocks and earth, the berries were very large and thick. The party had become much scattered, each selecting his own place of picking, and designing to come together again at a spring further down on the mountain. The young lady I have before mentioned had wandered away entirely alone. On one of those big moss plats so common, under the lee of an overhanging cliff, she found the berries uncommonly thick and large, and, suspecting no danger, sat down, and, in her eagerness to gather the whole, commenced a most rapid picking. How long she thus remained she does not remember; but, suddenly feeling something move in her apron, she looked, and in her lap was coiled up a monster rattlesnake! The spiral form was already assumed, and, with head erect, almost at her very throat, he already was vibrating his huge body, and commencing his fatal rattle. Springing, with a piercing shriek as she perceived her danger, she threw him many feet from her, and fell, unconscious, to the ground. The cry brought others immediately to her assistance, and, more dead than alive, she was led from the spot which had been so near witnessing her death.

In Upper Bartlett, near the old "Hall Stand," so well known to travellers, stands a neat little building, known as the "Chapel of the Hills." Its conception and erection has in it much of interest. A party of Boston people, tired of the dust and heat of the city, sought relief up among the mountains of New Hampshire. While stopping at the "Old Crawford House," daily becoming more and more impressed with the wonderful works of God around them, and feeling their hearts drawn out more, each day, in adoration to so great a Being, suddenly the thought occurred to them, What is the religious condition of these people around whose habitations God has so displayed his power and might? On inquiring, they learned that much might yet be done to advance their religious interests. An article was prepared by one of the party, on the subject, for the Christian Witness, of Boston, which met the eye of Mrs. Snow, a warm friend of the American Sabbath School Union, and, as special attention had been called to the *children* of the mountains, she offered two hundred dollars to aid in building a Sabbath School Chapel at some eligible point high up the valley of the Saco.

Rev. Mr. Souther, an agent of the Union, and an earnest and efficient laborer in the cause of Sabbath Schools, immediately made known the offer to the people of Upper Bartlett, and urged upon them the importance of its acceptance and their active coöperation. He labored with much zeal to stimulate them to raise the amount necessary to build such a building, and soon saw his labors blessed in the erection of a neat house of worship, every way adapted to their wants, and which, in its style, finish and appointments, is exceedingly creditable to their public spirit.

Mrs. Snow died two or three months before the chapel was completed. Her last act was to direct the payment of fifty dollars, completing her appropriation; thereby showing how much her heart was enlisted in the matter. "But, though dead, she yet speaketh." Eloquently she is yet speaking to those who visit these hills not to forget the spiritual wants of the dwellers among these mountains. Eloquently she is yet pleading with those inhabitants themselves to prize highly the privilege which they already enjoy, and to be ever ready for that glorious voice:

> "Sink down, ye mountains; and ye valleys, rise!
> With heads declined, ye cedars, homage pay!
> Be smooth, ye rocks; ye rapid floods, give way!
> The Saviour comes!"

And to the one who may minister within the walls of this little chapel she appeals most earnestly:

> "To the young, in season vernal,
>   Jesus in his grace disclose;
> As the tree of life eternal,
>   'Neath whose shade they may repose,
> Shielded from the noontide ray,
> And from evening's tribes of prey;
> And refreshed with fruit of love,
> And with music from above."

The account of the dedication of this chapel we give in Mr. Souther's own words:

"The dedication took place Jan. 21, 1854. Some ten

days previous, a missive reached me, so remarkable for its brevity and explicitness, that I transcribe it:

'BARTLETT, *Jan.* 7, 1854.
'To the REV. SAM. SOUTHER:
  'Our house is done, and we are going to dedicate it two weeks from this day, and we want you to attend, without fail.
  'Yours, truly,
  'SPENSER KENISON.'

"The twentieth was stormy. Leaving home in the midst of the whirling snow, it seemed exceedingly doubtful whether I should be able, the next day, to make my way up our snowy valley in season for the dedication services. The ministers expected to lead in the exercises failed; and when I reached the house, at about eleven, a crowded congregation was anxiously awaiting what turn affairs would take. Though taken thus unawares, I could not hesitate, when pressed into the novel service of preaching the dedication sermon. Ps. 122 : 1 — 'I was glad when they said unto me, let us go into the house of the Lord' — furnished an appropriate expression of my feelings, in being called to aid in setting apart this humble edifice to the worship of God, and it was a joyful occasion.

"There, at the foot of the dark gorge from which the Indian recoiled in terror as the abode of the Great Spirit, we had met to seek the presence of the God we worshipped, and to ask him to make His dwelling-place with us in the house we had built.

"Among these frowning heights around and above us, He had often manifested himself in the tempest and the fire. We asked that in the house we now consecrated to the ministrations of the word, He would come often by the still, small voice, that convinces of sin, and leadeth to repentance and faith in Jesus.

"The fact was not forgotten that the chapel owed its existence to the affectionate interest of a pious heart, in the religious instruction of children, and we left it in charge of the dwellers among the mountains, as the gathering point, on God's holy day, not only for themselves, but their children and their children's children through successive generations."

CHAPTER XII.

JACKSON.

THE VALLEYS OF THE MOUNTAINS. — THE DIRECTIONS IN WHICH THEY RUN. — MOOSE POND. — MOOSE BATHING. — MOOSE. — THE CONWAY HUNTER. — THE LEAP OF A MOOSE OVER A HORSE AND SLEIGH. — EAGLE LEDGE. — MINERAL RESOURCES. — GENERAL FEATURES OF JACKSON. — BENJAMIN COPP. — HIS ENDURANCE. — MR. PINKHAM'S ACCOUNT OF HIS FIRST ENTRANCE INTO JACKSON. — THE HOG. — THE HOUSE. — SCARCITY OF SALT. — INCIDENT OF CAPTAIN VERE ROYCE. — TORNADO. — EXPEDIENT TO SAVE CHILDREN. BEAR STORY. — FREEWILL BAPTIST SOCIETY. — ELDER DANIEL ELKINS.

"Princes and lords may flourish, or may fade ;
*　　*　　*　　*
But a bold peasantry, their country's pride,
When once destroyed, can never be supplied."

LIKE streets in some vast city, the high walls on either hand so completely overshadowing them that the sun but peeps into them in his course, and is gone; so the valleys run round among the many spurs and ranges of these mountains, into the vast depths of many of which he penetrates not deep enough to melt away the winter's snow. Most of the snow in the lowest ravines, it is said, is carried away by the little streams which run through them. These thaw out in the sunshine further up on the mountains, and, swollen to twice their original size, by the melting of the snow in the spring, go rushing and foaming through the drifts in the ravines. Long, dark caverns are thus formed in many of the valleys, one of which we have described in a previous chapter.

Bartlett is the plaza, or central square, of this city of mountains. Leading into it from the south is the Saco valley, the Broadway of the mountains. Before reaching the bend of the Saco, where it turns so gracefully to the left, the little valley of the east branch of the Saco runs off to the right, separating Dundy and Pequawket Mountains, and itself dividing, one branch separating Tin Mountain from Double Head, and the other holding in its bosom one of those beautiful little sheets of water, so common in this region, called Mountain Pond. Into three great sheets this Broadway loses itself in the central plaza. The Ellis river valley runs off to the north, itself sending off another valley at Jackson, a second square in the city, the Wildcat Brook valley. Rocky Branch, starting from the same point, but running further to the south and west of Ellis river, separates Iron Mountain from Mount Crawford and Giant's Stairs, and ends, at the very foot of the highest peaks, in what is called Oakes' Gulf. The Saco valley continues on from its turning point in Bartlett at right angles with its former course for many miles, when suddenly it turns again short round to the north, separating the whole vast cluster.

Jackson, as we have said, is a second plaza, or square, in this city of hills. Near a mile above a little settlement in this town, known familiarly as "Jackson City," is a little pond, quite half a mile in length, and about as broad as it is long, where moose formerly resorted in great numbers.

Paths led to it from all the great valleys and little glades; and each morning the huge monsters might be seen stalking thither to perform their daily ablutions. In winter, as in summer, they came each morning to bathe, and, breaking the thick ice with their feet, plunged fearlessly into the cold water.

Hunters took advantage of their habit of resorting daily to such places, and would there collect in great numbers to hunt them. Like most huge monsters, they are not quick-tempered, and, until sorely provoked, are very mild and peaceable. They shun contests with man and the lesser animals of the forest, and are non-resistants as far as it is prudent to be. But, once provoked, there is nothing equal to their ire. Woe betide the unfortunate hunter who wounds without killing them. With terrible wrath they turn upon him. They run him down, and, with their monster hoofs, administer such ponderous blows, that scarcely an atom of the poor fellow is left. An early settler in Conway once barely escaped from the hot pursuit of one by climbing into the topmost boughs of a tall tree. After every means to bring him down was exhausted which the moose could devise, he took his stand at the foot of the tree, and through the whole of a winter's night kept the poor man shivering in its top. The speed and agility of these animals are almost incredible. Over Sawyer's Rock one sprang at a leap, and bounded away on the other side. One, passing up the valley above the "Crawford House," during the deep snows of winter, chanced to meet a horse and sleigh, containing a man and his wife. One must turn out. Very kindly the moose, perceiving how difficult it would be for the man to do it, and not wishing to do it himself, jumped over the whole concern, horse, sleigh, man and woman.

Not far from this little pond is a high, craggy ledge, far up whose inaccessible side, on a shelf of the rock, an eagle for many years built her nest, and reared her young. The fierce mother became a terror to the region, and many a bold heart has quailed at her scream. Her nest, consisting of sticks and twigs woven strongly together with rushes, measured more than two yards square. No hunter dared attack her alone.

Jackson is rich in mineral resources. Iron ore exists in inexhaustible quantities on Bald-face Mountain, between the rocky branch of the Saco and Ellis river in Bartlett, near the south line of the town of Jackson.

Bald-face Mountain is composed of granite, having a few dykes of greenstone trap cutting through its midst. The elevation at which the iron ore occurs is fourteen hundred and four feet above the rocky branch of the Saco, and about one mile distant. One of the veins at the upper opening measures thirty-seven feet in width in an east and west, and sixteen feet in a north and south, direction.

The second opening, two hundred feet lower down the slope of the hill, exposes the ore, maintaining the same width. Three hundred feet lower down the vein is observed to narrow, and is but ten feet wide; and four hundred feet further down the width increases to fifty-five feet.

Five hundred and forty-six feet lower still there is a small opening, or cave, twenty feet deep, where the ore narrows again. A small quantity of bog iron ore has also been discovered, five miles north from Chesley's Tavern, in the midst of the forest.

Near the house of Captain J. Trickey occur several dykes of greenstone trap, which are so highly charged with carbonate of lime, as to effervesce strongly with acids.

On Thorn Mountain occur several veins of magnetic iron ore, which are contained in a kind of granite, consisting of felspar and quartz, without any mica; being, so far as it respects its mineralogical composition, a porphyry; but not marked by squares of felspar, like a true porphyritic rock.

The iron ore is found near the top of the mountain, and on its western side. The veins are from a few inches to two and a half feet wide.

Tin ore was unknown in the United States anterior to the discovery in Jackson, and here but four veins have thus far been discovered. Here, also, are found phosphate of iron, arseniate of iron, tungstate of manganese and iron, fluor of spar, mispickel, copper pyrites, purple copper, and a native copper.

Jackson is bounded north by unlocated lands, and south by Bartlett. "It is watered principally by the two branches of Ellis river, passing from the north, and uniting on the southern border, near Spruce Mountain. The principal mountain elevations are Black, Bald-face, and Thom Mountains." When first settled, this town was called New Madbury, from the fact that most of its early settlers came from Madbury, in the lower part of the state. It retained this name till the year 1800, when it was incorporated by the name of Adams. Some years after, it was again changed to Jackson, its present name. This was done to suit the politics of the times; all of its voters but one being for Jackson, when the question was whether he or Adams should be president.

This town was first settled by Benjamin Copp. He moved into it in 1778, and, with his family, resisted the terrors of the wilderness quite twelve years before any other inhabitant moved into it. During this time, his hardships and privations must have been great. No one can well conceive of them unless he has had some acquaintance with a forest residence. Living at the present day amid a sparse population will not give one such conceptions, much less will a residence in a city or larger village do it. To be surrounded in every direction by a dense forest, extending for miles, with no neighbors to whom you might resort in times of want or sickness — with no one to whom you could speak, for months, — these form a condition in life, such as those not acquainted with them can appreciate but poorly. Mr. Copp knew what they were, and was the very man to meet them, being healthy, strong and courageous in his nature. His powers of bodily endurance were wonderful. They must have been so, or he could never have sustained the various hardships and privations he encountered.

Poor food at best, together with seasons of scarcity for articles of living, such as they were, must have worn him out soon unless he had had what we sometimes call an "iron constitution." As a specimen, to illustrate his powers of bodily endurance, it is said that he has been known often to go ten miles to mill, with a bushel of corn on his shoulders, and never take it off from the time he started from his door till he put it down in the mill. He did the same, too, on his return home. And when he stopped to talk with any one by the way, he seldom relieved himself of his burden. He rested with the bag on his shoulders.

In the year 1790, five other families came into this town from Madbury, that of Captain Joseph Pinkham, Clement Meserve, Jonathan Meserve, John Young, and Joseph D. Pinkham. Daniel Pinkham, then ten years of age, a son of the first of the above named, and the builder of the road, called by his name the "Pinkham road," thus describes the moving of his father and his family from Madbury to Jackson:

"In company with my father, mother, two brothers and one sister, I came to the town now called Jackson, the 6th day of April, 1790. I was then ten years of age. At that time the snow was five feet deep on a level. There was no road from Bartlett, about eight miles, and we travelled on the top of the snow, which was sufficiently hard to bear us. Our entire stock of provisions, household furniture and clothing, was drawn upon a hand-sled.

"I remember one incident, connected with this first trip, which shows the extent to which boys' ingenuity will go to avoid labor. We had a hog with us, which constituted our entire stock of animals. Thinking that this hog, though not very well trained to the harness, might still afford us some aid in getting the sled along, we contrived a harness for him, and hitched him on. He worked much better than we expected, and, though less fleety than the horse, and less powerful than the ox, he did us good and sufficient service.

"Arrived at our destination, we found the log-house, erected the autumn previous, half buried in the snow, and had to shovel a hole through to find a door. It had no chimney, no stove, no floor, and no windows, except the open door, or the smoke-hole in the roof. We built a fire-place at one end, of green logs, and replaced them as often as they burned out, till the snow left us, so that we could get rocks to supply their place. We had but two chairs, and one bedstead. Thus we lived till the summer opened, when we moved the balance of our furniture from Conway, where we left it on first moving to the town."

Mr. Pinkham says, further, in regard to things generally in the town, at the time his father moved into it: "At the early period of the settlement of this town, there was much poverty, and great scarcity as to means of living. Some families had cows, and could afford the luxury of milk-porridge, while others, who had no milk, were obliged to eat their porridge without milk, made of water and meal only.

"The river afforded trout, and these constituted a large portion of the living for a number of families quite a length of time. These trout were first dried in the sun, and then roasted by the fire. When salt could be had, this was used with them, to give them relish. But often, not only the fish and the meat, such as they could get, were cooked and eaten without salt, but even porridge was eaten without it. This was the best they could do in relation to sustenance. For transportation they used only hand-sleds for a number of years. For barns they built hovels of logs covered with bark. Want and hard labor were familiar to them; but hope in the future sustained them, and in time they were surrounded with sufficient luxuries of life to make them comfortable and happy."

Soon after Captain Pinkham, the father of the man giving us the above account, moved into this town, an event transpired, near his residence, of thrilling interest. He lived near a river. One night he heard, some distance below his house, on the river, what he thought was the hallooing of a bear. It resembled that of a man; but, as it was a time when men were seldom abroad, and as bears often halloo very much like a man, he thought it was one of these, especially as they were plenty in the region. Acting under this impression, he took his gun, and went out to shoot him. Coming near to the spot whence the voice sounded, and wishing not to disturb the bear, he crept softly till he came in sight of him, as he supposed, and prepared to fire. Just at this instant he heard a coughing. It was a man he was preparing to fire at, — a Captain Vere Royce. He was a surveyor, from Fryburg, come into town to survey some land; but, being late in his arrival, and intercepted by the river, he went to that point on it where he was first seen, and hallooed for assistance to get across. Waiting for somebody to come and aid him in crossing, he escaped the peril to his life we have just recited. He coughed at an instant to save him from death.

At an early period in the history of this town, one of those terrible tornadoes passed over it, which are occasionally experienced in New England. It was so strong that scarcely anything could stand before it. Houses and barns were levelled to the ground, and trees were whirled about in the air like sticks. Men and children were caught up and carried along by its resistless force for many rods. Unlike most of the other violent winds which have passed over New England, this took place in the winter. The fearful tornado, which so desolated Warner and New London, in 1821, occurred in September, and was preceded by some of the hottest weather of the season. During the prevalence of this wind in Jackson a most ludicrous expedient was adopted by one of its inhabitants to save his children from being torn from him, and borne away on its current. His house had been razed by it to the ground. Chairs, beds, bedding, tables and children, were all flying in the wind. Snatching his babes with almost superhuman strength from the embraces of the rude monster, he thrust their heads between two rails of fence, and left them thus secured, and their legs dangling in the wind, to look after his other property. The five little children remained fast to their fastening, and, uninjured, outrode the tempest.

The hill-sides in this town afford excellent grazing, and hundreds of cattle are driven here yearly for pasturing. The great number of sheep scattered upon the mountains make it the principal place of resort for what bears and wolves are yet left among these hills. Occasionally one is killed, but rarely. Several years since, a Mr. Meserve accidentally came upon one, coiled up under the roots of an up-torn tree. His little son, a lad of some eight or ten years, was with him, and first espied the monster. The boy could not make out what it was, and, much frightened, retreated precipitately to his father, exclaiming that he saw something under the tree. Trembling through fear, he could only say that it looked awful ugly, had great glaring eyes, and that he guessed it was the devil. Advancing to see what it was that had so frightened his little son, the father saw, rolled up under the roots, a large she-bear. He had with him only a gun loaded with a small charge of shot for a partridge. The prize was, however, too tempting to be lost. He had with him a huge jack-knife, which he opened and gave to his son to reach him when he should want it. He then fired directly into the face of the bear. "The old woman did n't like the treatment; but Meserve loaded, and gave another dose, when the bear starting to run, he seized his knife, jumped on to her back, caught her by the head, threw her over, and cut her throat. She was a monstrous beast, and so fat she could hardly waddle."

A Freewill Baptist church was formed in this town in the year 1803, which has existed to the present time, and flourished. Elder Daniel Elkins was its first minister. He was an honest, good man, and labored much and successfully for the good of the church and town. Nor were his labors confined to these alone. For years he was a sort of bishop in all the region. In our earlier years we have often seen his smiling face, and heard his full, earnest voice at funerals, and on other occasions, in Conway and Bartlett. We remember him, as he appeared at such seasons, very distinctly; and if we could put on canvas the exact image of him, such as now exists in our minds, we could furnish a portrait of him true to life.

His pretensions to learning were small, and, yet, he seldom failed to interest those truly learned, by his honest simplicity and meekness. He can hardly be better described than in the words of the ancient poet, Chaucer:

> " Benign he was, and wondrous diligent,
> And in adversity full patient.
> *   *   *   *   *
> Wide was his parish, and houses far asunder,
> But he never felt nor thought of rains or thunder,
> In sickness and in mischief to visit
> The faithful in his parish much and oft,
> Upon his feet, and in his hand a staff;
> This noble example to his sheep he gave,
> That first he wrought, and afterwards he taught.
> Out of the gospel he the words caught,
> And this figure he added yet thereto,
> That if gold rust, what should iron do?
> And if a priest be foul, on whom we trust,
> No wonder if a common man do rust.
> Well ought a priest example for to give,
> By his cleanness, how his sheep should live."

CHAPTER XIII.

CONWAY.

BEAUTIFUL SCENERY OF CONWAY. — AUTUMNAL FOLIAGE. — ATTRACTIONS OF CONWAY TO HUNTERS AND EARLY SETTLERS. — ELIJAH DINSMORE. — EXPEDIENT TO KEEP FROM STARVING. — STORY OF EMERY. — GREAT FRESHET. — MAPLE SUGAR. — MR. WILLEY'S ENCOUNTER WITH A BEAR. — STEPHEN ALLARD'S BEAR STORY. — SCHOOLS. — BOYS AND THE HOGS. — CONGREGATIONAL CHURCH.— DR. PORTER. — BAPTIST CHURCH. — CHATAUQUE. — NORTH CONWAY. — LEDGES. — FAMILY BURYING-PLACE. — NAMES OF THE FAMILY DESTROYED AT THE NOTCH.

> "My own green land forever!
> Land of the beautiful and brave."

"ONE who visits the Conway meadows, sees the original of half the pictures that have been shown in our art-rooms the last two years. All our landscape painters must try their hand at that perfect gem of New England scenery. One feels, in standing on that green plain, with the music of the Saco in his ears, hemmed in by the broken lines of its guardian ridges, and looking up to the distant summit of Mount Washington, that he is not in any county of New Hampshire, not in any namable latitude of this rugged earth, but in the world of pure beauty — the *adytum* of the temple where God is to be worshipped, as the infinite Artist, in joy."

The mountains in Conway, and those on her borders, are among the most important things pertaining to her location. They help, essentially, to make her what she really is, one of the most delightful spots on earth. They surround her, particularly North Conway, almost as entirely as the mountains surround Jerusalem. To appreciate this fully you have but to take a position somewhere on the main road, about three miles south of Bartlett, standing with your face to the north. On your right will stretch up a line of mountains from Rattlesnake Mountain, situated about south-east, to Pequawket or Kearsarge on the north-east. Sweeping round from this, you pass over Thorn, and Double-head, and Black Mountains, till you come, at length, to the long range of the Motes that separate Conway from Upper Bartlett. From this point you follow them down on your left till you come to their terminus, a point in the heavens about south-west from where you stand. It is a grand post of observation to occupy at any time of the year, but keep it through the season, and for majesty and beauty you get a view of scenes such as can be obtained scarcely anywhere else. In winter you will see a parapet of mountains around you, shorn, indeed, of their summer attractions, but still commanding your attention from the naked and unadorned sublimity of their appearance. Pequawket will rise up before you, like an old sentinel who has stood his post for centuries amidst the many lightnings and storms that have beat on his defenceless head.

On either side of him will be his companions, reposing soberly and solemnly under their mantle of snow. In spring you will see nature in her loveliness — the hill-tops and mountain-sides blooming in their greenness; and especially on the smooth, beautiful intervales, skirting along close under your feet, you will see grasses and flowers in such abundance as completely to cover the surface of them with their strong luxuriance. In summer, you will see the plains and the valleys, less cheerful with swelling buds and blossoms, and fresh leaves of trees, and plants, but fragrant with fruit, the cornfields ripening towards the harvest, and the golden wheatfields reddening for the sickle. In autumn, you may see the sober, mournful change upon the trees, on the mountain tops and sides, the bright green verging to the solemn carmine, and almost every other sombre pallid hue of which an American forest is susceptible. The Rev. T. Starr King thus writes to the Boston *Transcript*, in the fall of 1852:

"The only way to appreciate the magnificence of the autumnal forest scenery in New England is to observe it on the hills. I never before had a conception of its gorgeousness. The appearance of the mountain-sides, as we wound between them and swept by, was as if some omnipotent magic had been busy with the landscape. It was hard to assure one's self that the cars had not been switched off into fairy land, or that our eyes had not been dyed with the hues of the rainbow. No dream could have had more brilliant or fantastic drapery.

"Now we would see acres of the most gaudy yellow heaped upon a hill-side; soon a robe of scarlet and yellow would grace the proportions of a stalwart sentinel of the valleys; here and there a rocky and naked giant had thrown a brilliant scarf of saffron and gold about his loins and across his shoulders; and frequently a more sober mountain, with aristocratic and unimpeachable taste, would stand out, arrayed from chin to feet in the richest garb of brown, purple, vermilion, and straw-color, tempered by large spots of heavy and dark evergreen. It did not seem possible that all these square miles of gorgeous carpeting and brilliant upholstery had been the work of one week, and had all been evoked, by the wand of frost, out of the monotonous green which June had flung over nature. The trees seemed to have bloomed into roses, or rather to be each a nosegay, done up into proper shape, and waiting to be plucked for the hand of some brobdignag belle."

Darby Field says that he "found ten falls on that (Saco) river, to stop boats, and there were thousands of acres of rich meadow to Pegwagget (Conway), an Indian town." Attracted by the glowing accounts which hunters gave of these "rich meadows," settlers early came to Conway from the lower towns. The extensive tracts of intervale, from fifty to two hundred and twenty rods wide, and extending through the entire length of the town, were then covered with a thick growth of white pine and maple. Game was nowhere so plenty; fish and fowl and animals were almost as thick as in the jungles of Africa. Settlers came mostly from Durham and Lee, following an easterly course until they reached the Saco, and then going north guided by the stream. Indian villages were thickly scattered along its banks, poor and small, however, in comparison with the once flourishing settlements of the Pequawkets. This tribe had received its death-blow, and nothing but deep hatred was left them. Fear alone prevented them from murdering the hardy pioneers following up their beautiful river to take possession of the rich hunting-grounds of their fathers.

The first settlement was made in this town in 1764. James and Benjamin Osgood, John Doloff and Ebenezer Burbank, were the first settlers. Their hardships in reaching their northern homes were similar to those we have related in the history of most of these towns. One Elijah Dinsmore and wife performed the journey in the dead of winter, travelling on snow-shoes from Lee, a distance of eighty miles. A huge pack contained all their furniture, which he carried on his back. They spent their nights in the open air, and slept, if they slept at all, upon the "cold, cold snow."

An expedient of the settlers to sustain their strength, during times of great scarcity of provisions, is worth noticing. A wide strap of some skin was fastened around them; each day, as they grew more emaciated and thin, the strap being drawn the straiter. Often the buckle was drawn almost to the last hole, the wearer anxiously eying and counting the number of holes, beyond which was complete prostration.

One persevering man, named Emery, had actually buckled into the last hole, and, hardly able to stand, tottered round, expecting on the morrow to be unable to rise. A neighbor, in nearly as bad a condition as himself, crept to his door, and informed him that a moose was not far from his cabin. The poor neighbor himself would have killed him had he had a gun. The intelligence brought a little strength to Emery, and could his strap be drawn a little tighter they yet might live. They cut a new hole, and, with all their strength, the skeleton men tightened the strengthening strap. As noiseless as a shadow he crept out, and, steadying his aim with great effort, killed the moose. Together the two famished men sat down to their repast, and before the close of the following day, *it is said*, their straps would hardly reach round them.

In 1675 the town was granted to Daniel Foster, the grantees agreeing to pay one ear of Indian corn each annually for ten years. Most of the early settlers built their cabins on the intervales along the banks of the river. They regarded as of little consequence the sudden rises of the Saco until the year 1800, when the "great freshet" taught them the folly of their course, and drove them back upon the high land. Houses and barns were all swept away by this sudden rise of water. Water ran many feet deep over the whole wide intervale. On the day following the storm houses and barns were seen sailing quietly down the current, the cocks crowing merrily as they floated on. This storm occasioned great loss of property.

The extensive growth of maple afforded for many years almost the entire support of the inhabitants. Maple sugar, in almost incredible quantities, was yearly manufactured. These meadows have gradually been cleared of their growth, but even to this day orchards of this noble tree may be seen on many of the islands around which rush the waters of the turbulent Saco. The operation of making the sugar is so well described by the authoress of the "Backwoods of Canada," that we extract it in this place:

"A pole was fixed across two forked stakes strong enough to bear the weight of the big kettle. The employment during the day was emptying the troughs and chopping wood to supply the fires. In the evening they lit the fires, and began boiling down the sap. It was a pretty and picturesque sight to see the sugar-boilers, with their bright log-fire among the trees, now stirring up the blazing pile, now throwing in the liquid, and stirring it down with a big ladle. When the fire grew fierce, it boiled and foamed up in the kettle, and they had to throw in fresh sap to keep it from running over. When the sap begins to thicken into molasses, it is brought to the sugar-boiler to be finished. The process is simple; it only requires attention in skimming, and keeping the mass from boiling over, till it has arrived at the sugaring point, which is ascertained by dropping a little into cold water. When it is near the proper consistency, the kettle or pot becomes full of yellow froth, that dimples and rises in large bubbles from beneath. These throw out puffs of steam, and when the molasses is in this stage it is nearly converted into sugar. Those who pay great attention to keeping the liquid free from scum, and understand the precise sugaring point, will produce an article little if at all inferior to Muscovado."

Two bear stories illustrate the life of the early inhabitants. The first was an encounter with a bear near my father's dwelling in Conway; one which I faintly recollect, and one, too, in which my father was the principal actor. We give this in the language of my eldest brother, who was the son referred to in the description : —

"One night, in the summer of 1800, my father was waked from his sleep, by the noise of the sheep running furiously by his house. Springing from his bed to a window, he discovered, by the light of the moon, an enormous bear in close pursuit of them. Calling me instantly, then a boy about fourteen years old, we sallied forth with the gun, and nothing on but our night-clothes, to pursue this fell destroyer. By this time the sheep had made a turn, and were coming down toward the house, with the bear at their heels. Secreting ourselves a moment in a shed back of the house, until the sheep had passed, my father sprang forth with his gun. Old bruin, stopping to see what his ghostly visitor meant, was instantly fired at, and severely wounded. My father and myself, with our axes, offered him a closer combat, and he readily accepted the challenge. After two or three charges, we considered it the better part of valor to retreat to the house, which we did, closely pursued by the bear. While we were in the house, reloading the gun, the enraged animal crept up to the window, near the head of my father's bed. My mother, supposing the bear to be on the other side of the house, in attempting to look out through the window, put her head within a few inches of his nose. On discovering her perilous situation, she gave one of those piercing female shrieks which make the welkin ring, and fell back on the floor. By this time we had reloaded the gun, and now issued forth to renew the combat. But, owing to the bad state of the powder, we were unable to fire the gun again. Perceiving the bear to be gaining strength, and showing signs of an intention to retreat to the woods, after a few moments' consultation, we determined to make another desperate effort to kill him with our axes. My father, after receiving strong assurances that I would stand by him, approached the bear the second time, and drove the axe into his head up to the eye, and so finished him." This was a remarkable bear for size and boldness. He measured fourteen inches between his ears, was nine feet long from his nose to his tail. Though lean, he weighed seventy-five pounds a quarter. It was judged at the time that, if he had been fat, he would have weighed six hundred pounds. Instead of travelling in the woods, as most do, when he went from place to place, he often travelled in the public highway. On the very night in which my father had the encounter with him, and killed him, he was met by a man on horseback, on the main road."

A mile south of Conway Corner, on the road to Eaton, a small hill rises up very abruptly from a little pond of water. An early settler of Albany, a stout, athletic man, was ascending this hill one intensely dark night. Near the summit, he came suddenly and unawares into the warm embrace of a big bear. The bear, more on the alert than himself, had snuffed his approach, and, to give him a cordial welcome, had risen on her hind legs and spread out her fore ones. The man immediately knew his antagonist, and a regular contest in wrestling commenced between the two. The bear hugged, and the man tripped. By a dexterous trip, he at last threw the bear from her feet, and the two went down together. The hill was so steep that they commenced to roll over, first one top, and then the other, nothing stopping them until they tumbled splash into the pond. Crawling wet out of the water, neither felt inclined to renew the contest. The name of this man was Stephen Allard, a kind, peaceful citizen, or else certainly the neighborhood to him could never be an object of desire.

A view of some of the schools of our boyhood so well illustrates the difficulties and privations of the first settlers in educating their children, that we can but refer to them. We presume other towns might have afforded instances of as great or greater disadvantages than this town; but let Conway speak for the whole.

The first that now occurs to us was kept, literally, in a small opening in the woods. To reach it, most of the scholars had always to go in paths cut through the thick forest, and in "bad weather" on sleds drawn by oxen; and when, by such means, they reached the house of instruction, it was very poor, and illy adapted to the end for which it was designed. It was contracted in dimensions, and rude in its construction. The walls were built of rough hemlock logs, grooved together at their ends, and covered with the bark of trees, and rude boards. The something that answered for a fire-place and chimney was constructed with poor bricks and rocks, together with sticks, laid up so as to form what was called a "catting," to guide the smoke. It was lighted by panes of glass placed singly in its wall. Rude, however, as it was in structure, many a contest in "spelling and ciphering" has taken place within its walls; and many tears have been shed, and bursts of applause shaken the very bark on its roof, at the successful performance of the "Conjurer," and "Neighbor Scrapewell."

Another school, and the last we shall specify, to illustrate the general character of schools half a century since, was kept, about that time, near the place of my birth. It was kept by a veteran teacher, peculiar in his habits and aspect, keen, fearless, and practised in his business. He kept in a house we shall not describe at great length. In a few words, it was contracted in its dimensions, uninviting in its general appearance, and open on its walls and floor, so that both the light and the winds of heaven could pass freely through it. Under the house the hogs had as free access as the light and the winds of heaven had into it above. This was their cherished place of resort; and they were there, too, every day, as regularly as the scholars were to the school. They greatly annoyed the teacher, but were as acceptable to most of the scholars as they were troublesome to him. Many were the scenes of amusement, during that school, which took place with these hogs. Sometimes, after lying and rolling on the ground awhile, grunting and growling as they rooted each other's sides, they would rise up, and, brushing along under the floor, carry their bristles up through the large cracks into plain sight of the scholars. Seeing these, one of them would creep along, when the master's eye was turned, and give them a sharp pull. Then immediately would come a squeal, and after that sharp words from the teacher. "Boys! let those hogs alone; mind your studies." For a moment they would put their faces into their books, and seem content; but they wouldn't "stay put." There was a working of humor that must be gratified, and now was a good time to gratify it. Presently the bristles would be seen moving along again in the crack of the floor, and then would follow another pull, and then immediately another squeal. Now would come stronger, sterner words from the teacher. "Boys! I say, let those hogs alone. If you don't, I'll give it to you!" This, it might seem, would stop them, and it did seem to affect them awhile. But still the itching in them for fun was not yet allayed. Their fingers worked nervously to be hold of those bristles again, and provoke another squeal. Nor did they wait long before another opportunity came to indulge their craving. Soon the bristles appeared again, and then came another pull, and immediately another squeal. Now things became more serious, and the teacher must put more authority and power into his words than he had in either of the preceding cases. "Consumption, boys!"—that was the word he often used—"Consumption, boys! what do you mean? If you don't let these hogs alone I'll tan your jackets for you! I'll make your backs smoke!"

The early settlers of Conway, true to the puritan spirit of their fathers, under which they were trained, were not unmindful of religious and moral institutions. They took seasonable means toward planting these among them, for the benefit of themselves and their descendants after them.

A Congregational church was formed in this town, October 28th, 1778, consisting of Timothy Walker, Abiel Lovejoy, Thomas Russell and Richard Eastman. Soon after its formation, Noah Eastman, Abiathar Eastman, with their wives and others, were added to it. Rev. Nathaniel Porter, D. D., was the first pastor of this church, installed over it at the time of its formation. In this relation he labored with the church and people for the space of thirty-seven years; and to say that he labored well through many privations and hardships, would be saying no more than we ought to say. It is not the place here to attempt any extended view of his ministerial character. That has been given already, better than we can give it in this place. We have the opportunity, however, to say a few things respecting him here, and our heart would reproach us if we did not say them. We knew him well, being for a season his colleague in the ministry. And we knew him only to admire him; his keen, sharp eye, and his sharper intellect; his salient wit; his original thoughts, exhibited in conversation or writing; and, above all, his manifested regard, in every place, for what was the plain teaching and design of the Bible. He was a doctor, made such by one of the most discriminating, learned institutions in the land. The title was well conferred. He deserved it, not because he studied books very extensively, but because he read the few choice ones he had carefully; not because he studied classics much, or the fathers, but because he studied nature in the forests, in the grand mountains surrounding him, together with his own heart, and the hearts of others, especially in the light of God's revealed truth. Doctor Porter was poor through all his life, often, for the want of other lights, writing his sermons by the blaze of pitch knots. In going to his meetings on the Sabbath, which were always miles from his home, he generally went, in early times especially, on horseback, often facing a stiff north-west wind. The same was true in relation to the funerals he attended, and his weddings, and his visitings. He never knew much about the luxury of an easy carriage. To this it may be owing, partly at least, that he lived to so great an age — ninety-three years. In the best days of his manhood he scarcely ever failed to impress one with the deep penetration and force of his mind. Said a preceptor of Fryburg Academy once, "I had rather see anything come into my school than those keen, piercing eyes," referring to Doctor Porter. "I am afraid of them." This he said, not because he especially disliked him, but because, in connection with a few others, the doctor was deputed by the trustees to visit his school, and correct some of its irregularities. This impression had of him, by the preceptor, from a slight acquaintance, would be deepened by a larger intercourse with him. This would affect you with a feeling similar to that possessed by the poet, when he said, referring to a certain person,

> "He is a man of grave and earnest mind,
> Of warm heart, yet with a sense of duty —
> As how he must employ his powerful mind —
> That drives all empty trifles from his brain,
> And bends him sternly o'er his solemn tasks;
> Things nigh impossible are plain to him.
> His trenchant will, like a fine-tempered blade,
> With upturned edge, cleaves through the baser iron."

A Baptist church was formed in this town, August 26th, 1796. Among their ministers have been Richard Ransom Smith, father of the present Mayor of Boston; Roswell Mears, and others.

There are two villages in Conway. Chatauque, or Conway Corner, is a small village situated near the junction of the Saco and Swift rivers. It commands a fine prospect of Mount Washington and the other White Mountains, which are distinctly seen up the valley of the Saco. A splendid and capacious hotel, called the "Conway House," has recently been opened here. It is under the charge of Mr. Eastman. It is not surpassed by any hotel in the state.

North Conway, five miles further north, is pleasantly situated near the beautiful intervales of the Saco. Many families resort to this village, in order to avoid the noise, bustle and expense of the large hotel. This village is also the favorite resort for artists. Pequawket Mountain is ascended from this place. There are several fine hotels. On the western bank of the Saco, opposite North Conway, are two very high mountain ledges. The most northerly, sometimes called "Hart's Looking-glass," rises up about perpendicular six hundred and fifty feet. The other is nine hundred and fifty feet high. They stand on a level fine plain, and rise up so abruptly that you can ride to their very base. One of them is so interspersed with white quartz and bushes, as to present the illusion of a white horse ascending its side. Hence it is known as the "White Horse Ledge."

"One cannot help being struck, at North Conway, with its capacity of improvement. It might be made as lovely a spot as it is possible for this planet to hold. If some duke or merchant prince, with his unlimited income, could put the resources of landscape taste upon it, gem it with cottages, hedge off the farms upon the meadows, span the road with elms, cultivate the border hills as far up as there is good soil, the village might be made a new Eden. Or even if the inhabitants would consent to remove their barns from the most sightly places, tear down the fences from the intervale, and sod the sandy banks that fret and heat the eye on a sultry day when it turns towards the cool verdure below, the general effect would be vastly better. The beauty of the place is measured by the fact that people so seldom notice the entire lack of everything like taste which is shown in the arrangement of the houses and grounds.

On the boundary between Conway and Bartlett, near the homestead of my father, on the high bank overlooking the intervale and the Saco, is the burying-place of my family. Here rest the remains of the bodies of my brother's family recovered from the avalanche. In one wide grave they sleep, — father, and mother, and two children. Three yet sleep among the ruins of the storm. A broad stone near the entrance of the yard marks their resting-place. The following are the names of those destroyed: —

Samuel Willey, jr., aged	. .	38
Polly L. Willey,	" . . .	35
Eliza Ann,	" . . .	13
Jeremiah L.	" . . .	11
Martha G.,	" . . .	9
Elbridge G.,	" . . .	7
Sally,	" . . .	5
David Nickerson,	" . . .	21
David Allen,	" . . .	37

Two first, parents; five next, children; two last, hired men. The three first and three last have been found.

CHAPTER XIV.

FRYBURG.

THE IMPORTANCE OF FRYBURG IN EARLY TIMES. — THE GRANT OF TOWN TO GEN. FRYE. — CONDITIONS OF THE GRANT. — FIRST SETTLERS. — THEIR HARDSHIPS. — OLIVER PEABODY. — INDIANS. — SABATIS. — ENCOUNTER WITH A CATAMOUNT. — LOVE OF THE WATER. — INDIANS' LOVE FOR MR. FESSENDEN. — OLD PHILIP. — FRYBURG. — EXPEDITION TO SHELBURNE. — FRYBURG ACADEMY. — BUILDINGS. — PRECEPTORS. — PAUL LANGDON. — DANIEL WEBSTER. — AMOS J. COOK. — REV. WILLIAM FESSENDEN. — MARION LYLE HURD.

"Where the hunter of deer and the warrior trod."

FRYBURG was, in early times, the principal, and, in fact, the only village of the White Mountains. It was, for long years, the centre whence came all the fashions, and to which tended all the trade. Its favorable situation, in respect to the seaboard towns, and the rapidity with which the village grew, gave it great prominence in its early days. Every neighborhood and settlement sent its representatives, weekly, to the village, to trade, and its one long street was then a busy scene of bustle and activity. Unlike most of our villages, it sprang up, in a comparatively few years, to its full size. It stands on a broad, level plain, slightly elevated above the intervales of the Saco, which encloses it in one of its huge folds. On a broad, straight, beautiful sheet the village is principally built.

The "old Province of Maine," says Williamson, the king had no right to give away. But, in violation of all right, he did give to Gen. Joseph Frye a grant of land since called Fryburg, from its grantee. Gen. Frye had been an officer in the king's army, and received the grant in consideration of his gallant deeds on the frontiers. He had been at Fort William Henry, and escaped, with the gallant Monro, the fearful carnage which cast such a stain upon the honor of Montcalm. He was an officer in command of a company, and, it has been faintly hinted, opposed the surrender of the fort. On his return he was presented with an elegant silver-mounted sword and tankard.

The grant was made in the year 1762. The conditions of the grant were that he should give bond to the province treasurer to have the township settled with sixty good families, each of which should have built, within the term of five years, a good house, twenty feet by eighteen, and seven feet stud, and have cleared seven acres for pasturage or tillage. He should reserve one sixty-fourth of the township for the first Protestant minister, one sixty-fourth for a parsonage forever, one sixty-fourth for a school fund forever, one sixty-fourth for Harvard College forever. A Protestant minister was to be settled in the township within ten years.

The first settler was a Mr. Nathaniel Smith, a sort of *squatter*, led hither of his own free will and inclination. His cabin was reared, and his family moved into it the year succeeding the grant, in the summer of 1763. In the fall of this year, influenced by the glowing representations of Gen. Frye, came Samuel Osgood, Moses Ames, John Evans, and Jedediah Spring, from Concord, N. H. "Their path," says a true son of Fryburg, "was through the woods for sixty or seventy miles. For this distance no friendly house of entertainment on the way, in which to rest their weary limbs, or satisfy the demands of appetite — no, not even the hut of an humble peasant could be seen.

These were they who encountered the hardships, the fatigues, the sufferings, the losses attendant on the first settlers of a land so remote from the benefits of knowledge and refinement — who enjoyed the fruits of friendship even in society so narrow in its bounds — who established themselves in the bosom of an extensive wilderness, and constituted the *first civil family* on its desolate plain.

In this romantic retreat, from these small beginnings, a beautiful village has arisen ; and the population of it and the surrounding country has been beyond calculation. To those venerable fathers, therefore,

"Patient of toil ; serene amidst alarms ;
Inflexible in faith ; invincible in arms ;"

to those worthy matrons, who, with heroic courage, and fortitude of soul, set hardships and dangers at defiance, who raised with tender, fostering care, a race of hardy sons ; to their spirit of patriotism are we indebted, next to Divine Providence, for the enjoyment of this goodly land.

The nearest *white neighbors* whom they, for a long time, had, were at Saco ; and, even with those there were no means of communication. Sanford was their place of resort to obtain those articles of necessity which they could not forego ; and this was nearly sixty miles off. The only mode of conveyance was on horses, and their guides were the marked trees of the forest. If there our fathers were parched with drouth, the sallying spring would slake their thirst. If their stomachs craved food, the cold luncheon of beef or venison would satisfy the appetite. If their weary limbs demanded repose, the moist ground was the bed on which it was sought, and on which it was usually found.

After the settlement began, the town settled very rapidly. Among the long list of proprietors, we find the name of that almost ubiquitous person, Oliver Peabody, who seems to have had a hand in settling most of the towns in this region. A deed of *rights* of two sixty-fourths he obtained; one sixty-fourth better off than most of those who helped to settle only this town.

This was a favorite resort of the Indians; and, for many years after the dispersion of the Pequawket tribe, solitary members continued to linger around their old home. Old Philip, Sabatis, Tom Hegon, and Swarson, are familiar names with the old people yet. Sabatis was a great favorite with the whites, and many are the stories yet told of him. A little cross, we think, at times, perhaps when in liquor; for we have heard it said that sometimes he had to sleep out doors. The old man was a hydropathist, and always slept on such occasions with his feet in water. He was a little timid withal, and the sudden appearance of any wild animal when alone, especially during the last years of his life, would set his teeth to chattering quite merrily. A catamount caused him a dreadful fright; the adventure with which he chattered off in broken English to every one who would listen to his story. The huge fellow lay couched in a tree, and the first that Sabatis saw was his fierce eyeballs glaring full upon him. "Me hold up the gun," said he; "but me tremble so, afraid to fire; me take the gun down. Then me try it again. Hold up, but still tremble so, afraid to fire.

Afraid the gun would not go; or, if it did go, that I shouldn't hit. So me greatly troubled about it. Afraid to go away and leave her, cause then she jump on me; so must fire, or be killed. Dreadfully troubled; so me try it. By and by, hold up the gun little more steady; not so much tremble. Then I more steady, and fire. Catamount drop. She no come upon me."

Another of his hydropathic tricks was swimming among the cakes of ice, as they came down the Saco in the cold waters of the spring, diving among them, and coming up crying, "See otter! See otter!" The boys admired old Sabatis.

The Rev. Mr. Fessenden was very popular with the Indians. His son says he has seen a dozen cooking their meat in his father's fire-place at once.

> "His house was known to all the vagrant train,
> He chid their wanderings, but relieved their pain."

Major Rogers was aided in his expedition against St. Francis by old Philip, and by the few Pequawkets, of whom he was chief. During that expedition, two little Indian boys were captured by Philip and his Indians, one of whom was named Sabatis, the same probably referred to above. Old Philip joined the American army during the revolution, saying "he was a whig Indian." Swanson, a companion of Philip, was of such service to the American cause, that he was presented with an elegant sword.

At the time of the "Shelburne massacre," which we have given at length in the chapters on Shelburne and Segar's narrative, when the settlers seemed just on the eve of being all butchered by the savages, a man was dispatched to Fryburg in hot haste for assistance. Nobly did the gallant little settlement respond to the call. The messenger arrived at Fryburg a little past noon; immediately two men mounted their horses, and, proceeding up both banks of the Saco, summoned all the men, with their guns, to repair at once to the house of one Nathaniel Walker. Quickly they assembled, and learned from the messenger the terrible fate which seemed pending over their neighbors. When the call was made for volunteers to march at once to their assistance, thirty brave men stepped forward — thirty brave men, but in no condition to undertake such an expedition. Many of them were barefooted, some bareheaded, and a few nearly as destitute of clothing as the foe they designed to encounter. Before nightfall, however, the thirty men were all armed and equipped, and comfortably prepared for the march. In long Indian file they marched, Sabatis, the guide, leading the way, followed by the commander, Stephen Farrington, on horseback. Nathaniel Walker, junior officer of the expedition, himself on horseback, brought up the rear of the long file. Just after dark they forded the Saco, some two miles above the village, and, bidding adieu to their friends, struck out into the wilderness. As the sun rose over Bethel Hill the following morning, they reached the house of Capt. Twitchell. Sabatis had already discovered the Indian trail. Stopping but a few moments at Capt. Twitchell's for food, they immediately commenced their pursuit of the savages.

The Indians had the start of them more than twelve hours; how they had employed these hours may be learned from Segar's Narrative.

By the aid of Sabatis, who could track them where the whites could see no traces whatever, the party followed the Indians, till, coming to a rocky hill, even old Sabatis was at fault. "Me find um quick," said the Indian, and struck round the hill. Here they met Clark, whom the Indians had permitted to return, on condition that he should stop any party of whites who might pursue them, by representing the determination of the Indians to kill the prisoners as soon as they should find any party in pursuit.

But the men would not be persuaded; their blood was up, and, though Clark told them they could not reach the Indians till every prisoner was slain, they would not yield.

The party, old Sabatis having found the track, pushed on. They soon found the piece of *spruce bark* pegged on to a hemlock tree, to which Segar has thus referred:

"Here an Indian pulled off some *spruce bark*, untied my hands, and told me to write that, if ever we were overtaken by Americans, they, the Indians, would kill the prisoners. This bark he stuck on a tree, and then bound my hands again."

Still, Captain Farrington was for passing on, but at length yielded to the unanimous voice of the men, who voted to return. "We came back," says one of the company, "buried poor Pettingill, staid over night at Bethel, and the next day returned to Fryburg."

What a truly heroic expedition, when we consider the circumstances! A little settlement, less than twenty years of age, fifty miles in the forest, that had already spared the flower of its strength for the army, gathers, in less than half a day's notice, a corps of thirty men. This little band plunges into the woods at nightfall, and, after a hard night's march, follows the trail of a wily, savage foe, that has marked his track with devastation and blood, and are persuaded to give up the pursuit only when convinced that it will be an injury rather than a benefit to those whom they would succor.

"In November, 1791, a grammar-school was established in Fryburg, which, in February, 1792, was incorporated with academic privileges, and endowed by the legislature of the commonwealth of Massachusetts with twelve thousand acres of land. By the vigilance and instrumentality of the trustees, these lands have become productive, and the funds thus arising secured, in most instances, according to human calculation, beyond a possibility of failure, including the tuition of the students, give an annual interest of nine hundred dollars."

The first building was but little larger, or of much higher finish, than the ordinary school-houses of the times. After that, a more costly, spacious, and fitting structure was reared. This stood quite a long season, but at length, some ten years ago, was burnt down. Near the spot where this stood there is now a building, reared at great expense, not inferior in any respect to its predecessor, perhaps superior on the whole, which we hope will remain for a long time to come the light and ornament of the place where it stands.

The first preceptor of Fryburg Academy was Paul Langdon, son of Doctor Samuel Langdon, once president of Harvard University. He was a good scholar, and graduated with the highest honors of that ancient and learned institution. Few ever left it leaving behind them a higher reputation for intellect and mental acquirements. He bid fair to mark a brilliant course in life. But things that promise most in the outset do not always succeed best in the end. The destroyer often lingers around the fairest flower in our gardens. It was so in his case. The habit of drinking freely intoxicating drinks, formed in early life, darkened his worldly prospects, and checked his opening career of greatness. This was his easily-besetting sin, beguiling him in his professional course, and one but for which he might have filled as splendid a page in history as any other man.

Soon after leaving college he was induced to go and take charge of Fryburg Academy, his friends hoping, by removing him from the temptations of Portsmouth to such a quiet retreat as Fryburg, to break up this habit. But he disappointed them. He found rum in Fryburg, as he had in Portsmouth and Cambridge, and drank it. This rendered him unfit, at times especially, for the proper management of his school. The trustees of the Academy for a long time bore with him, and sought to save him by counsel and admonition; but all to no purpose. At length, after many trials, when forbearance ceased to be a virtue, they discharged him. After this he occasionally taught public town-schools in the vicinity of Fryburg. He was employed on condition that he should drink only a certain quantity of spirits per day. This was dealt out to him by his employers, and he assented to it all cheerfully. He was willing to be in the hands of others, knowing that he was not capable of governing himself. It was in one of these schools that I first became acquainted with him, and acquired all the knowledge of him, by personal intercourse, I ever had. I never saw him after that school closed; but, during that school, I acquired impressions of him, as a teacher and a man, such as time never can efface. These were all of the happiest character. Even his occasionally leaning to folly cannot essentially darken them, more especially because he never justified himself in any errings from this source, but always lamented them. His manner and spirit as an instructor were such as to make almost every one admire him. Many times, as he has stood over me while reciting some lessons, have I felt the magic of his tone and action. His deep, earnest breathing I can now seem almost to hear. His long fore-finger, he used to say, humorously, had a good deal of Latin and Greek in it; and the manner he used it certainly gave force to the remark. It did seem to me that the presence of that fore-finger aided me in my recitations.

Mr. Langdon, through most of his life, with a large family on his lands, struggled hard with poverty. At length his sons grew up, and, going into successful business, furnished him with a plentiful home in the state of New York. Thither he removed from Fryburg, near the close of his life, reforming entirely his habit of drinking; and, professing religion, he died, after a few years, under its inspiring consolations.

Daniel Webster succeeded him in the Academy, though not immediately, where he taught nine months. Of him we need say but little here, as the world is full of his fame. That little shall be that, comparatively, his success as a teacher was much inferior to that in the law and in the forum. He was eminent in the latter sphere, but just respectable in the former. If he had pursued the business of instructing, and made it the main occupation of his life, we should probably never have heard of him much beyond the precincts of the school-room.

Amos J. Cook was his successor. He continued in the place of preceptor for years. Under his care the Academy grew in reputation and numbers; it drew in scholars from a wide circle of towns. When we first entered it, fifty years ago, there were scholars in it from all the larger towns on the nearest seaboard.

Mr. Cook was a good man. Some prize smart men very much; they think it a great thing to say of a man, he is shrewd in his movements. And, indeed, these are not unimportant qualities in a person. But, if we must make distinctions in the traits of a man's character, or give prominence to any of them, let it be one of a moral, solid nature. If the question be, Shall we look merely for smartness or goodness in a man? we say, give us goodness. Now, Mr. Cook was not at all deficient in proper smartness or intellect; he had enough of these to make him a good teacher. The distinguishing thing about him, however, was goodness; we do not say perfection of character, — one entirely free from moral infirmity or weakness, — but prevailing conformance to the rules of moral rectitude in conduct and feeling. He always carried about with him an apparent deep regard for what was due to God and his fellows. We never saw him but when reverence to the one and kindness to the others were clearly marked on his face; and we never heard anything of him but what indicated a deeply kind and forgiving disposition of soul.

In October, 1774, the Rev. William Fessenden was invited to settle in the town; the invitation was accepted, and, in October, 1775, he was ordained to the work of the ministry. This good man, says a correspondent, continued for many years in a happy union with his people. When he became the minister of Fryburg the town was new, with but few inhabitants, and the most of these in indigent circumstances. The sum agreed upon as a compensation for his services was small — less, I think, than two hundred dollars per annum; and this pittance, in consequence of the poverty incident to the people of a new settlement, was never promptly or fully paid. With a young and increasing family depending upon him for food and raiment, the first years of his ministry were years of severe toil, hardship, and privation. He cleared and cultivated a little farm, and studied his sermons, as best he could, while his hands were employed in procuring means of subsistence for his household, and in hours which should have been given to sleep. His library at this time was small indeed, consisting of the Bible, and perhaps a volume or two of theology and history. I think it might all have been carried in a common-sized satchel.

The book of Inspiration he daily and carefully studied, and from it learned his theology, and drew most of the arguments and illustrations which he used to establish and elucidate the truths which he inculcated in his public discourses, As a speaker, his manner was dignified and graceful, his voice clear, commanding, and musical.

He was courageous, energetic, and persevering. I think the most prominent traits of his character were benevolence, integrity, and frankness. He was generous almost to a fault. He ever kept open doors, and always bade a hearty welcome to all the hospitalities he was able to furnish; not merely to acquaintances and friends, but to the stranger and passing traveller, and all who sought a temporary asylum under his roof.

> "The long-remembered beggar was his guest,
> Whose beard, descending, swept his aged breast;
> The broken soldier, kindly bade to stay,
> Sat by his fire and talked the night away."

Our Sunday school libraries contain the life of a little girl, daughter of the present minister of Fryburg, and a native of this town. Marion Lyle Hurd is the most wonderful instance of precocious development on record. Though but four years and twenty-one days old when she died, her conversation and deportment were more like that of one fourteen, than one so young. The books of her library were the following, as given by her father, near the commencement of her fourth year. "They were a Bible and Testament, Child's Book on Repentance, Life of Moses, Family Hymns, Union Hymns, Daily Food, Lessons for Sabbath Schools, Henry Milner, Watts' Divine Songs, Nathan W. Dickerman, Todd's Lectures to Children, and Pilgrim's Progress." These, with her various other books, were kept during the day in one part of the room in which she slept, and in the midst of them she passed hours daily; and at night she would carefully gather them up in her boxes, and place them beside her bed.

She began to compare ideas in her mind obtained from her reading; to exercise the reasoning faculties, and to make inferences; and often did her countenance indicate a reflecting and thoughtful state of mind. Sometimes it was said to her, "Tell me of what you are thinking." Once, observing her in this state of mind, the question was put, "Marion, what are you thinking about?"

"I am thinking," she said, "whether the angels have wings!"

"Well, what do you think of it?"

"I think they have; for Apollyon, who fought with Christian, had wings; and, if wicked angels have wings to do hurt with, good ones must have, to do good with."

Passages innumerable might be quoted, showing her remarkable maturity; but one more must suffice.

Her reading and love of poetry, probably, led Marion to attempt clothing her own thoughts in a kind of poetic dress. This she began to do. Sometimes, at the table, she would utter one or two lines, and then, covering her face, would say,

"John is laughing at me."

This she could not endure. Very frequently the other children would say to us,

"Hark! hark! hear Marion's rhymes."

Some of these are still remembered; and, to show the operations of her mind, and the mental efforts she was putting forth during the last month of her life, we give you an example or two.

Marion, at times, anticipated the return of summer, when she could go out and gather flowers, and wished that the winter was over, asking how long before the spring and the birds would come. On one of these occasions she said:

> "By and by the spring will come,
> And flowers again will bloom;
> To the woods and fields I'll run,
> And gather flowers till noon."

The following was addressed to her doll:

> "My darling little miss,
> How good you've been to-day;
> I'll give you a sweet good kiss,
> And lay you snug away."

Reference has been made to the strong attachment Marion felt toward those little girls who were her companions at school; and to be separated so much from their society, as she necessarily was in winter, was a painful sacrifice to her feelings. Often, the last winter, would she amuse herself by weaving their names into rhyme; and, in her way, singing them over, as she was engaged among her books and playthings. The following are productions of this kind:

> "Anna, Sarah, Abby,
> And dear Louisa too;
> Who have been in to-day,
> To ask me how I do;

I send my love to you,
    This cold and wintry day ;
'T is faithful love and true,
    'T will never die away.

For you I make this song ;
    With me to school you went ;
And fast we ran along, —
    On learning we were bent.

I 've pretty things to see,
    And many things to say ;
So come and visit me
    When mothers come to pray ! "

CHAPTER XV.

LOVEWELL'S FIGHT.

VIEW FROM PEQUAWKET MOUNTAIN. — LOVEWELL'S POND. — SUFFERINGS OF THE EARLY SETTLERS IN DUNSTABLE. — EXPEDITION TO WINNIPISEOGEE LAKE. — EXPEDITION OF LOVEWELL TO PEQUAWKET. — HIS COMPANY. — ENCAMPMENT ON THE SHORE OF THE POND. — SITUATION OF THE INDIAN VILLAGE. — "CARRYING-PLACE." — DISCOVERY OF THE FIRST INDIAN. — KILL THE INDIAN. — THE BATTLE. — RETREAT OF LOVEWELL'S MEN. — CHAMBERLAIN AND PAUGUS. — COUNCIL AT NIGHT. — RETREAT. — ENSIGN WYMAN AND COMPANIONS. — MR. FRYE. — JONES. — FARWELL AND DAVIS. — TRACES OF THE BATTLE. — THE OLD BALLAD.

" Nor, Lovewell, was thy memory forgot,
Who through the trackless wild thy heroes led,
Death and the dreadful torture heeding not,
Mightst thou thy heart-blood for thy country shed,
And serve her living, honor her when dead.
O, Lovewell! Lovewell! nature's self shall die,
And o'er her ashes be her requiem said,
Before New Hampshire pass thy story by,
Without a note of praise, without a pitying eye."

STANDING upon the summit of Pequawket Mountain, one beholds in the south-east, and apparently but a short distance from the base of the mountain, the beautiful village of Fryburg, encircled by the circuitous windings of the Saco. Directly beyond, and in the immediate neighborhood of the

INCIDENTS IN WHITE MOUNTAIN HISTORY. 205

village, lies Lovewell's Pond, the scene of one of the bloodiest combats in the Indian history of New England.

It is a small pond, embosomed amid slightly elevated hills, and with thickly wooded shores. It contains two or three islands, and the quiet stillness of its waters but little reminds you of the terrible encounter which once took place upon its borders.

Throughout the year 1724 the Indians had been more than commonly bold and savage. The more exposed settlements were in constant alarm and excitement, from their almost daily depredations and barbarous massacres. The Massachusetts General Court, startled by the sad reports which were continually being brought to them, had passed a bill, offering a bounty of £100 for every Indian's scalp.

Dunstable, one of the border towns of Massachusetts, was much exposed, and had suffered greatly from the attacks of the Indians. In September of this year, the Indians had carried away two men, and killed nine of the ten men who had gone out in search of the missing ones. Farwell, who afterward accompanied Lovewell on his expedition to Fryburg, was the only one of his company of ten who escaped with his life. Among the numerous expeditions from this town, those commanded by one Captain John Lovewell seem to be the most successful.

"In December," succeeding the September above, "he made an expedition, with a few followers, to the north-east of Winnipiseogee Lake, in which he killed one, and took another prisoner. For these he received the bounty offered by government." But the most important excursion that Lovewell made, previous to the one to Fryburg, in which he was killed, was that to the head of Salmon Falls river, now Wakefield, in New Hampshire, in February, 1725. Of this, Drake says: "With forty men, he came upon a small company of ten Indians, who were asleep by their fires, and, by stationing his men advantageously, he killed all of them. This bloody deed was performed near the shore of a pond, which has ever since borne the name of Lovewell's Pond. After taking off their scalps, these forty warriors marched to Boston in great triumph, with the ten scalps extended upon hoops displayed in the Indian manner, for which they received £1000. This exploit was the more lauded, as it was supposed that these ten Indians were upon an expedition against the English upon the frontiers; having new guns, much ammunition, and spare blankets and moccasons, to accommodate captives. This, however, was mere conjecture; and whether they had killed friends or enemies was not quite so certain as that they had killed Indians."

The last and most memorable expedition, commanded by Captain Lovewell, left Dunstable on Friday, April 16th, 1725, to attack the Pequawket tribe at their home on the Saco. He had in his command forty-six men, volunteered from the adjoining towns. It was an arduous and perilous undertaking; and it has been truly remarked by an old writer, that "to attempt a march of more than one hundred miles into the wilderness, where not a friendly hut or civilized inhabitant were to be met with — where savages and wolves were 'lords of the soil' — where 'dangers prest on every side,' was a desperate adventure, reserved for the daring spirit of an intrepid Lovewell. Though he fell in the contest, he opened a road into a wide-extended country, rich in soil, healthy in climate; and pointed the way to the settlement and civilization of this pleasant and populous country."

They proceeded up the Merrimack toward Winnipiseogee, the direction Lovewell had taken the preceding winter. They were but a short distance from Dunstable when Toby was suddenly taken sick. He was a valuable member, and could hardly be spared. To return, however, and wait his recovery, or for him to go on, were equally impossible. He was accordingly dismissed, and with great reluctance returned. At the mouth of the Contoocook river, near Duston's Island, Mr. William Cummins and a relative of his were dismissed and returned. Mr. Cummins had been wounded some time previous by the Indians, and the long and wearisome march had so inflamed the wound as to make it impossible for him to proceed. From the grounds of the powerful Pennacook, their route lay to the north-east, and the next we learn of them is on the shores of Ossipee Pond. Here Mr. Benjamin Kidder, of Nutfield, was taken sick, and they halted while they could construct a shelter for him till their return. They built a small fort for "a retreat in case of emergency, and to serve as a deposit of part of their provisions, of which they disencumbered themselves before leaving it." Here they left the doctor, a sergeant, and seven other men, to take care of Kidder. Their company was now reduced to thirty-four; all brave men, except one, who, in the language of the Rev. Mr. Symmes, "ran from them at the beginning of the engagement, and sneaked back to the fort, and whose name is unworthy of being transmitted to posterity." These are the names of those brave fellows, who boldly and successfully contended with more than twice their number, viz. : —

Captain John Lovewell, Lieutenant Josiah Farwell, Lieutenant Jonathan Robbins, Ensign John Harwood, Sergeant Noah Johnson, Robert Usher, Samuel Whiting, all of Dunstable. Ensign Seth Wyman, Corporal Thomas Richardson,

Timothy Richardson, Ichabod Johnson, Josiah Johnson, all of Woburn. Eleazer Davis, Josiah Davis, Josiah Jones, David Melvin, Eleazer Melvin, Jacob Farrah, Joseph Farrah, all of Concord. Chaplain Jonathan Frye, of Andover. Sergeant Jacob Fulham, of Weston. Corporal Edward Lingfield, of Nutfield. Jonathan Kittridge, Solomon Kies, of Billerica. John Jefts, Daniel Woods, Thomas Woods, John Chamberlain, Elias Barron, Isaac Lakin, Joseph Gilson, all of Groton. Ebenezer Ayer, Abiel Aston, of Haverhill.

They were still some forty miles from the Pequawket encampment, all the distance through an unbroken wilderness; but, rested by their halt at Ossipee, and nerved on by the hope of soon meeting the enemy, they commenced the last stage of their lengthened march, and reached Saco pond on Thursday, May 6th, 1725. They were now in the very heart of the hunting-ground of Paugus. Traces of the powerful foe they had come out to conquer could be seen on every hand. Indeed, so near did they come in their march on Thursday to the settlement of the tribe, that the noise of the unseen village made them apprehensive they were discovered and dogged. They encamped upon the westerly side of the pond, and prepared themselves for an encounter. Thirty-four men, fifty miles from any white settlement, in the depth of an unbroken wilderness, preparing themselves to encounter a warlike enemy of hundreds! Excited by the near vicinity of the Indians, and undecided what course it was best to take in attacking them, they remained at their first stopping-place from Thursday night until Saturday morning. Friday night they were much alarmed by the stealthy marching of large numbers of Indians, as they thought, in their near vicinity; but it was very dark, and they could see nothing, nor make any further discovery than the hushed footsteps of these unseen foes hovering about their camp.

> "No clattering hoof falls sudden and strong ;
> No trumpet is filled, and no bugle is blown ;
> No banners abroad on the wind are thrown ;
> No shoutings are heard, and no cheerings are given ;
> But they speed, like coursers whose hoofs are shod
> With a silent shoe, from the loosened sod ;
> And away they have gone, with a motionless speed,
> Like demons abroad on some terrible deed.
> The last one has gone ; they have all disappeared ;
> Their dull echoed trampings no longer are heard ;
> For still, though they passed like no steeds of the earth,
> The fall of their tread gave some hollow sounds birth ;
> Your heart would lie still till it numbered the last,
> And your breath would be held till the rear horseman passed ;
> So swiftly, so mute, so darkly they went,
> Like spectres of air to the sorcerer sent,
> That ye *felt* their approach, and might guess their intent."

Leaving awhile our heroes upon the margin of the pond, it may be necessary here to speak of the tortuous windings and turnings of the Saco river at this point, and its relation to Lovewell's Pond and Fryburg village, the then headquarters of Paugus. With a bold sweep, the Saco changes its course, near Chatauque, in Conway, New Hampshire, to the north-east, nearly at right angles with its former course. It passes in this direction Weston's Bridge, the rendezvous, as we have said, of the Indians, and, continuing on, traverses a distance of forty miles, within a space of six miles square, now north, now south, now east, now west, till it comes at last to Lovewell's Pond, only one mile and a half from Weston's Bridge. It was the choice hunting-ground, the garden of the Pequawkets. Starting from their very door, they could sweep round on its current the whole length, filling their boats with game from its well-stocked shores, and, reaching at last the pond; could shoulder their canoes, and, ere the long "file" should be formed, their chief would be in his wigwam. The distance between the pond and their settlement was called a "carrying-place."

It seems that, at the time of which we write, Paugus, with eighty of his men, had been scouting down the river, and had arrived, on the Saturday morning above referred to, at their landing-place on the pond.

This Saturday morning had dawned none too soon for the excited men of Lovewell. All night they had listened through the dense darkness to the distant barking of the dogs and the silent creeping of the Indians, till they grew eager for the light. Breakfasting, they were assembled upon the beach for their accustomed morning devotion.

> "Then were men of worth,
> Who by their prayers slew thousands, angel like."

And their chaplain had scarcely uttered the significant words, "We came out to meet the enemy; we have all along prayed God we might find them. We had rather trust Providence with our lives, yea, die for our country, than try to return without seeing them, if we might, and be called cowards for our pains," when a gun was fired, and they espied an Indian on a point of land that ran into the pond on the opposite side from them. A hurried consultation was held, and they concluded that the design of the gun and the Indian discovering himself was to draw them that way; but that the main body of the enemy was to the north of the pond. Clamoring now eagerly to be led forward, the "Captain readily complied, though not without manifesting some apprehensions." Their march lay along the margin of the pond, just glistening in the first rays of the rising sun. Near the north-western shore they crossed the Indians' "carrying-place." At the north-east end of the pond the land rises very gradually to a slight elevation, and then falls off again to the north into a thickly-wooded morass, covered with high brakes. Here, on this slightly elevated plain, where the trees were thin and the brakes small, they divested themselves of their packs, and commenced a more cautious march. They had gone but a short distance, when " Ensign Wyman discovered an Indian, who was out hunting, having in one hand some fowls he had just killed, and in the other two guns." Immediately a signal was given, and they all "squatted." He came unsuspectingly towards them, and, when near enough, "several guns were fired at him, but missed him. Seeing that sure death was his lot, this valiant Indian resolved to defend himself to his last breath; and the action was as speedy as the thought. His gun was levelled at the English, and Lovewell was mortally wounded. Ensign Wyman, taking deliberate aim, killed the poor Indian." Mr. Samuel Whitney was also wounded by the shot of the Indian. The operation of scalping the Indian was performed by the chaplain, Mr. Frye, and another man. From this point they commenced their return to where they had left their packs. Paugus, as we have said, had arrived with his warriors at their landing-place on the shores of the pond; and scarcely had Lovewell crossed the "carrying-place," in search of his foe, when the wily sachem, pursuing the well-beaten path to his village, came upon signs of the white man's moccasons. Instantly, the long "file" was hushed, and,

"With a slow and noiseless footstep,"

they followed the track. Coming upon the packs, they were counted, and the number of the whites was known. Adopting their usual mode of warfare, they instantly sprang into the morass as an ambush. Thus concealed, they could bring their whole force to bear in an instant upon the whites, and, by the celerity of the movement, could so surprise them as to cause them to surrender at once. This undoubtedly was the thought of Paugus. Scarcely had the last brake ceased to move above the crouching forms of the Indians, when Lovewell and his men came up, and commenced searching for their packs. Now is the time; and, springing from the thicket, with a horrid yell, the savages fired their guns directly over the heads of the whites, and ran towards them with ropes, demanding if they would have quarter.

"Only at the muzzles of their guns," replied the intrepid Lovewell and his men, and the fight commenced.

> "Wild and more wild the tumult grew
> Amid the crazed, demoniac crew;
> Knives flashed, and man to man opposed."

Lovewell and his party, seizing the advantage, "rushed towards the Indians, fired as they pressed on, and, killing many, drove them several rods." But they soon rallied, and, maddened by the unexpected resistance, rushed furiously on, killing nine, and wounding three with their first fire. Captain Lovewell, Mr. Fullam (only son of Major Fullam, of Weston), Ensign Harwood, John Jefts, Jonathan Kittridge, Daniel Woods, and Josiah Davis, were killed, and Lieutenants Farwell and Robbins, and Robert Usher, wounded by the assault. The English, thus in number reduced, and seeing the Indians about to surround them, commenced to retreat. It was done in good order, fighting bravely all the way, and manfully contesting each inch of ground. Directly back of them was a point of rocks which ran into the pond, and a few large pine trees standing on a sandy beach. Here they came to a stand. On their right was the mouth of a large brook, at this time unfordable; on their left, this sharp ridge of rocks, while the pond guarded them in the rear. Here " the fight continued, very furious and obstinate, till towards night; the Indians roaring, and yelling, and howling like wolves, barking like dogs, and making all sorts of hideous noises; the English frequently shouting and huzzaing, as they did after the first round." Thus they fought from ten in the morning "till the going down of the sun, and till but nine of their company remained uninjured. Wahwa could lead but twenty Indians uninjured from the field; and, though they had the advantage, at sunset they fled, leaving the dead unburied. Paugus, the brave chief, had been slain, and thirty-nine of his bold followers had been killed and wounded. Paugus had been killed in single combat, by one Chamberlain, of Groton. Wearied by the protracted contest, each had come to opposite sides of the brook to quench their thirst and wash their guns, which had become foul by so frequent firing. Their guns could almost touch, so narrow was the space between them. As they washed their guns, conversing familiarly with each other, Chamberlain assured Paugus that he should kill him. Paugus returned the threat, and bade him defiance. Carefully drying their guns, they commenced loading at the same time. Their movements exactly corresponded, and the balls of each were heard as they were sent home by the rods at the same instant. But the gun of Chamberlain primed itself, and Paugus' did not. Striking the breech upon the ground, it primed, and, raising it with deliberate aim, he fired, and Paugus fell dead upon the bank, and, as he fell, the well-aimed ball from his rifle passed through the thick locks on the top of Chamberlain's head, but left him unwounded.

About midnight, it being certain the Indians would not renew the contest, the shattered remnant of the brave English assembled themselves together to examine into their situation. Nine of their company, including their captain, were dead. Three were unable to move on account of their wounds; eleven, though wounded, thought themselves able to travel. Nine remained untouched.

What now should be done? To remain in the very centre of an enemy's country, maddened by the loss of their brave chief, and destitute of all food, was impossible; but to return, they must leave, not only their dead unburied, but their wounded companions unprotected, to die by the torture of the savages. Farrar, one of the wounded, expired during the consultation. Robbins and Usher urged and commanded their companions to return, and leave them to their fate. "Lieutenant Robbins even desired his companions to charge his gun and leave it with him, which they did, he declaring that, 'as the Indians will come in the morning to scalp me, I will kill one more of them, if I can.'" As the moon was rising they bade adieu to their companions, and, taking a last look of the scene of their dreadful encounter, commenced their memorable return. They had gone but a mile and a half, when four of the men, Farwell, Frye, Davis and Jones, declared themselves unable to go on; and, like the brave fellows they had already left, they were unwilling to detain the company, and desired them to proceed. Their number, now reduced to sixteen, they divided into three parties, fearing to make too large a track, by which the Indians might pursue them. One of these parties reached the fort at Ossipee, but found it deserted. "The coward, who fled in the beginning of the battle, ran directly to the fort, and gave the men posted there such a frightful account of what had happened, that they all fled from the fort, and made the best of their way home." The main party of eleven, leaving the Ossipee fort, continued on, and reached Dunstable, May 13th, in the night.

Let us now return to those we have left by the way. One Solomon Kies " had fought in the battle till he received three wounds, and had become so weak, by the loss of blood, that he could not stand; he crawled up to Ensign Wyman, in the heat of the battle, and told him he was a dead man; ' but,' said he, 'if it be possible, I will get out of the way of the Indians, that they may not get my scalp.' Kies then crept off by the side of the pond, where he providentially found a canoe, when he rolled himself into it, and was driven by the wind several miles towards the fort. He gained strength fast, and reached the fort as soon as the eleven before mentioned; and they all arrived at Dunstable on the 13th of May, at night.

" On the 15th of May, Ensign Wyman and three others arrived at Dunstable. They suffered greatly for want of provisions. They informed that they were wholly destitute of all kinds of food from Saturday morning till the Wednesday following, when they caught two mouse-squirrels, which they roasted whole, and found to be a sweet morsel. They afterwards killed some partridges and other game, and were comfortably supplied till they got home."

Farwell and Davis, Frye and Jones, whom we left but a short distance from the scene of the encounter, remained some time in the helpless condition in which they were left; but at length, "though their wounds were putrefied and stank, and they were almost dead with famine, yet they all travelled on several miles together, till Mr. Frye desired the others not to stop on his account, for he found himself dying, and he laid himself down, telling them he should never rise more ; and charged Davis, if it should please God to bring him home, to go to his father, and tell him that he expected in a few hours to be in eternity, and that he was not afraid to die. They left him; and this amiable and promising young gentleman, who had the journal of the march in his pocket, was not heard of again."

He was a young man of a liberal education, who took his degree at college in 1723, and was chaplain to the company, and greatly beloved by them for his excellent performances and good behavior, and who fought with undaunted courage till he was mortally wounded. But when he could fight no longer, he prayed audibly, several times, for the preservation and success of the residue of the company.

Jones, being separated from his companions by some accident, "traversed Saco river, and, after a fatiguing ramble, arrived at Saco (now Biddeford), emaciated, and almost dead through the loss of blood, the putrefaction of his wounds, and the want of food. He was kindly treated by the people of Saco, and recovered from his wounds."

Farwell and Davis suffered exceedingly from hunger. They were entirely destitute of provisions, and subsisted upon the spontaneous vegetables of the forest. "Lieutenant Farwell held out, on his return, till the eleventh day, during which time he had nothing to eat but water and a few roots, which he chewed; and by this time, through his body he was so mortified, that the worms made a thorough passage. On the same day, Davis, who was with him, caught a fish, which he broiled, and was greatly refreshed by it; but the lieutenant was so much spent that he could not taste a bit.

Then, at Farwell's earnest entreaties that he would provide for his own safety, he left him to his own fate. Previous to this, he had taken Farwell's handkerchief and tied it to the top of a bush, that it might afford a mark by which his remains could the more easily be found. After going from him a short distance, Farwell called him back, and requested to be turned upon the other side. Davis being now alone, in a melancholy, desolate state, still made toward the fort, and the next day came to it; there he found some pork and bread, sustained by which, he was enabled to reach Berwick, and then Portsmouth, where he was carefully provided for, and had a skilful surgeon to attend him."

Thus ends the battle of Lovewell's Pond. After the fear had subsided, Colonel Tyng, with a small company, went to the place of action, and buried the dead. Paugus and a few other Indians had been buried.

Trees perforated by the balls may be seen to this day on the shore of the pond; and the older citizens of Fryburg will relate to the visitor the bloody engagement of early Pequawket with all the ardor of youth.

Standing upon the summit of Pequawket Mountain, one sees before him the pond, so peacefully glittering in the rays of the sun, near the quiet village of Fryburg. But the Indians are gone. The bold Paugus no longer raises the shrill war-whoop, starting the echoes of the hills, and Wahwa no longer leads the scout upon the beautiful windings of the Saco.

"Where is their home, — their forest home? the proud land of their sires?
Where stands the wigwam of their pride? where gleam their council-fires?
Where are their fathers' hallowed graves? their friends, so light and free?
Gone, gone, — forever from our view! Great Spirit! can it be?"

The following ballad stanzas were printed originally in the work entitled "Collections, Historical and Miscellaneous, and Monthly Literary Journal," published at Concord, N. H., and edited by J. Farmer and J. B. Moore. The author's name is not given; but it is conjectured that they were written by a personal friend of the learned and excellent editors, who was then young and not much practised in writing, and who is said to be still living somewhere in the State of Maine:

" 'T was Paugus led the Pequot tribe:
   As runs the fox, would Paugus run;
   As howls the wild wolf, would he howl;
   A huge bear-skin had Paugus on.

But Chamberlain, of Dunstable,
   One whom a savage ne'er shall slay,
Met Paugus by the water-side,
   And shot him dead upon that day.

What time the noble Lovewell came,
   With fifty men from Dunstable,
The cruel Pequot tribe to tame,
   With arms and bloodshed terrible.

With Lovewell brave John Harwood came; —
   From wife and babes 't was hard to part;
Young Harwood took her by the hand,
   And bound the weeper to his heart.

' Repress that tear, my Mary dear,'
   Said Harwood to his loving wife;
' It tries me hard to leave thee here,
   And seek, in distant woods, the strife.

' When gone, my Mary, think of me,
   And pray to God that I may be
Such as one ought that lives for thee,
   And come at last in victory.'

Thus left young Harwood babe and wife;
  With accent wild, she bade adieu;
It grieved those lovers much to part,
  So fond and fair, so kind and true.

John Harwood died, all bathed in blood,
  When he had fought till set of day;
And many more we may not name
  Fell in that bloody battle fray.

When news did come to Harwood's wife,
  That he with Lovewell fought and died,—
Far in the wilds had given his life,
  Nor more would in his home abide,—

Such grief did seize upon her mind,
  Such sorrow filled her faithful breast,
On earth she ne'er found peace again,
  But followed Harwood to his rest.

Seth Wyman, who in Woburn lived,—
  A marksman he, of courage true,—
Shot the first Indian whom they saw;
  Sheer through his heart the bullet flew.

The savage had been seeking game;
  Two guns, and eke a knife, he bore,
And two black ducks were in his hand;
  He shrieked, and fell, to rise no more.

Anon, there eighty Indians rose,
  Who hid themselves in ambush dread;
Their knives they shook, their guns they aimed—
  The famous Paugus at their head.

John Lovewell, captain of the band,
  His sword he waved, that glittered bright;
For the last time he cheered his men,
  And led them onward to the fight.

'Fight on, fight on!' brave Lovewell said,
  'Fight on, while Heaven shall give you breath!'
An Indian ball then pierced him through,
  And Lovewell closed his eyes in death.

Good Heavens! is this a time for prayer?
  Is this a time to worship God,
When Lovewell's men are dying fast,
  And Paugus' tribe hath felt the rod?

The chaplain's name was Jonathan Frye;
  In Andover his father dwelt;
And oft with Lovewell's men he 'd prayed,
  Before the mortal wound he felt.

A man was he of comely form,
  Polished and brave, well learnt and kind;
Old Harvard's learnèd halls he left,
  Far in the wilds a grave to find.

Ah! now his blood-red arm he lifts,
  His closing lids he tries to raise,
And speak once more before he dies,
  In supplication and in praise.

He prays kind Heaven to grant success,
  Brave Lovewell's men to guide and bless,
And when they 've shed their heart's blood true,
  To raise them all to happiness.

'Come hither, Farwell,' said young Frye;
  'You see that I 'm about to die;
Now for the love I bear to you,
  When cold in death my bones shall lie,

'Go thou and see my parents dear,
  And tell them you stood by me here;
Console them when they cry, Alas!
  And wipe away the falling tear.'

Lieutenant Farwell took his hand,
  His arms around his neck he threw,
And said, 'Brave chaplain, I could wish
  That Heaven had made me die for you.'

The chaplain on kind Farwell's breast,
  Bloody and languishing, he fell;
Nor after that said more but this,
  'I love thee, soldier; fare thee well!'

Good Heavens! they dance the powwow dance;
  What horrid yells the forest fill!
The grim bear crouches in his den,
  The eagle seeks the distant hill.

'What means this dance, this powwow dance?'
  Stern Wyman said; with wondrous art
He crept full near, his rifle aimed,
  And shot the leader through the heart.

Then did the crimson streams that flowed
  Seem like the waters of a brook,
That brightly shine, that loudly dash
  Far down the cliffs of Agiochook.

Ah! many a wife shall rend her hair,
  And many a child cry, 'Woe is me,'
When messengers the news shall bear
  Of Lovewell's dear-bought victory.

With footsteps low shall travellers go,
  Where Lovewell's Pond shines clear and bright,
And mark the place where those are laid,
  Who fell in Lovewell's bloody fight.

Old men shall shake their heads, and say,
  'Sad was the hour and terrible,
When Lovewell brave, 'gainst Paugus went,
  With fifty men from Dunstable.'"

CHAPTER XVI.

GILEAD.

SITUATION OF GILEAD. — SOIL. — WILD RIVER. — EARLY SETTLERS. — MINISTERS. — FIRST CHURCH. — SLIDE. — BEARS. — ENCOUNTER OF ONE BEAN. — YORK'S WARM RECEPTION BY A BEAR. — OLIVER PEABODY'S LOOSE OX. — FAMINE AMONG BEARS. — BEAR AND HOG STORY. — HORRIBLE TRAGEDY.

> "My wife! my wife! What wife? I have no wife;
> O, insupportable! O, heavy hour!
> Methinks it should be now a huge eclipse
> Of sun and moon."

GILEAD, formerly called Peabody's Patent, took its name from a great Balm of Gilead tree, still standing near the centre of the town. It lies on both sides of the Androscoggin river, which runs through its entire length from east to west, the town being six miles long, and three wide. On the borders of this river is some of the best land in the region, producing very bountiful crops. One farm, some years since, under the cultivation of a very skilful, industrious farmer, when a premium was offered by the State of Maine for the best crop of wheat on a given portion of land, secured the premium. Large crops of corn and potatoes have been raised on it. Some of the former have equalled one hundred bushels to the acre. The more usual crop is from forty to sixty bushels. Potatoes have gone up as high as one thousand six hundred bushels to the acre; and one man, for a number of years in succession, raised one thousand five hundred bushels to the acre.

The town is so situated as to escape almost entirely the early frosts of autumn. Ranges of high mountains bound the valley in which it is situated, completely shutting it in on the east and west. A continual current of air is thus formed, preserving the crops in the valley and on the hillsides, while the frost is busily at work in the adjoining towns. Shaggy and rude in the extreme are the mountains which so completely wall in this fertile valley. One has remarked that "the expense of transportation of fuel down the mountains, in a slippery time, is very trifling."

Wild river, one of those impetuous mountain streams, empties into the Androscoggin in this town. "It is a child of the mountains; at times fierce, impetuous and shadowy, as the storms that howl around the bald heads of its parents, and bearing down everything that comes in its path; then again, when subdued by long summer calms, murmuring gently in consonance with the breezy rustle of the trees, whose branches depend over it. An hour's time may swell it into a headlong torrent; an hour may reduce it to a brook that a child might ford without fear."

This town was settled about the time Shelburne was, whose brief history we have just given. The settlers came generally from Massachusetts and the southern part of New Hampshire. They were Thomas Peabody, Capt. Joseph Lary, Isaac Adams, Eliphalet Chapman, Capt. Eliphalet Burbank, George Burbank, Ephraim and Seth Wight, John Mason, Stephen Coffin, and Samuel Wheeler. After this soon came Phineas Kimball, Henry Philbrook, Peter Coffin, and Joseph Lary, jr. These were all exemplary good men, giving a character of energy to the place. They regarded religious institutions, and helped sustain them by their property and example. They were a church-going people, always attending the worship of God on the Sabbath.

From the earliest time of its settlement it has enjoyed more or less steadily the preaching of the gospel. Before any Christian church was planted in it, it had a succession of missionaries, sent from different sources, who were instrumental of great religious benefit to the people. Among these were the Rev. Jotham Sewall, or, as he is often called, "Father Sewall," and the Rev. Samuel Hidden, of Tamworth.

In 1818, a Congregational church was formed, consisting of Melvin Farwell and wife, Abraham Burbank and wife, Widow Susannah Burbank, Betsey Philbrook, John Mason, jr., H. Ingalls, Rhoda Styles, Mary Peabody, and Ephraim and Seth Wight. This church, sometimes through its own efforts, and sometimes in connection with Shelburne, has had preaching most of the time since its formation. Its regularly settled pastors have been Rev. Henry White, and Rev. Henry Richardson. Besides those, Rev. Daniel Goodhue and others have been supplies for different portions of time. There is a Methodist church, also, which has been instrumental of great religious and moral benefit to the place.

During the terrible storm of 1826, when my brother's family was destroyed at the Notch, slides also took place on many of the mountains around this town. From Picked Hill came rushing down thousands of tons of earth, and rocks, and trees, and water, destroying all that lay in their path. No lives were lost, but the consternation of the inhabitants was great. The darkness was so intense as almost to be felt. The vivid lightnings and long streams of fire, covering the sides of the mountains, caused by the concussion of the rocks, only served to make the darkness more visible. Amid the deluge of rain, the terrific crashings of the thunder, and, over all, the deafening roar of the descending slides, it was impossible to make one's self heard. The valley rocked as though an earthquake was shaking the earth. The frightful scene did not last long; but, during its continuance, more terror was crowded into it than during an ordinary lifetime. The inhabitants under these mountains alone can appreciate the awful scene through which my brother and his family passed on that terrible night.

This region has been very much infested with bears, especially during the summer months. Many live now on the mountains, preventing entirely the raising of sheep. Though much of the land, especially on the mountains, is well adapted to grazing, still it is never safe to trust sheep and young stock far from the settlements. So late as the summer of 1852, a most desperate encounter took place between one of the farmers in this vicinity and a large black bear of the white-face breed — the most savage of that variety.

A Mr. Bean was to work in his field, accompanied by a boy twelve years of age. The bear approached him, and having his gun with him, charged for partridges, he fired, but with little effect. The bear bore down upon him; he walked backwards, loading his gun at the same time, when his foot caught by a twig, which tripped him up, and the bear leaped upon him. He immediately fired again, but with no visible effect. The bear at once went to work,— seizing his left arm, biting through it, and lacerating it severely. While thus amusing himself, he was tearing with his fore paws the clothes, and scratching the flesh on the

young man's breast. Having dropped his arm, he opened his
huge mouth to make a pounce at his face. Then it was that
the young man made the dash that saved his life. As the
bear opened his jaws, Bean thrust his lacerated arm down
the brute's throat, as far as desperation would enable him.
There he had him! The bear could neither retreat nor advance, though the position of the besieged was anything but
agreeable. Bean now called upon the lad to come and take
from his pocket a jack-knife, and open it. The boy marched
up to the work boldly. Having got the knife, Bean with his
untrammelled hand cut the bear's throat from ear to ear, killing him stone dead, while he lay on his body! It was judged
the bear weighed nearly four hundred pounds. One of his
paws weighed two pounds eleven ounces.

The earlier annals of this town are full of adventure,
nearly equalling this in daring and bravery. The older inhabitants can recall many a scene of thrilling interest which
took place within sight of their very cabins.

A man by the name of York, living in the woods, one day
came rather suddenly upon a full-grown bear. They both
stopped and looked each other steadily in the face. Neither
seemed disposed to retreat. The bear bade defiance in her look,
and York did the same. An encounter seemed unavoidable,
partly because he dare not retreat now if he might, and
partly because he had the pluck not to do it if he could. So
they both addressed themselves to the battle. The bear raised
herself on her hind feet, standing upright, and spread her
fore legs to receive her antagonist. York responded by opening his arms, and a close grip succeeded. Then followed a
struggle for dear life, the issue of which no one could have
decided but for one circumstance. York had the advantage
in it from having an open, long-bladed jack-knife in his right

hand when it commenced. This, of course, he used in the best way he could, not stopping to ask whether it was fair or not. Making a little extra exertion on the first good opportunity, he drew the blade across the bear's throat, and she relaxed her hold and soon bled to death. The victory was his.

One dark night Mr. Oliver Peabody, living in a log hut, was disturbed by his cattle in the hovel near by. Supposing that one of them had broken from his fastening, and was goring the rest, he arose from his bed, and, with nothing on but his night-dress, ran towards the hovel to search out the cause of the trouble. As he came to the entrance, which was merely a hole in its side, he espied some black creature standing just inside, and, thinking it one of his cattle, stepped forward a little, and struck it on the rump with a stick he had in his hand, crying, "Hurrup! hurrup there!" The creature, deeming this rather a rough salutation, turned round, and, with the full force of his huge paw, gave him a heavy slap on the side. By this time he began to imagine that he was in no very delicate, refined company, and must look out for himself. The salutation he received from the creature was a little more unceremonious and rude than the one he first gave him. He was fully aware, now, that sometimes a person must take blows as well as give them, and hard ones, too. Certain it was, he had no disposition to repeat his stroke, or his cry of "Hurrup! hurrup!" and, perceiving that the bear was about to repeat the blow, he sounded a retreat, and made haste back to his hut. Whether the bear kept his ground, and proceeded to annoy the cattle further, we were not informed.

In the autumn of 1804, it required all the vigilance and courage of the inhabitants to preserve their cattle and hogs from the ferocious creatures. The nuts and berries, their usual food, had failed them, and, driven on by hunger, the infuriated beasts would rush almost into the very houses of the settlers. Young hogs were caught and carried off in sight of their owners, and within gunshot of their pens. A huge, growling monster, seized a good-sized hog in his paws, and ran off with it, standing on his hind legs, satisfying his hunger as he went.

One dark night Mr. Oliver Peabody, the same we have spoken of before, was disturbed by the loud squealing of his hogs. As unsuspecting as before, he rushed out in his nightdress to the yard where they were kept, back of his barn. Scarcely yet fully awake, he placed his hands upon the top rail, and stood peering out into the darkness, shouting lustily to whatever might be disturbing his hogs. So intent was he on driving away the intruder, that he was conscious of nothing until he felt the warm breath of a large bear breathing directly in his face. The huge monster had left the hogs on his first approach, and, rearing herself on her hind legs, placed her paws on the same rail, near his hands, and stood ready for the new-year salutation of the Russians — a hug and a kiss. Realizing fully his danger, he darted away for his house, the bear following close at his heels. He had barely time to reach his door, and throw himself against it as a fastening, when Madam Bruin came rushing against it. The frail thing trembled and squeaked on its wooden hinges, but his wife had placed the wooden bar across it, and thus it withstood the shock. Opening the door slightly, on the first opportunity, he let out his dog. The dog, used to the business, seized the bear fiercely by the throat, as she sat on her haunches eying the door. Not so easily driven off, however, she threw the mastiff with tremendous force against the house, and leaping a fence near at hand, sat coolly down. The noble dog, as soon as he could recover from the stunning blow, again attacked her. With still more force she threw him this time against the cabin, displacing some of its smaller timbers, near where some of the children were asleep in a truckle-bed. Bounding away, she ran some eighty rods, to the house of one Stephen Messer, seized a large hog, and leaping a fence three feet high with it in her arms, ran thirty rods, and sat down to her feast. Before Messrs. Peabody and Messer could reach her, she had finished her repast and walked slowly off into the woods.

About the middle of June, 1850, one of the most tragical scenes transpired in this town that ever took place in any region. Happily the principal actors in it were not natives of the town or region, but foreigners. A contractor on the Atlantic and St. Lawrence Railroad, which was then being constructed through the Androscoggin valley, after burying his wife in Bethel, went to board with a Mr. George W. Freeman, a blacksmith. This man was in the employ of the contractor, helping him build a very expensive bridge over Wild river. Mr. Freeman's family consisted of a wife and three children. He had been somewhat remarkable as a kind and faithful husband and indulgent parent, and nothing had ever occurred to mar the peace of the family until the advent of the contractor into it. Mrs. Freeman, young and beautiful, was very attractive in looks and address, but in all respects, heretofore, had shown herself an exemplary woman and devoted wife. Freeman, unable to harbor the thought of anything wrong in his wife, for a long time passed by many things which caused him much uneasiness. The particular attentions of the contractor to his wife he tried long and hard to construe as only the civilities due from a gentleman to a lady. As each day the attentions became more marked, and the evident partiality of the two for each other's society became more manifest, the loathed suspicion worked itself gradually into the terrible conviction that his companion was yielding to the wiles of the seducer. So bold had they become in their course, that scarcely a day passed but they rode out together, sometimes extending their rides to late hours in the night. At last they went to Bethel, a distance of nine miles, to attend a ball, and did not return until near morning. This fully roused Mr. Freeman from his heretofore almost stupid forbearance. He undressed and put his children to bed, and then calmly awaited the return of the guilty pair. Not in anger, but intensely in earnest, he expostulated with them, warning them of the consequences of their guilty course. Passionately he besought his wife to remember their hitherto happy life, and spare himself and her babes the disgrace and loss of such a companion and a mother. It was all, however, to no purpose.

Shortly after the ball at Bethel, Mrs. Freeman threw off all restraint, and asked her husband for a divorce. Her affection, she said, for him was gone, and it was better for them to separate. She could never again love him as she had, and to live with him in her present state of mind was unendurable. She not only asked him for divorcement, but told him that, with or without it, she should certainly leave him. That she was in earnest was clearly manifest. She commenced her preparations for a journey, proceeding even so far as to pack some of her things.

The contractor's office was in Freeman's house, and his clerk was almost constantly employed in it. By chance Freeman overheard one day a conversation between his wife and the clerk. She had come for advice, and imagining no opposition from the clerk, disclosed to him her plans. Contrary to her expectations, the noble young man reprimanded her severely for her conduct, and warmly advised her for her good. Freeman heard all, and it confirmed his worst suspicions.

Previous to these active preparations of Mrs. Freeman for her departure, the contractor had left for New York. Before leaving, it seems, it had been arranged between them that Mrs. Freeman should soon follow to meet at some place yet to be agreed upon. Freeman learned these facts but too soon. Not long after the contractor had left, a beautiful trunk, marked for Mrs. Freeman, was one day left at the door, when Mrs. Freeman chanced to be out. With a shop-key Freeman opened the trunk in his shop, and there full evidence of the intentions of the pair was manifest. Beautiful dresses and jewelry for herself and children were the contents, and under all a letter disclosing the plans. She was to meet the contractor at Syracuse, N. Y. There were minute directions as to the routes to travel, and particular caution to fasten the door of her bedchamber, at night, in the different hotels. The day for her departure was named. He concealed from his wife the trunk and letter, and she never probably knew of its arrival.

The day for Mrs. Freeman's departure was already fixed, and the night preceding her leaving in the morning had arrived. Calmly Freeman sat among his family during the evening, and on their retiring had embraced and kissed them according to his usual custom. Long he lingered near his wife, but at length, bidding her the last good-night, retired to his room. They had not slept together for some time, a servant-girl occupying the bed with his wife and young child. Stillness had settled down upon the house, when suddenly a piercing shriek broke upon the night, startling every sleeper from his slumbers. "I am murdered! I am murdered!" was all that could be distinguished in the confusion which ensued. Each hurried whence the voice proceeded, and there, in Mrs. Freeman's room, weltering in blood, lay the unhappy wife, shrieking in paroxysms of terror. She rose up in bed, as they entered, the mutilated, bleeding arm hanging at her side. Medical assistance was soon at hand, the wounded limb amputated and carefully dressed, but to no effect; from loss of blood the murdered woman died but a few hours after. A few buckshot were taken from the head. The shattered condition of the arm, and the broken window, made it evident in what manner the poor woman had been murdered. Sleeping on her side, the murderer had aimed directly at her heart, but, missing, had discharged the whole contents of the gun into her arm. He had accomplished, however, his purpose as well as though he had not missed his aim.

The murdered wife was conscious who had murdered her. Her husband was the only one of the large family who gathered not around her bedside at her fearful summons. "It was my husband," were her words. And the full weight of her great guilt bursting upon her too late, she could but groan and ejaculate, "O, my own dear husband! And will he not come! O, George, my husband, shall I not see him, to be forgiven!" She died, not suspecting that her husband was dead, but that he avoided seeing her from grief. Fully forgiving him, she died with his name upon her lips.

But to turn from the sad spectacle of the wife to the still sadder sight of her husband. Instant search was made for him as the murderer of his wife, and after long hours of hunting, about a mile from his house, he was found dead, lying in a pool of his own blood. His throat was cut from ear to ear, his hand still grasping the fatal razor. By him lay his gun and a piece of rope. The gun, it seems, he had tried, but it had not done its work, merely bruising badly one cheek.

A jury of inquest was holden on his body, and a verdict rendered according to facts. On examination of his affairs, letters were found, written by his own hand, giving directions in regard to his children, and the disposition he wished to be made of his property when he was dead. It is supposed, from some things in his case, especially one important incident, that until a late period in his life, he did not intend to kill his wife, but the contractor.

He asked the clerk of the contractor, one day, which side of the bed they held in common he, the contractor, slept? giving an occasion by this for an inference that he had some design upon him. But the contractor leaving before the design could be executed, and determined, as he had declared, that the contractor should never enjoy his wife, he made up his mind to kill her, and did actually perform the dreadful deed we have rehearsed. How strongly this whole affair impresses upon us the importance of watching against the first emotions of any great sin, and praying earnestly the prayer taught us by the Saviour, "Lead us not into temptation, but deliver us from evil," we certainly need not say. There being no minister in Gilead at this time, Rev. Mr. Leland, of Bethel, attended the funeral on the occasion. He preached to a very large concourse of people on the text, "When lust hath conceived it bringeth forth sin; and sin, when it is finished, bringeth forth death."

CHAPTER XVII.

SEGAR'S NARRATIVE.

ATTACK ON BETHEL. — SEGAR. — INDIANS. — CAPTURE OF SEGAR AND COMPANIONS. — MRS. CLARK. — THE JOURNEY TO CANADA. — PETTENGILL'S HOUSE. — HOPE AUSTIN. — CAPT. RINDGE. — MURDER OF POOR. — CLARK'S ESCAPE. — ENCAMPMENTS AT NIGHT. — UMBAGOG LAKE. — SUFFERINGS FROM HUNGER. — ARRIVAL AT ST. FRANCIS RIVER. — INDIAN DANCE. — BRITISH PROTECTION. — RETURN HOME.

"With hearts unbent, and spirits brave,
They sternly bore
Such toils as meaner souls had quelled."

On the third of August, 1781, a party of six Indians from Canada, in the employ of British officers, made an attack upon Bethel, then Sudbury, Canada, and Shelburne, killing three men, and carrying as many more into captivity. It was the last of a long series of outrages upon the frontier settlements, commencing with King Philip's war, and ends the bloody Indian history of this region.

Segar, one of the three men captured, who published an account of this surprisal and captivity after his return, and whose narrative we have more particularly followed, had early removed to Sudbury, Canada, from Massachusetts. He had been a soldier in the revolutionary army on the breaking out of war, had retreated from Bunker Hill, and had helped to garrison the fort at Ticonderoga.

With three others he had built a hut, and at the time of his capture was residing six miles from any white settlement. No danger was apprehended from the Indians. Since the decisive victories of Norridgewock and Pequawket, they had appeared perfectly subdued, and lived on the most friendly terms with their more powerful neighbors. Since the breaking out of war there had been some indications of returning hostility, but not enough to excite alarm. Frequently they had come to the settlements, painted and decorated for war, and occasionally, for a moment, assumed their old demeanor of insolent brutality; but their generally kind and frank manner quieted all fear, and no one imagined harm.

On the day above stated Segar and two others, Jonathan Clark and Eleazer Twitchell, were at work in the field some distance from any house. Suspecting nothing, they were entirely unarmed. Suddenly six Indians, headed by one Tomhegan, a bold, impudent fellow, well known to the settlers, painted and armed with guns, tomahawks and scalping-knives, with a shrill war-whoop, sprang from a piece of woods near by, and made captives of the three.

Having secured their prisoners they marched them to Clark's house, the nearest to the party. Here they bound them down, and, with threats of killing them if they attempted to escape, commenced plundering the premises. Clark's wife, a courageous, resolute woman, did not admire the operation, and determined by stratagem or fight to oppose it. While they were filling their bottles with some rum they had found in the cellar, she took her husband's valuable watch and hid it in the ashes. Some old clothing she allowed them to take, without making any objection; but when they demanded the gold necklace on her neck, she plainly told them they could not have it, and summoned all her strength to fight it out. In the struggle which ensued, the string broke, the beads flew about the floor, and the Indians were never the richer by one. Not succeeding in obtaining the beads, they next demanded the silver buckles on her shoes; but the undaunted woman gave them to understand, in plain words and a shrill voice, that her feet and the buckles on them were her own, and their safety lay in not meddling with them; and so thoroughly were the fellows frightened, that they made no more attempts on her.

While this was going on, her husband and the others were quaking with fear that the Indians would become infuriated, and kill the whole party together. Says one of the trembling captives: "My fears were that they would kill her; she was very bold towards them, and showed no fears."

During the struggle with Mrs. Clark, another Indian joined the party with Mr. Benjamin Clark, whom he had just taken. Him they secured, and sat down to count their gains, and make their arrangements for escaping undetected with their prisoners. Twitchell, seeing them thus engaged, and somewhat emboldened by the courageous bearing of the woman and the timidity of the savages, slipped his fastenings, and left suddenly for the woods, where, hiding himself among the logs, he escaped the search made for him.

The Indians, having determined on their course, packed up their plunder into large, heavy bundles, which they fastened on the backs of their prisoners. Whether fearing to take Mrs. Clark or not, they left her unharmed, simply remarking, as the fearless matron followed her husband to the door, that, if she remained in the house, she would not be molested; but, if she attempted to follow, she would be killed, for there were hundreds of Indians in the woods. Numbers, they might have thought, would terrify her, who, if they had undertaken to lead her off with them with their present forces, would have been quite likely to have turned upon them with

> "Nay, then,
> Do what thou canst, I will not go to-day;
> No, nor to-morrow, nor till I please myself."

It was now late, and they could go but a few miles before it would be dark. With heavy hearts the poor men trudged on under their heavy burdens, their hands bound closely behind them, and their captors continually hurrying their speed, fearing their booty might be taken from them. Continuing on as long as they could see, the darkness at length compelled them to halt for the night in the hut of one Peter Austin, who, fortunately, chanced to be from home. Here they found but little to plunder. Two guns,— one of them not good for anything, which they broke to pieces,— and a little sugar, were all they could find.

Tightening the cords with which they were tied until their hands were benumbed, they compelled their captives to lie down, and, surrounding them, the savages went to sleep. Says our narrator: "Here we spent a gloomy night, which none can realize except those who have been in a like condition." At daylight the Indians were astir, and lading their captives for the march. In Gilead, then Peabody's Patent, they stopped at the house of one Pettengill. Pettengill himself was not in the house, but some distance from it, in sight; and, the Indians calling him, he instantly came in. They searched the house, as usual, and found sugar and some cream in a tub, on which they breakfasted, "eating like hogs," but gave none to the prisoners.

After finishing the repast, they told Pettengill he must go with them, and to make himself ready. But he pleaded his want of shoes; and fearing, perhaps, resistance, or the danger of having too large a number of captives, they left him, but strictly charged that he should not leave the house. Mrs. Pettengill and the children, remaining quiet, received no abuse.

They had gone but a short distance from the house when two of the Indians returned, captured and bound Pettengill, and gave him his load among the others. But, for some reason, they feared him. They dared not take him with them, and they dared not leave him free. But one course was left, and, after having proceeded but a little way, they killed him on the spot. His wife, a few days after, discovered his body, and friends from Bethel buried it.

At Shelburne the Indians became greatly alarmed. Questioning some children, whom they found at play near a small brook, concerning the number of men in an adjoining house, they replied there were ten, and that they all had guns. This so terrified them that they placed all the packs on the prisoners, and prepared themselves to take to their heels if attacked. The poor fellows, thus loaded down, were ordered to cross the Androscoggin river at a place where "it was never forded before or since." None of the men could swim, and how they succeeded in getting over, our narrator says he "cannot imagine." The fright, however, was groundless, as not a man was in the house. At the house of Hope Austin, which they passed, they found money, and other booty of less value, but left Mrs. Austin unharmed, bidding her remain in the house.

They were now on the very outposts of the scattered frontier settlements. Some miles after leaving the house of

Austin, Tomhegan, the instigator of these barbarities, left the party, and struck out into a by-path. He had not been gone long, when a gun was heard, and, soon after, Tomhegan returned with a negro, named Plato. He had been lurking round the premises of a Capt. Rindge, and, as one Poor and Plato were going out to work, Tomhegan had called to them to come to him. Poor, suspecting treachery, turned to run, when Tomhegan instantly shot him, and captured the black.

After learning from Plato that there was no one to fear but Capt. Rindge and wife, it was determined to march the captives to the house. Rindge was exceedingly terrified. He not only submitted patiently to the plundering of the savages, but even brought them articles they would never have found. Here the poor prisoners fared well. While they were eating, the Indians went out and scalped Poor. A boy named Ingalls was seized, but, by the persuasion of Rindge, was left.

Having satisfied their cupidity, they started on. Finding the number of captives too large to manage safely, they told Jonathan Clark he might return, provided he would keep the path they had travelled. Suspecting something was wrong, after going a short distance out of sight of the Indians, he left the path, and struck out into the woods. As he afterwards learned, it was the saving of his life; for, not long after he had taken the woods, two Indians who had been left behind came along the path, and would undoubtedly have killed him as a deserter.

Capt. Rindge's was the last house on the frontier, and an unbroken wilderness now lay between them and Canada. Shortly after leaving the house, the Indians took a large piece of spruce bark, and ordered Segar to write on it, that if they were taken by Americans the prisoners would all be killed. This they fastened to a tree.

At the encampments at night the savages amused themselves by their brutal dances. Says our author, of one of these scenes: "During our tarry in this place, we were permitted to sit down and rest ourselves; but they would not permit us to sit together. This was a very rocky place. Here they took the hair of their scalps in their teeth, and began to shake their heads, to whoop, to jump from rock to rock, and conducted and acted in such a hideous and awful manner, as almost to make our hair stand upright upon our heads, and to fill us with fear and trembling. I had heard of an Indian powwow; but what tongue can tell, or imagination can describe, the looks and actions of these savages on such occasions? Such scenes are beyond description. Their actions are inconceivable. It would seem that Bedlam had broken loose, and that hell was in an uproar."

After reaching Umbagog Lake, the remaining distance was made in canoes, carrying them on their shoulders across the carrying-places. During the whole march the captives suffered exceedingly from hunger. For days nothing would be given them to eat; and, when so worn down that they could with difficulty move, old moccasons of moose-skin, tainted by the heat, would be broiled, and bits of it given them. But once after leaving the settlements until they reached the St. Francois river was anything eatable given them, and this was moose-meat dried in the smoke. Most of this distance, too, they travelled with their hands tied fast behind them.

After reaching the St. Francois they fared better. Fish were plenty in these waters, and easily taken. Sturgeon were taken in large quantities by torchlight. As they came among the remote settlers, milk frequently was obtained, and occasionally, says our narrator, "we had good bread and milk to eat, which was a very luscious dish, and highly pleasing to us, and we ate as much as we wanted."

But a short distance from their village the Indians commenced loud demonstrations of rejoicing. As they entered the encampment, it was dark; but the Indians made it as light as day with their torches. There were seventy Indian warriors at this place. "When we came near the shore, an Indian clinched me by the arm, and violently pulled me to him, swaggering over me as though he would have killed me. I was surrounded by the Indians on every side, with terrible countenances, and of a strange language which I did not understand. At this time there were great rejoicings among them over the prisoners, scalps and plunder, which they had taken in this nefarious enterprise."

The captives were readily given up to the British officers, except Clark. No abuse was offered them amid the wild carousal of their captors. Black Plato stood awhile as a mark at which they threw firebrands; but, crying lustily, was released uninjured.

Clark had completely taken the fancy of the Indians, or, perhaps, of the squaws. They determined on making him their chief, and had already "cut off his hair, painted him, and dressed him in an Indian dress," when they were prevailed upon to give him up. A bounty was paid the Indians by the British officers of eight dollars for a scalp, or for a prisoner.

"We were here under guard two days. After this, we were given up by the British guard to the Indians, with an interpreter, to carry us in their canoes to Montreal. About ten Indians took the charge of us. On account of contrary head winds, we were many days in going up the river St. Lawrence. The prisoners were sometimes ordered to march by land, with a number of Indians to guard them. When we were in the canoes we were not permitted to wear our shoes. The canoes, as soon as we were on the land, left the shore even before I could pick up my shoes. When the Indians came up again, I immediately went for my shoes; but I could not find them. I asked for them, but an Indian told me they had sold them for pipes. I found some fault with them for their conduct; but they told me the king would find me shoes. These were the last things they could take from me. They had ordered me to give them my shirt before, and they gave me an old frock for it without giving me any back. I could not help myself, for I was a prisoner, and in their power.

"We at length arrived at Montreal, and were conducted to the commander. There were three of us. They examined us, and asked us many questions; — where we were taken prisoners; how long we had been in the American service, and many other like questions.

"The Indians requested the commander that they might keep Mr. Clark; but he would not grant their request. The Indians then took off all the ornaments from him, and every rag of clothes, except a very short shirt. They now received their bounty money for the prisoners and scalps. They took Plato away with them, and sold him to a Frenchman in Canada. Afterwards he was sent back to his old master, Capt. Rindge. The rest of us were given up to the British. We were ordered to go with a man, who conducted us to the jail, and delivered us to the guard, where were ten prisoners, and some of them confined in irons. Our situation now was truly distressing. We had been so worn down with hunger and a fatiguing journey through the wilderness, and distressing fears in our minds, that we were almost ready to despond. Our allowance was not half sufficient for us. In this place were multitudes of rats, which would devour the whole allowance that was granted to us, and was of itself too small for us; but we took every measure to secure it from the rats. The lice which we caught of the Indians were a great annoyance to our bodies. We were, therefore, afflicted on every side."

After remaining in this situation some forty days, they were sent with others to an island, fifty miles up the St. Lawrence. Here they remained till the close of the war in 1782, enduring much from the extreme cold and want of food. On the general exchange of prisoners attendant upon peace, they were returned to Boston, after suffering sixteen months' captivity.

"I tarried at Newton some time to refresh myself, after I returned from captivity; and, soon after the peace, I returned to Bethel, and have made me a small farm, where I have resided ever since, and have reared up a large family. I have undergone all the hardships and self-denials which are incident to those who are engaged in settling new countries; but have lived to see the town rise from a howling wilderness into fruitful fields, and in flourishing circumstances, and peace and order promoted therein for the rising generations and those yet unborn."

CHAPTER XVIII.

SHELBURNE.

SITUATION OF SHELBURNE. — MOUNTAINS. — EVENING DRIVE AMONG THE MOUNTAINS. — MOUNT MORIAH. — MOSES' ROCK. — GRANNY STARBIRD'S LEDGE. — WHY SO CALLED. — MINERAL WEALTH OF THIS TOWN. — EARLY SETTLERS. — MR. DANIEL INGALLS. — MOSES INGALLS. — KILLING THE DEVIL. — ROBERT FLETCHER INGALLS. — SUFFERINGS OF THE EARLY SETTLERS. — INDIAN MASSACRE. — TERRIBLE ENCOUNTER WITH WOLVES. — THE FAMISHED SOLDIER.

> "Long since that white-haired ancient slept; but
> Still *   *   *   *   *   *   *
> *   * his venerable form again
> Is at my side, his voice is in my ear."

THIS town, situated in Coös County, was chartered as early as the year 1668. It was rechartered by George III., King of England, to Mark H. Wentworth and six others. It then included what was called Shelburne Addition, now incorporated into a town called Gorham. This new charter was given in the year 1771, and the town surveyed by Theodore Atkinson the same year. The town is bounded north by Success, east by Maine and Bean's Purchase, and west by Gorham. The population in 1820, when it was incorporated, was 205. In 1850 it was 430, indicating a fair increase. The Androscoggin river passes through the centre of the town, into which fall the waters of Rattle river and many smaller streams. The soil on each bank of the river is very good, producing in abundance grain and grass; but, as we rise from the river, the land becomes mountainous and unfit for cultivation. Besides the ranges of mountains bordering on the river, many isolated peaks stand within its bounds. Mount Moriah, the highest of the several summits, lies in the southern part of the town. "It was so named, by one of the early settlers of the region, because its shape or position coincided with some conception he had formed of its Scripture namesake." A writer in the Boston *Transcript* thus describes the beauty of this and other mountains lying within an evening's drive of the Alpine House, in Gorham:

"About six in the evening is the time for a drive. Nature, as Willis charmingly said, pours the wine of her beauty twice a day — in the early morning, and the evening when the long shadows fall. Here the saying is more literally true, not only as to the shadows, but in regard to color. Her richest flasks are reserved for the dessert-hour of the day's feast. Then they are bountifully poured. Herr Alexander and Wizard Anderson, when they perform the trick of turning many liquors from one bottle, to an astonished crowd, meanly parody the magic of the evening sun shedding over these hills the most various juices of light from his single urn. Those strong, substantial, twin-majesties, Madison and Jefferson, have a steady preference for a brown-sherry hue; the Androscoggin Hills take to the lighter and sparkling yellows, hocks and champagne; but the clarets, the red hermitage, and the deep purple Burgundies, are reserved for the ridge of Mount Moriah. This wine for the eye does not interfere with the temperance pledge; and the visual flavor is so delicious, that one is eager all through the day for the evening repast."

Mount Moriah is much visited by travellers. The view

from its summit is beautiful and extensive. To the east can be seen Umbagog Lake, embosomed amid high hills, the highest of which is Saddleback Mountain, and still further to the eastward the Blue Mountains in Temple, Bald Mountains in Carthage, Mount Abraham in Kingfield, and beyond all Mount Bigelow in Franklin County. South-easterly, when the atmosphere is clear, Portland and the ocean beyond may be distinctly seen with a good glass. More to the south lie Pleasant Mountain, amid numerous small sheets of water, and Lake Winnipiseogee, still further to the right. The White Mountains shut in the view on the west.

Near the centre of the town is a steep, precipitous ledge, named Moses' Rock. It is sixty feet high and ninety long, very smooth, and rising in an angle of fifty degrees. Tradition says that a hunter once drove a moose over the steep descent, and his dog, in close pursuit, followed close at his heels, both mingling together in one common mass at the foot. During the early survey of the town, the best lot of land in the township was offered to the man who would climb this ledge. One Moses Ingalls, stripping off his shoes, accomplished the daring feat, running up its smooth front like a cat. This circumstance gave it its name.

Not far from this ledge is another, called Granny Starbird's Ledge. An immense boulder, many thousand tons in weight, a great portion of which has been blown to pieces and used on the railroad, formerly rested on a shelf of this ledge. Under this large rock an old lady, named Starbird, many years ago, took shelter from a heavy, desolating storm of rain. On her way, on horseback, to see a sick person, being a doctress by profession, she took shelter under this rock, one night, as some protection against the storm. The ground was too wet to lie down; so, to protect herself and

INCIDENTS IN WHITE MOUNTAIN HISTORY.   247

horse from the pelting of the rain, she stood and held him by the bridle all night. In this condition, with sleepless attention she realized all the terrors of the storm. She saw every flash of lightning, heard every peal of thunder that broke over her, and keenly felt every gust of the tempest that swept by her shallow retreat. Her situation was anything but desirable. She bore, however, her exposure with a hardy spirit, and awaited the light of morning with a calmness such as few beside herself could exhibit. At length the light of day began to appear, but there was no cessation of the storm. This continued in its strength, and the rain fell in torrents on the projection of rock over her head. Still the wind howled around her. About noon the clouds retired, the sun shone out, and she resumed her journey. It is not strange that, from such a circumstance, the ledge under which she rested that fearful night should ever since bear the name of " Granny Starbird's Ledge."

A lead mine was discovered a few years since in the northwest part of this town, on a hill-side, and in the bed of a small mountain rivulet. The ravine is a deep gap in the mica-slate rocks which form the principal mass of the mountain, and in this are numerous veins of quartz and brown spar, with veins of lead, zinc and copper ore. The veins of ore contain much brown spar, or carbonate of lime, and iron in the form of rhomboids and in foliated masses. The black blende fills the narrow parts of the vein, and the swells or pockets are filled with very pure and heavy masses of the argentiferous galena, almost free from the zinc ore. Sixteen hundred and eighty grains of this Shelburne lead yield three grains of fine silver.

On a Mr. Burbank's farm, in this town, where the Androscoggin river cuts through the intervales, are large numbers of forest trees buried in the alluvial soil at the depth of from ten to twelve feet. The trees project from the bank into the river, and are generally found to lie in a nearly horizontal position, the tops pointing to the northward. The wood is but little altered, and is sufficiently sound to be sawed, many of the maples having been dug out and manufactured into wheels for wagons. From the magnitude of the stumps of trees that are found on the surface, which are estimated to be at least two hundred years old, and from the fineness of the strata of alluvial matter covering the buried trees, it is evident that they must have been buried there for a great length of time. The prevalence of clay over and around them accounts for their not having undergone decomposition; the exclusion of air and the prevention of the circulation of water having contributed to their preservation.

Some of the first settlers in the town of Shelburne were Hope Austin, Benjamin and Daniel Ingalls. These moved into it in the year 1770. In 1772 came Thomas Green Wheeler, Nathaniel Porter and Peter Poor, who was afterwards killed by the Indians.

In 1780 came Moses Messer, Capt. Jonathan Rindge, Jonathan Evans and Simeon Evans, all valuable men, who left a good impress on the general character of their posterity. One of them was particularly a worthy man, and conspicuous in his day for the many moral virtues he exhibited. His name was fragrant with piety in all the region about him. Mr. Daniel Ingalls was generally known and highly esteemed in all the vicinity of the White Mountains. A sense of the divine mercy seemed to be ever present with him, whether he sat in the house, or walked by the way. In his journeyings, he has been heard frequently, on alighting from his horse, and while drinking at some spring by the roadside, to ejaculate, "How good the Lord is, to furnish so plentifully this refreshing water to drink!" He exhibited religion in its best light. In his conversation and general deportment he presented it in a manner to show its real character. He was cheerful, and yet you would very seldom say he verged to levity; sober when he should be, and yet seldom seen with an aspect of sadness or gloom on his face. He was a man of much prayer, and always attached as much importance to the duties as he did to the doctrines of religion; as much to what commended its practice as he did to its precept. Many interesting anecdotes have been told of him in our hearing, some of which we shall here relate. He once took a journey of considerable length with Col. David Page — a cotemporary of his living in Conway. In the course of it they tarried together during a night at the house of a friend. On rising, the colonel suggested to Mr. Ingalls whether he had not better, that morning, omit family worship, which it was his usual practice to perform, and make the most of the day, by taking an early start. In his opinion this omission of worship would be best, because in the time required to perform it they might catch their horses, and be ready the sooner to start after breakfast. To all this Mr. Ingalls, often called Deacon Ingalls, kindly replied, "No, colonel, no! let us worship first." This was enough. The colonel, highly respecting the deacon, submitted. They took breakfast, and then had worship, and while they worshipped, the horses both came up to the bars of the pasture, near the house, and stood there waiting to be taken.

Another slight incident, transpiring after his death, clearly shows how Mr. Ingalls was esteemed in his life. His death made a deep sensation in the region where he was known, and that was widely extended. At Conway the news was received by all with sadness. Said a man in this town, as the news was announced to him in the field where he was at work with others, "How straight Deacon Ingalls went up to heaven when he died!" and, pointing upward with his extended arm, he continued, "No eagle ever went up straighter into the sky than he did when he breathed his last breath." This very serious appearance and language was the more noticeable, because previous to this he had generally been a very rude man, and seemed often to take pleasure in annoying the deacon with infidel cavils.

Moses and Robert Fletcher Ingalls, the two eldest sons of Deacon Ingalls, came to Shelburne soon after their father. They were both valuable men, yet quite different in their general characteristics. Their days were spent near each other, in the discharge of mutual kindnesses, and still you would seldom see two brothers more unlike. Moses was quick and irritable naturally, while Fletcher was more cool and even in his disposition. Moses was all life and energy in whatever he undertook — a grand pioneer for a new country. No hardships or discouragements seemed, in the least, to repress his energies. He was bold to a proverb, as his ascent of the ledge called by his name fully proves. Nor were his wit and shrewdness less than his courage. He was especially fond of hunting moose and bears.

One Sabbath morning, unknown to his father, he joined his companions and started on a hunt. They followed down the Androscoggin a few miles, when they espied a large moose in the river eating water-grass. Ingalls gave him a shot. The moose escaped, as they supposed, uninjured. On his return home, being asked by his father where he had been, he replied that he had been out hunting, seen a moose, and had a shot at him, but did not kill him. To this his father replied, with false discretion we think, "No, Moses! that was the devil you shot at, instead of a moose. How dare you so break the Sabbath?" Some few days after this, Moses, passing down the river, found the moose dead, killed by the shot he had given him the previous Sabbath. Returning home, with exultation marked on his countenance, he said, "Father, the devil is dead!"—"What do you say?" replied his father. "Why, Moses, what do you mean?"—"Mean, father!" said he in return, "mean, why I mean as I said, the devil is dead. You said the creature I shot at the other day was the devil, and, if so, he is dead, because I have just found the creature I know to be the one I shot at, and he is dead enough." Long after that the report went, Moses *shot* the devil.

Robert Fletcher Ingalls, familiarly called "Uncle Fletcher," to whom we have already referred as the younger brother of Moses, resided, all his days, in the first framed house ever built in Shelburne. This house is still standing, owned by his son-in-law, Barker Burbank, Esq. Some of the boards on it, still to be seen, were cut with a whip-saw, an instrument much used in early times.

In his youth, this Mr. Ingalls was very mirthful, but afterwards became more manly and serious in his deportment. He was respected, by all that knew him, as a man of genuine piety and Christian benevolence. He aimed at all times, and everywhere, to be doing good. To the cause of temperance, especially, he was an early and ardent friend. The first temperance meeting, we think, ever had under the shadow of these mountains, was under his direction and appointment. Among the various means he took to stay the evil, was the formation of a body, called the "Cold Water Army," designed to embrace especially the youth of both sexes in that region. By dint of much effort, he brought most of these in town, under fifteen years of age, into it. He regarded it as a sort of child in his old age, and spared no toil in laboring for its extension and prosperity. On the fourth of July, the year before his death, in a procession formed for celebrating the day, he was put at the head of his army and marched to the meeting-house to listen to an oration. After the oration, by request, he addressed the young soldiers of the army. And it was an address, as we have been told, worth hearing; kind, instructive and pathetic. Scarcely an eye in the assembly was free from tears when the old man sat down.

Among many impressive counsels and expostulations, he uttered on this occasion, these were a few: "I charge you," turning himself to the parents of the children, and the citizens of the town, "I charge you, in the name of Heaven, to bring up these children right. Train them in the good way of temperance and sobriety; guard them from evil as you would the most precious jewels put into your hands." He spoke in this way till there was not an unfeeling heart in the assembly. And now he is dead we may suppose he is still speaking to some of the survivors of that tearful assembly through the sweet and clear recollections of his looks and words.

The history of Shelburne is strikingly diversified with scenes of toil and hardships endured by its early settlers. Mr. Hope Austin with his family, consisting of a wife and three children, moved into this town April 1st, 1781. At that time there was five feet of snow on the ground. All the way from Bethel they waded through this depth of snow, occasionally going on the ice of the Androscoggin river, along which their path lay. The furniture was drawn by Mr. Austin and two hired men, on hand-sleds. Mrs. Austin went on foot, carrying her youngest child, nine months old, in her arms, with Judith the eldest girl, six years of age, and little James, then four years, trudging by her side. They went, in this way, at least twelve miles to their place of residence. When they arrived at their new home, they found simply the walls of a cabin without floor or roof. To make a shelter from the rains and snows, they cut poles and laid them across the walls to serve as the support of a roof. On these they laid rough shingles covering a space large enough for a bed. With no more covering on its roof, and with only some shingles nailed together and put into one of the sides for a door, they lived till the next June.

Then they covered all its walls, and gave it an entire roof. For something to shelter their cow, they dug a large square hole in the snow, down to the ground, and covered it over with poles and boughs. This served as a house till the snow went off, and then the poor cow needed no shelter but the open heavens. Thus they lived quietly and happily, if not very comfortably, till August, the time of the Indian massacre.

An account of this has been given, in part, in the narrative of the captivity of Nathaniel Segar. What was omitted by him, not coming under his observation, we shall here give. Segar tells us that a party of Indians from the woods, painted and armed with tomahawks, came upon him and some others while in a field at Bethel, bound them, and after plundering the house and making a rude assault upon the wife of one of the prisoners, started them off, saying they were prisoners and must go to Canada. The first halt they made was at Gilead, where they killed and scalped Mr. James Pettengill. After this they crossed the Androscoggin with these prisoners, and went to the house of Hope Austin in Shelburne.

Here they searched for plunder. Mr. Austin being away

254   INCIDENTS IN WHITE MOUNTAIN HISTORY.

from home, they told his wife to remain in the house, and she should not be hurt. Hurrying on, they went to the house of Capt. Rindge, further up the river. Here they killed and scalped Peter Poor, and took Plato, the colored man, prisoner. So far Segar, in his narrative, has traced their course, though much more minutely in its various details. Now, leaving him to pass on his way to Canada with the Indians, we shall take up those parts of the sad scene which he did not witness. Hope Austin, who was at Capt. Rindge's at the time the Indians and their prisoners went into his own house, when they approached Capt. Rindge's, after seeing Poor killed, and Plato taken prisoner, fled immediately across the Androscoggin. Following down this river a mile or two, he came to the house of Mr. Daniel Ingalls. Here he found his three children. His wife had been here, brought over the river in a boat by Mr. Ingalls, but had just gone back to her house on an important errand. The children came, one with a Mrs. Wentworth, who waded the river with it in her arms, and the other two in the boat with their mother. Mrs. Austin had gone back to her house just before her husband came, in company with Mrs. Wentworth, to get some meal and bring it to Ingalls', she having more of that article than any other one in the vicinity. Very soon after Austin arrived at Mr. Ingalls', most of the neighbors came hurrying in, excited by the news of the sad affair that had just taken place near Rindge's house.

Mrs. Austin and Mrs. Wentworth not returning so soon as they were expected, the whole company crossed the river and went to Mr. Austin's house. Here they found them making all haste to gather the meal and return to Mr. Ingalls'. But after consulting awhile, and reflecting that there might be danger in all the houses, they concluded to take the meal and some maple sugar, and go to the top of a mountain near by, and spend the night. They did this, and, after ascending its precipitous side, spent the night on the summit, in full hearing of the whoopings and shoutings of the Indians. From this circumstance the mountain has since been called "Hark Hill."

Finding, on their return from this mountain the following morning, that there were signs of Indians still in the neighborhood, they fled to Fryburg, all the way through the forest, fifty-nine miles from Shelburne. Here they remained till the danger was passed. Then again they sought their home in the wilderness. The season being unpropitious, the return company, numbering about twelve persons, old and young, made their way back through many hardships and sufferings. It was March, and a large quantity of snow was on the ground. Their journey about half accomplished, they encountered a terrible storm of rain. The men were compelled to stand out in the open air, and buffet its force through one whole night, while the women and children were protected from it only by ticks of beds drawn over poles. These exposures they endured with noble courage, and at length reached the end of their journey.

One of the most terrible encounters with wolves ever put on record is said to have taken place in this town. A Mr. Austin, returning home on a time with his team, overtook an Indian, bent almost double with the heavy pack on his back. Kindly he offered the Indian a ride, which the weary man gladly accepted. During the ride, Austin asked the Indian his name. He replied, somewhat facetiously, that John Peter or Peter John suited him, just which it pleased the fancies of others to call him. At the junction of two roads they separated, the Indian shouldering again his heavy load, and going in an opposite direction to the team. After leaving Mr. Austin, a pack of famished wolves attacked the poor Indian with all the fury of starvation. How long the battle lasted we know not, nor how many remained of the hungry pack to devour the Indian; but when the spot was visited not long after, seven carcasses of huge wolves lay beside the clothes and bones of their slayer. Seven of the monsters he had slain ere he himself yielded the struggle.

Leaving the Atlantic and St. Lawrence railroad at Strafford, and following up the Connecticut river to the boundary between New Hampshire and Canada, you come to a little river, one of the tributaries of the Connecticut, called "Hall's Stream." On its bank a poor soldier named Hall was drowned. The starved man dragged his skeleton body to the bank of the stream to drink. His head hung over a little descent, and, unable to raise it, he drowned, the water playing with his long hair when he was found.

At the time of the deplorable situation of the American army near Quebec, especially after the fall of the lamented Montgomery, the commander in the unsuccessful attack upon it, things became so distressing, that desertion among the famished soldiers was deemed almost a virtue. Twelve of them made their appearance in Shelburne in the autumn of 1776. They were first discovered by a negro in the employment of Capt. Rindge, who succeeded, after much persuasion, in inducing them to follow him to the house of his master. Here, so far exhausted were they with hunger, that they required the strictest attention in order to be kept alive.

As soon as they were sufficiently recruited, they gave an account of the scenes through which they had passed. They told how they succeeded in getting away from the army near Quebec. They followed the course of the Chaudiere river for a long distance, till at length they crossed the high lands and came to the Magallaway river, down which they passed to its confluence with Clear Stream, at a place called Enrol. Here they left one of their number, too feeble to follow them any further. On receiving this information, Capt. Rindge immediately prepared himself with provisions and other things necessary for a journey in the wilderness, and started in quest of the soldier left behind. He took with him Moses Ingalls, to whom we have already referred, then a young man about twenty years of age. With great speed and toil they pursued their course till they came to the place designated by the soldiers in Shelburne as the one where they left their fainting comrade. After looking round, they soon found him. He had moved but little from the spot where he had been left. He lay nearly across his gun, with his long hair in the water, dead. They buried him on the shore of the stream, and, as a memorial of the poor fellow, changed the name of the little river from Clear to "Hall's Stream."

CHAPTER XIX.

GORHAM.

WHITE MOUNTAIN INDIANS. — COL. CLARK. — MOLLY OCKETT. —PEOL SUS-UP. — INDIAN ELOQUENCE. — GORHAM. — INFLUENCE OF THE RAILROAD UPON IT. — ALPINE HOUSE. — GLEN HOUSE. — MOUNT WASHINGTON ROAD. — CARRIAGES. — BUILDING OF THE "SUMMIT HOUSE."— WEATHER ON THE SUMMIT IN MAY. — ORIGIN OF PEABODY RIVER. — WONDERFUL ENDURANCE OF COLD.

A FEW things remain yet to be said concerning the White Mountain Indians. Amid the obscurity and uncertainty which shroud the many traditions respecting them, we think the following facts to be authentic. During the last years of the American Revolution, the northern Indians seem to have determined to make a final struggle for their hunting-grounds and home, and Pennacook, or Rumford Falls, in Maine, was selected as the scene of their resistance to white encroachments. No general battle was fought, but after committing many murders and barbarities on the settlers, and greatly annoying them, they retired, forgetting their revenge in the sad and weak condition of their tribe. One Tom Hegan, whom we have before mentioned, was particularly active in waylaying and killing the whites. He figures conspicuously in all the cruel Indian stories of this region. Sometimes in the employ of the British, and sometimes impelled onward by his own deep hatred, he was very bold, and bloody, and barbarous, and for a long time a terror to the settlers.

A Col. Clark, of Boston, had been in the habit of visiting annually the White Mountains, and trading for furs. He had thus become acquainted with all the settlers and many of the Indians. He was much esteemed for his honesty, and his visits were looked forward to with much interest. Tom Hegan had formed the design of killing him, and, contrary to his usual shrewdness, had disclosed his plans to some of his companions. One of them, in a drunken spree, told the secret to Molly Ockett, a squaw who had been converted to Christianity, and was much loved and respected by the whites. She determined to save Clark's life. To do it, she must traverse a wilderness of many miles to his camp. But nothing daunted the courageous and faithful woman. Setting out early in the evening of the intended massacre, she reached Clark's camp just in season for him to escape. Tom Hegan had already killed two of Clark's companions, encamped a mile or two from him. He made good his escape, with his noble preserver, to the settlements. Col. Clark's gratitude knew no bounds. In every way he sought to reward the kind squaw for the noble act she had performed. For a long time she resisted all his attempts to repay her, until at last, overcome by his earnest entreaties and the difficulty of sustaining herself in her old age, she became an inmate of his family, in Boston. For a year she bore, with a martyr's endurance, the restraints of civilized life; but at length she could do it no longer. She must die, she said, in the great forest, amid the trees, the companions of her youth. Devotedly pious, she sighed for the woods, where, under the clear blue sky, she might pray to God as she had when first converted. Clark saw her distress, and built her a wigwam on the Falls of the Pennacook, and there supported her the remainder of her days. Often did he visit her, bringing the necessary provision for her sustenance.

It is the tragical end of this same Tom Hegan, we think, which is so commonly remembered by many of the old inhabitants in Maine, even to this day. "He was tied upon a horse, with spurs on his heels, in such a manner that the spurs continually goaded the animal. When the horse was set at liberty, he ran furiously through an orchard, and the craggy limbs of the trees tore him to pieces."

A daughter of this Molly Ockett married one Peol Susup, we think the one who was afterwards tried for murder at Castine. This Peol Susup was a Penobscot Indian; but the northern and eastern tribes freely intermarried, we believe. "All the tribes between the Saco and the St. John, both inclusive, are brothers."

As a specimen of Indian oratory, the speech of John Neptune, the chief of the tribe, at the trial of Susup, may not be uninteresting. "The case was nearly as follows : — On the evening of the 28th of June, 1816, this Indian was intoxicated, and at the tavern of one Knight, at Bangor (whether he had procured liquor there with which to intoxicate himself, we are not informed) ; and being noisy and turbulent, Knight endeavored to expel him from his house. Having thrust him out of doors, he endeavored to drive him away, and in the attempt was stabbed, and immediately died. On his arrest, Susup acknowledged his guilt, but said he was in liquor, and that Knight abused him, or he had not done it. Being brought to trial in June, the next year, at Castine, by advice of counsel he pleaded not guilty ; and, after a day spent in his trial, a verdict was rendered according to the defence set up, manslaughter.

"After the sentence was declared, Susup was asked by the court if he had anything to say for himself; to which he replied, 'John Neptune will speak for me.' Neptune rose up, and, having advanced towards the judges, deliberately said, in English:

"'You know your people do my Indians great deal wrong. They abuse them very much, — yes, they murder them. Then they walk right off; nobody touches them. This makes my heart burn. Well, then, my Indians say, "We will go kill your very bad and wicked men." No, I tell 'em, never do that thing — we are brothers. Some time ago, a very bad man about Boston shot an Indian dead. Your people said, surely he should die; but it was not so. In the great prison-house he eats and lives to this day. Certainly he never dies for killing Indian. My brother say let that bloody man go free — Peol Susup too. So we wish. Hope fills the hearts of us all. Peace is good. These my Indians love it well. They smile under its shade. The white men and red men must be always friends. The Great Spirit is our father. I speak what I feel.'

"Susup was sentenced to another year's imprisonment, and required to find sureties for keeping the peace two years in the penal sum of five hundred dollars, when John Neptune, Squire Jo Merry Neptune, of his own tribe, Captain Solmond, from Passamaquoddy, and Captain Jo Tomer, from the river St. John, became his sureties in the cognizance."

Gorham is a rough, unproductive township, lying on the northerly base of the mountains. It was formerly called Shelburne Addition; but was incorporated by its present name, June 18th, 1836. Numerous streams descend from the mountains, through this town, into the Androscoggin.

The opening of the Atlantic and St. Lawrence Railroad brought this little town out from the greatest obscurity, and it has become one of the great resorts for the travelling community. Its peculiarly favorable situation for viewing the mountains was never known, until travellers, posting through its borders for other destinations, were compelled to admire its beauties.

Immediately on the completion of the railroad to this point, the Alpine House was erected, and the announcement made that the cars set passengers down at the very base of the White Mountains. People, for a moment, were dumb with astonishment. It had never been supposed that there was any north or south, or east or west, to these old heights; but that every one who visited them must make up his mind for a long stage-coach ride through Conway or Littleton, and ultimately be set down at the Crawford or Fabyan's. That the cars should actually carry visitors to the base of the mountains was something which every one had supposed would take place in the far-off future, but not until they themselves had ceased to travel; but it was certainly so; and the Alpine House and Gorham had become familiar words to travellers.

The Alpine House is a large hotel, owned by the railroad company. It is some distance from the base of the mountains, which are seldom ascended from this point; but for quiet and comfort, and beautiful drives, it is surpassed by no house at the mountains. A beautiful little village has sprung up around it, consisting mostly of buildings owned by the company. The post-office is kept here, and the telegraph affords an excellent opportunity to business men to visit the mountains, and attend to their business at the same time. Mount Moriah, Randolph Hill, Berlin Falls, and Lary's, should all be visited before the traveller takes his departure.

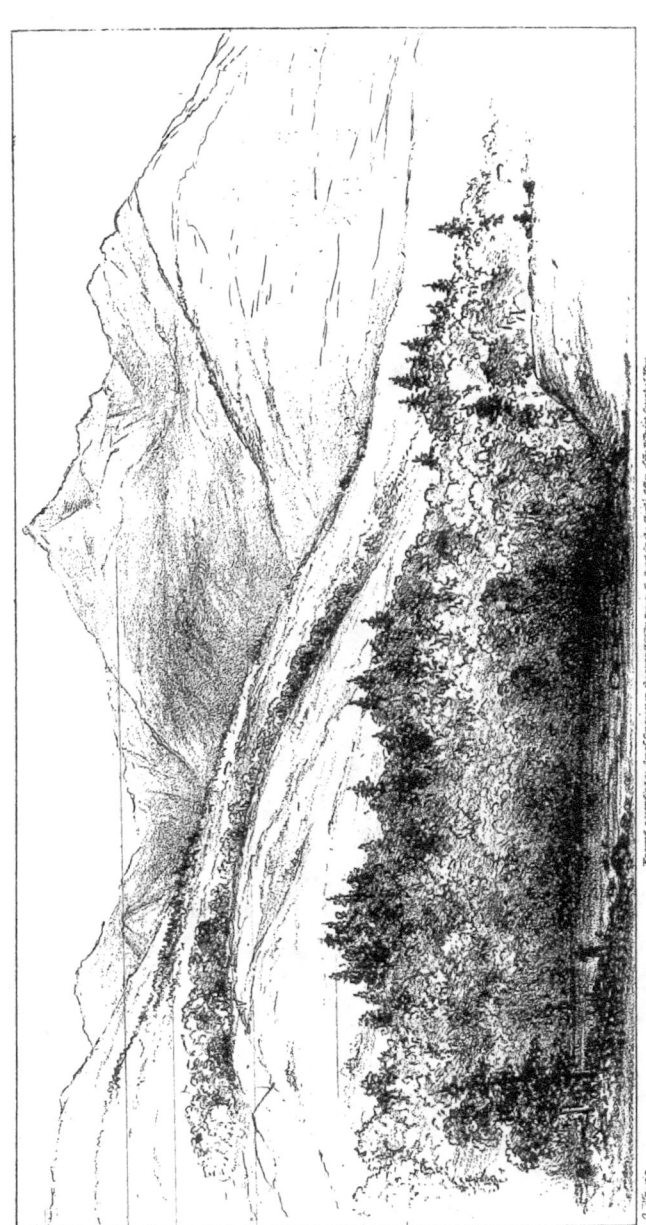

MT. JEFFERSON AND ADAMS FROM THE GLEN HOUSE.

The Glen House is seven miles from the Alpine House, in the valley of the Peabody river, immediately under Mount Washington, and in the midst of the loftiest summits in the whole mountain district. The house is situated in Bellows' Clearing, which contains about a hundred acres. For a base view of the mountains, no spot could be selected so good. Several huge mountains show themselves proudly to view, in front of the piazza, nothing intervening to obscure their giant forms. "You see them before you in all their noble, calm and silent grandeur, severally seeming the repose of power and strength. On the left is the *mountain* bearing the *worthiest name* our country ever gave us. Toward the right of its rock-crowned summit rise, in full view, the celebrated peaks of Adams and Jefferson — the one pointed, the other rounded. On both wings of these towering summits are the tops of lesser elevations. In an opposite direction, fronting the 'patriot group,' of gigantic forms, is the long, irregular rise of Carter Mountains."

The carriage road to the summit of Mount Washington starts from this point. We have described this road in a previous chapter, but find the following additional facts in a late Boston paper. Such a gigantic enterprise cannot be too often referred to. "The Mount Washington Road Company are now pushing on the work of grading up the mountain, as rapidly as possible. Between two and three miles are finished, and the whole is to be completed this fall. The carriages, of which we have just seen a model, are to be of omnibus form, each to hold twelve persons. The vehicles are to be drawn by four horses. The passengers will not sit facing each other, nor facing the front, but half way between these two positions. A separate seat is arranged for each passenger, and each carriage has only twelve seats inside. The body of the carriage is so arranged as to be raised in front in ascending, and in the rear in descending the mountains, so as to always keep the body on a level. The brake is so applied to the wheels as to insure perfect safety, being operated much in the same way as railroad-car brakes. The only difference is, that these are moved by the feet of the driver instead of his hands. A safety-strap passes up into the carriage, and, by a ring lying on the bottom, the motion of the horses may be arrested by any one of the passengers, if necessary.

"The carriages are to be built by Downing and Sons, Concord, N. H., and with a view of embodying these improvements, which are all made by D. O. Macomber, Esq., President of the Road Company, they have constructed the model examined by us yesterday. The character of Downing and Sons, and their fame as omnibus and carriage builders, is a guaranty that the workmanship will be of a superior kind, and worthy of the *elevated* use of the vehicles."

The building of the Summit House, on the top of Mount Washington, was a noble undertaking. No one but a Yankee would ever have thought of building a house where heretofore men had hardly been able, on account of the cold, and wind, and storms, to remain long enough to obtain a satisfactory view of what surrounded them. The bold thought, we believe, is due to Joseph S. Hall, who was a guide from the Notch House for many years, and who saw the necessity of a shelter at the summit.

Mr. Hall disclosed his plans to a Mr. Rosebrook, a brother farmer of Jefferson, and together they determined to undertake the task. No one surely owned the top of Mount Washington; no one ever thought of owning it, save one

Nazro, a moon-mad Jew, who sought to establish tolls around the summit, and himself sat down to collect the fees. But to make all sure, a lawyer was employed to search the records at Concord, and it was fully ascertained that the State of New Hampshire had never granted to any one the acre of solid rock which crowned Mount Washington. J. M. Thompson, Esq., the landlord of the Glen House, granted them for a small compensation the use of his bridle-path, over which to transport their material; and the first day of June, 1852, they broke ground, or rather rock, for their house, and, the twenty-fifth day of July, sat down to dinner in it, with the outside completed. The state of the atmosphere on the summit, during these early months, may be imagined from an account of an ascent made in the month of May, the 9th instant, this year, 1855.

"The second and third miles we found the snow from two to four feet deep, and with sufficient crust for snow-shoeing. At the old 'half-way camp,' we left our snow-shoes, and proceeded on an icy crust, so solid that a heel stamp would scarcely dent it. All the high mountain streams are yet fettered by the strong chain of winter, and in several places we were compelled to cut stepping-places in the ice with our hatchets, that we might advance. In this manner we at last arrived at the foot of the highest crag, when, trumpeted along by the deafening roar of high wintry wind, a frost-cloud came over us, and shrouded us in white. We found our houses yet firmly resisting the destructive power that freely moves around them in this exposed latitude; and after much difficulty succeeded in entering the Tip-Top house by a back window. The doors and windows of both houses were securely covered with a glistening crust of thick frost, and against the doors snow was banked up so solid, that even with a good axe and spade, I think we could not have lived to cut away an entrance, with the wind and sleet so strong against us. I can say truly, that, entering as we did on one side sheltered by rocks from the wind, we were compelled to make constant and active exertion to keep from freezing, with thick gloves and heavy outside coats. In short, we went prepared with a thorough winter dress."

A camp was built about half way up the mountain, in the small growth of spruce and pine, which was to be their home while building the house. Several tough, scrubby mountain horses and pack-saddles were purchased, and a number of stout, able-bodied men were hired. Thus prepared, they at length commenced operations. A few commenced blasting heavy blocks of stone from the solid mountain itself, and laying up the walls of the house. A few were employed down at the camp in hewing timbers and riving shingles, and the remainder brought up from the valley below, on their own shoulders, and on the horses, boards and "*fixins*" for the finishing. Those on the summit could work but a few hours during the day, and some days not any. Occasionally, clouds of sleet and snow would come drifting over the summit, so frosty and biting, that the utmost exertion could only save them from being thoroughly numbed. Their only safety then was in fleeing to their camp. Thus whole days would be spent in going to and from their work. Around the summit it would appear all clear and comfortable, and up they would go to their labor. Hardly would they be fairly commenced, when some sudden storm would come upon them, and down they would be forced to go to their shelter. Seldom more than two or three consecutive hours could they work at once. The house was located under the lee of the highest rock on Mount Wash-

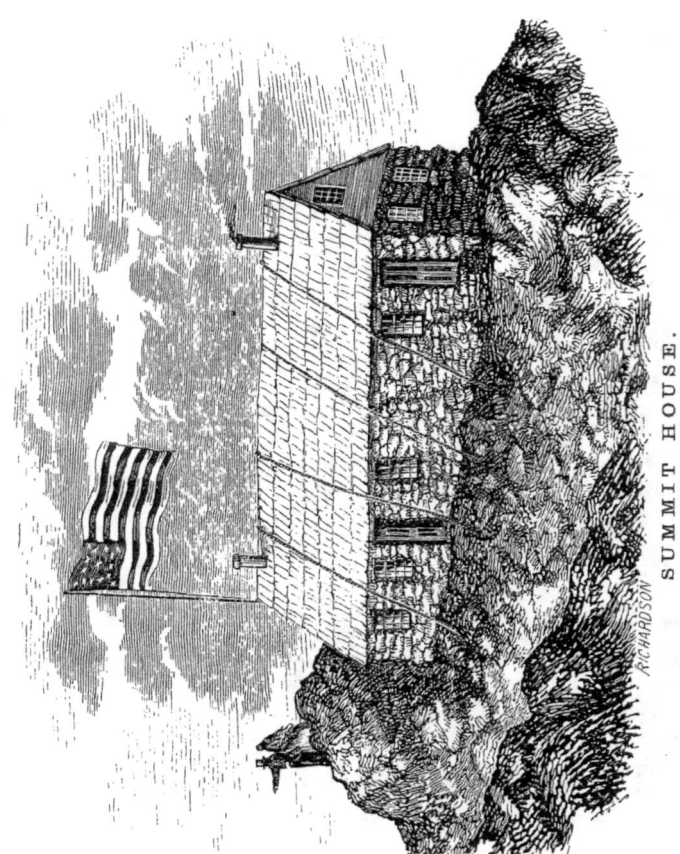

SUMMIT HOUSE.

ington, and was laid out forty feet long, and twenty-two feet wide. The walls were four feet thick, laid in cement, and every stone had to be raised to its place by muscular strength alone.

While these were laying the walls, the material for finishing and furnishing were being dragged up from the Glen House, a distance of six miles. Lime, boards, nails, shingles, timbers, furniture, crockery, bedding and stoves, all had to be brought up by piecemeal on the men's or horses' backs. No one ever went up without taking something — a chair, or door, or piece of crockery. Four boards (about sixty feet) could be carried up at once on a horse's back, and, but one trip could be made daily. Mr. Rosebrook, a *young giant*, carried up at one time a door of the usual length, three feet wide, three and one half inches thick, ten pounds of pork, and one gallon of molasses.

The walls were raised eight feet high, and to these the roof was fastened by strong iron bolts; while over the whole structure were passed strong cables, fastened to the solid mountain itself. The inside was thrown, primitive fashion, into one room, in which the beds were arranged, berth-like, for the most part on one side of the room, in two tiers, with curtains in front. A table, capable of seating thirty or forty persons, ran lengthwise of the room. At one end of the room a cooking-stove and the other furniture of a kitchen were placed, with a curtain between it and the table. At the other end was a small stove, in which was burned mountain moss. The walls are perfectly rough, outside and in; a little plaster upon the inside merely fills up the chinks. The house trembles and creaks in the gale, but stands strong. Says one: "The Summit House is quite as good a place as a 'cottage chamber,' wherein to listen to the strain,

> 'Which is played upon the shingles,
> By the patter of the rain.'

"It seems like the times of bygone days, when we used to sleep in a chamber with nothing overhead but the humble roof.

> 'Every tinkle on the shingles
> Has an echo on the heart,
> And a thousand dreary fancies
> Into busy being start,
> And a thousand recollections
> Weave their bright hues into woof,
> As I listen to the patter
> Of the soft rain on the roof.'"

"The father of Oliver Peabody, who resided at Andover, Mass., in one of his excursions into New Hampshire, met with an adventure, which has connected his name with the geography of the country, and which, for that reason, as well as for its singularity, may perhaps with propriety be mentioned here. He was passing the night in the cabin of an Indian, situated on the side of a mountain, in the neighborhood of Saco river. The inmates of this rude dwelling were awakened in the course of the night by a loud noise, and had scarcely time to make their escape, before their hut was swept away by a torrent of water rushing impetuously down the hill. On reconnoitring the ground, they found that this torrent had burst out suddenly from a spot where there was no spring before. It has continued flowing ever since, and forms the branch of the Saco which bears the name of Peabody's river."

A late number of the *State of Maine* contains the following narrative, which it almost curdles one's blood to read. We were in Shelburne, at the time it transpired, collecting materials for our work, and saw ourselves young Goulding, who was at the hotel under the care of a physician. Who besides these men would not have yielded to death in such an extremity?

"On January 31st, Nathaniel Copp, son of Hayes D. Copp, of Pinkham's Grant, near the Glen House, White Mountains, commenced hunting deer, and was out four successive days. On the fifth day, he left again for a deer killed the day previously, about eight miles from home. He dragged the deer (weighing two hundred and thirty pounds) home through the snow, and at one o'clock, P. M., started for another one discovered near the place where the former was killed, which he followed until he lost the track, about dark. He then found he had lost his own way, and should, in all probability, be obliged to spend the night in the woods, the thermometer at the time ranging from thirty-two to thirty-four degrees below zero.

"Despair being no part of his composition, with perfect self-possession and presence of mind, he commenced walking, having no provisions, matches, or even a hatchet; knowing that to remain quiet was certain death. He soon after heard a deer, and, pursuing him by moonlight, overtook him, leaped upon his back, and cut his throat. He then dressed him, and, taking out the heart, placed it in his pocket for a trophy. He continued walking twenty-one hours, and the next day, at about ten o'clock, A. M., he came out at or near Wild river, in Gilead, in Maine; having walked on snow-shoes the unparalleled distance of forty miles without rest, a part of the time through an intricate growth of underbrush.

"His friends at home becoming alarmed at his prolonged absence, and the intensity of the cold, three of them started in pursuit of him, viz., John Goulding, Mr. Hayes D.

Copp, his father, and Thomas Culbane. They followed his track, until it was lost in darkness, and, by the aid of dogs, found the deer which young Copp had killed and dressed. They then built a fire, and waited five or six hours for the moon to rise, to enable them to continue their search. They again started, with but the faintest hopes of ever finding the lost one alive; pursued his track, and, being out twenty-six hours in the intense cold, found the young man of whom they were in search.

"Goulding froze both his feet so badly that it is feared he will have to suffer amputation. Mr. Copp and Mr. Culbane froze their ears badly. No words can reward the heroic self-denial and fortitude with which these men continued an almost hopeless search, when every moment expecting to find the stiffened corpse of their friend.

"Young Copp seems not to have realized the great danger he has passed through, and, although his medical advisers say he cannot entirely recover the use of his limbs for from three to six months, talks with perfect coolness of taking part in hunts which he planned for the next week."

CHAPTER XX.

ALBANY, FRANCONIA, AND BETHLEHEM.

DRAKE'S VERSION OF CHOCORUA'S CURSE. — POPULAR LEGEND CONNECTED WITH THIS CURSE. — CAUSE OF THE DISEASE AMONG CATTLE IN ALBANY. — REMEDY FOR THE DISEASE. — BEAVERS. — MILITARY INCIDENT. — FRANCONIA. — IRON MINE. — EXTENT OF THE MINE. — KNIGHT'S MOOSE STORY. — VILLAGE OF BETHLEHEM. — VIEW OF THE MOUNTAINS FROM BETHLEHEM. — EARLY SETTLEMENT. — FIRST ROAD TO THE WHITE MOUNTAINS FROM BETHLEHEM. — EXPEDIENT TO KEEP FROM FREEZING. — FIRST TOWN MEETING. — BUILDING BRIDGE OVER AMMONOOSUCK. — SCARCITY OF PROVISION. — EXTREMITY TO WHICH INHABITANTS WERE DRIVEN. — BETHLEHEM OF THE PRESENT DAY.

"What a rich, sonorous word, by the way, that 'Chocorua' is! To my ears it suggests the wildness, freshness and loneliness, of the great hills. It always brings with it the sigh of the wind through mountain pines."

WE have given in another place what Drake, the author of the "History of North American Indians," considers the correct account of Chocorua's curse. There is, however, a beautiful story connected with it, whether true or not we cannot say, which should not be passed over unnoticed.

A small colony of hardy pioneers had settled at the base of this mountain. Intelligent, independent men, impatient of restraint, they had shunned the more thickly-settled portions of the country, and retired into this remote part of New Hampshire. "But there was one master-spirit among them who was capable of a higher destiny than he ever fulfilled.

"The consciousness of this had stamped something of proud humility on the face of Cornelius Campbell,— something of a haughty spirit, strongly curbed by circumstances he could not control, and at which he seemed to murmur. He assumed no superiority; but, unconsciously, he threw around him the spell of intellect, and his companions felt, they knew not why, that he was 'among them, but not of them.' His stature was gigantic, and he had the bold, quick tread of one who had wandered frequently and fearlessly among the terrible hiding-places of nature. His voice was harsh, but his whole countenance possessed singular capabilities for tenderness of expression; and sometimes, under the gentle influence of domestic excitement, his hard features would be rapidly lighted up, seeming like the sunshine flying over the shaded fields in in April day.

"His companion was one calculated to excite and retain the deep, strong energies of manly love. She had possessed extraordinary beauty, and had, in the full maturity of an excellent judgment, relinquished several splendid alliances, and incurred her father's displeasure, for the sake of Cornelius Campbell. Had political circumstances proved favorable, his talents and ambition would unquestionably have worked out a path to emolument and fame; but he had been a zealous and active enemy of the Stuarts, and the restoration of Charles II. was the death-warrant of his hopes. Immediately flight became necessary, and America was the chosen place of refuge. His adherence to Cromwell's party was not occasioned by religious sympathy, but by political views too liberal and philosophical for the state of the people; therefore, Cornelius Campbell sought a home with our forefathers, and, being of a proud nature, he withdrew with his family to the solitary place we have mentioned.

"A very small settlement in such a remote place was, of course, subject to inconvenience and occasional suffering. From the Indians they received neither injury nor insult. No cause of quarrel had ever arisen; and, although their frequent visits were sometimes troublesome, they never had given indications of jealousy or malice. Chocorua was a prophet among them, and, as such, an object of peculiar respect. He had a mind which education and motive would have nerved with giant strength; but, growing up in savage freedom, it wasted itself in dark, fierce, ungovernable passions. There was something fearful in the quiet haughtiness of his lips; it seemed so like slumbering power — too proud to be lightly roused, and too implacable to sleep again. In his small, black, fiery eye, expression lay coiled up like a beautiful snake. The white people knew that his hatred would be terrible; but they had never provoked it, and even the children became too much accustomed to him to fear him.

"Chocorua had a son, nine or ten years old, to whom Caroline Campbell had occasionally made such gaudy presents as were likely to attract his savage fancy. This won the child's affections, so that he became a familiar visitant, almost an inmate, of their dwelling; and, being unrestrained by the courtesies of civilized life, he would inspect everything, and taste of everything which came in his way. Some poison, prepared for a mischievous fox, which had long troubled the little settlement, was discovered and drunk by the Indian boy, and he went home to his father to sicken and die. From that moment jealousy and hatred took possession of Chocorua's soul. He never told his suspicions; he brooded over them in secret, to nourish the deadly revenge he contemplated against Cornelius Campbell.

"The story of Indian animosity is always the same. Cornelius Campbell left his hut for the fields early one bright, balmy morning in June. Still a lover, though ten years a husband, his last look was turned towards his wife, answering her parting smile; his last action a kiss for each of his children. When he returned to dinner, they were dead — all dead! and their disfigured bodies too cruelly showed that an Indian's hand had done the work!

"In such a mind grief, like all other emotions, was tempestuous. Home had been to him the only verdant spot in the desert of life. In his wife and children he had garnered up all his heart; and now that they were torn from him, the remembrance of their love clung to him like the death-grapple of a drowning man, sinking him down, down, into darkness and death. This was followed by a calm a thousand times more terrible — the creeping agony of despair, that brings with it no power of resistance.

'It was as if the dead could feel
The icy worm around him steal.'

"Such, for many days, was the state of Cornelius Campbell. Those who knew and reverenced him feared that the spark of reason was forever extinguished. But it rekindled again, and with it came a wild, demoniac spirit of revenge. The death-groan of Chocorua would make him smile in his dreams; and, when he waked, death seemed too pitiful a vengeance for the anguish that was eating into his very soul.

"Chocorua's brethren were absent on a hunting expedition at the time he committed the murder, and those who watched his movements observed that he frequently climbed the high precipice, which afterwards took his name, probably looking out for indications of their return. Here Cornelius Campbell resolved to effect his deadly purpose. A party was formed, under his guidance, to cut off all chance of retreat, and the dark-minded prophet was to be hunted like a wild beast to his lair.

"The morning sun had scarce cleared away the fogs, when Chocorua started at a loud voice from beneath the precipice, commanding him to throw himself into the deep abyss below. He knew the voice of his enemy, and replied, with an Indian's calmness, 'The Great Spirit gave life to Chocorua, and Chocorua will not throw it away at the command of the white man.' 'Then hear the Great Spirit speak in the white man's thunder!' exclaimed Cornelius Campbell, as he pointed his gun to the precipice. Chocorua, though fierce and fearless as a panther, had never overcome his dread of fire-arms. He placed his hands upon his ears, to shut out the stunning report; the next moment the blood bubbled from his neck, and he reeled fearfully on the edge of the precipice. But he recovered himself, and, raising himself on his hand, he spoke in a loud voice, that grew more terrific as its huskiness increased, 'A curse upon ye, white men! May the Great Spirit curse ye when he speaks in the clouds, and his words are fire! Chocorua had a son, and ye killed him while the sky looked bright! Lightning blast your crops! Winds and fire destroy your dwellings! The Evil Spirit breathe death upon your cattle! Your graves lie in the war-path of the Indian! Panthers howl and wolves fatten over your bones! Chocorua goes to the Great Spirit,— his curse stays with the white man!'

"The prophet sunk upon the ground, still uttering inaudible curses, and they left his bones to whiten in the sun. But his curse rested on that settlement. The tomahawk and scalping-knife were busy among them; the winds tore up trees, and hurled them at their dwellings; their crops were blasted, their cattle died, and sickness came upon their strongest men. At last the remnant of them departed from the fatal spot to mingle with more populous and prosperous colonies. Cornelius Campbell became a hermit, seldom seeking or seeing his fellow-men; and two years after he was found dead in his hut."

This disease among cattle at one time excited considerable interest among scientific men. Prof. Dana, of Dartmouth College, was appointed, in 1821, to visit the town of Burton, now Albany, and learn, if he could, the cause of the disease. After much investigation he found the difficulty to be in the water. It was a weak solution of muriate of lime. He recommended as a remedy or preventive *weak ley*, or *ashes*, or *soap-suds*. A certain kind of *mud*, however, had been discovered by the citizens, which was used with great benefit. " This mud is found on a meadow, and, during the summer, it is collected for use; it is made into balls as large as an ordinary potato, and forced down the animal's throat; by it the tonic effect of the muriate of lime is prevented, and the bowels are kept lax. I visited the spot where the mud is procured. A spring issues from the place, and the water brings with it a grayish-white matter, which is deposited in the rill leading from the spring. This whitish substance is the matter in question. After being heated to redness, it becomes snow-white; when digested in an acid, a slight effervescence occurs, a portion is dissolved, and the remainder has the character of fine, white, siliceous sand; the portion dissolved in the acid was found by appropriate tests to be *carbonate of lime.*"

Albany was much frequented by the Indians for the excellent hunting which it afforded. Its many streams abounded in otter and beaver, after they had begun to disappear in many of their old resorts. The beaver ever retires before the advance of civilization. Of the hundreds of ponds and dams which they had reared on these mountain streams, many of which were still existing in our boyhood, scarcely one now is to be found. Traces of their dams and houses are occasionally to be seen, but the ingenious builders are gone. The Indian considered them rich game, and hunted them as unsparingly as the whites, and still they seem to accompany the one in his wanderings, and shun the other. Our clattering mills and destruction of the forests are more unpleasant to them than the wild war-whoop and tomahawk of the Indian. A traveller thus remarks on the peculiar attractiveness of their young: "A gentleman long resident in this country espied five young beavers sporting in the water, leaping upon the trunk of a tree, pushing one another off, and playing a thousand interesting tricks. He approached softly, under cover of the bushes, and prepared to fire on the unsuspecting creatures; but a nearer approach discovered to him such a similitude between their gestures and the infantile caresses of his own children, that he threw aside his gun."

The population of this town was, for many years, very small. The superstitious fear of the Indian's curse, perhaps, — certainly the difficulty of keeping cattle, — kept its number of inhabitants much reduced. The soil is fertile, and along its streams are beautiful intervales, which, since the discovery of a remedy for the disease, are fast beginning to be occupied. A most amusing incident is told of one Farnham in the first legal meeting of its citizens. Warrants had been sent out for a "May training." Every soldier in town had assembled. Officers were chosen, and, after the choice, come to form the company, it consisted of only one private. "Looking wistfully upon his superiors, standing in terrible array before him, he said : ' Gentlemen, I have one request to make ; that is, as I am the only soldier, I hope your honors will not be too severe in drilling me, but will spare me a little, as I may be needed another time.' He could form a solid column, he said, ' but it racked him shockingly to display.' "

The objects of interest at Franconia we have described in a previous chapter. The town was granted, under the name of Morristown, in the year 1764, to Edward Searle and others. Permanent settlement was made in 1774 by Capt. Artemas Knight, Lemuel Barnett, Zebedee Applebee, and others. The town owes its rise and prosperity to the discovery of iron ore in its vicinity. There are two establishments for working it in town. The lower works are situated on the south branch of the Ammonoosuc river, and are owned by the New Hampshire Iron Factory Company. Their establishment is very extensive, consisting of a blast furnace, erected in 1808, an air furnace, a forge and trip-hammer shop. The ore is obtained from a mountain in the east part of Lisbon, three miles from the furnace, and is considered the richest in the United States, yielding from fifty-six to sixty-three per cent.

The vein has been opened and wrought forty rods in length and one hundred and forty-four feet in depth. The ore is blasted out. The mine is wrought open to daylight, and is but partially covered to keep out the rain. The first miners, ignorant of any other means of discovering the veins than such as the pickaxe afforded, wasted much labor and expense in fruitless search. At one place they cut a gulley one hundred and twenty feet long into the solid granite ; and at another there is a similar cut, seventy-one feet in length. Many curious and remarkable caverns have thus been formed in the rocky hill-side.

Numerous interesting minerals have been brought to light, and may be found among the rejected masses which have been thrown out. The most interesting and abundant are a deep brownish-red manganesian garnet, crystallized and granular epidote, prismatic and bladed crystals of hornblende.

Artemas Knight, whom we have mentioned as one of the first settlers of the town, during a severe famine which prevailed in its early history, one bleak December's day, shouldered his gun, and made his way through the deep snow to Round Meadows in Button Woods, a distance of ten miles or more. On his way he forded Gale's river, a tributary of the Ammonoosuc, his wet clothes almost instantly freezing as he came out of the water. The water was quite deep, and he was nearly in the same condition as though he had swam the stream. At Round Meadows he killed a moose weighing over four hundred pounds, skinned it with his jack-knife, cut it up with his hatchet, buried three quarters in the snow, and with the fourth on his back, returning to his hut in Franconia, again fording Gale's river, and reached home in the evening of the same day.

The village of Bethlehem is about seventeen miles west of the Notch of the White Mountains, on the road to Franconia and Littleton. The road here passes over a broad, undulating hill, in an open and airy situation, which gives the traveller an opportunity to admire, at his leisure, the view of the range of the White Mountains, the finest and most satisfactory to be anywhere seen. Mount Washington is here brought into its true place in the centre of the chain, and takes the precedence which belongs to its greatly superior breadth and height. The mountains on each side are well arranged in their proper and subordinate situations; the pointed peaks of Adams, Jefferson and Clay, contrasting finely with the smoother and flatter summits of Monroe, Franklin, Pleasant and Clinton.

Jonas Warren, Nathaniel Snow, Nathan Wheeler and others, made a permanent settlement in Bethlehem in 1790. It was then known by the name of "Lord's Hill." Like the early settlers of all these towns, privations, sufferings and hardship, were their daily lot. Now their cattle would wander away and be lost in the broad pasture in which they roamed, requiring days and sometimes weeks to find them. Without carts or carriages of any kind, they performed all their labor, piling the bags of corn upon the steers' backs, and marching them through the rough forest twenty-five miles to mill, when meal in the settlement got low. Capt. Rosebrook, not long after the settlement of the town, projected a road and with others cut out a decent path from his own lone hut in Nash and Sawyer's location, to his neighbors on Lord's Hill. A log bridge was built over the Ammonoosuc, but did not withstand long the many sudden rises of the rapid stream.

The settlers of this town were hardy, persevering men, more nearly resembling Capt. Rosebrook than any we have before met. To help out their small stock of provisions a party went at one time to Whitefield ponds for fish. On their return in the night a thick fog arose, completely hiding the trees which they followed as their guides, and, ere they were aware, they were lost. The cold was intense; they had no fire-arms, and life hung on their devising some method to keep themselves warm. Cutting down long, slender trees, they trimmed them, and, placing them across a log, with a man at each end, they commenced rapidly pushing them back and forwards, as men do a "cross-cut" saw. Diligently they plied their toothless saws all the night, working as only men work for their lives.

Lord's Hill was incorporated into a town by the name of Bethlehem, December 25th, 1799, and the first town-meeting was held in the house of Amos Wheeler. The following year the town voted to raise four dollars to defray town charges, twenty-four dollars for schooling, and sixty dollars for bridges and highways. In April of the same year the project of building a bridge over the Ammonoosuc was started, and the following month the town voted, in town-meeting convened, to build the bridge, and raised three hundred and ninety dollars to do it with. So scarce was provision during the construction of this bridge, that all the poor laborers, working in the water all day, had to eat was milk-porridge, carried to them hot by their wives. Eight cents were allowed per hour to the men for their services, and six cents for a yoke of oxen.

So great was the famine at this time that the citizens were obliged to desist from their labors, go into the woods, and cut and burn wood sufficient to make ashes enough to load a team of four oxen with potash. This load of potash they dispatched with a teamster to Concord, Mass., a distance of one hundred and seventy miles. It was four weeks ere the teamster returned with provisions. During his absence they saved themselves from starvation only by cooking green chocolate roots and such other plants as would yield them any nourishment.

The little settlement of early times is now a flourishing village. Two beautiful churches send their spires up to heaven from its midst. Five large mills for sawing lumber are in constant operation, and a large factory manufactures yearly one hundred and forty tons of starch, requiring thirty-three thousand bushels of potatoes.

CHAPTER XXI.

GEOLOGY.

INDIAN THEORY OF THE CREATION OF THE WORLD. — INDIAN IDEA OF THE
CREATION OF THE WHITE MOUNTAINS. — DR. JACKSON'S THEORY. — SIR
CHARLES LYELL'S THEORY.

THE rude Indian's idea of the creation of this world, with its hills and mountains, and the formation of the fearful Agiocochook, and the theories of scientific scholars concerning the origin and history of these mountains, we may be pardoned for placing in the same chapter.

"Water at first overspread the face of the world, which is a plain surface. At the top of the water a musk-rat was swimming about in different directions. At length he concluded to dive to the bottom, to see what he could find on which to subsist; but he found nothing but mud, a little of which he brought in his mouth, and placed it on the surface of the water, where it remained. He then went for more mud, and placed it with that already brought up; and thus he continued his operations until he had formed a considerable hillock. This land increased by degrees, until it overspread a large part of the world, which assumed at length its present form. The earth, in process of time, became peopled in every part, and remained in this condition for many years. Afterward a fire run over it all, and destroyed every human being except one man and one woman. They saved themselves by going into a deep cave, in a large mountain, where they remained for several days, until the fire was extinguished. They then came forth from their hiding-place, and from these two persons the whole earth has been peopled."

ORIGIN OF THE WHITE MOUNTAINS.

" Cold storms were in the northern wilderness, and a lone red hunter wandered without food, chilled by the frozen wind. He lost his strength, and could find no game; and the dark cloud that covered his life-path made him weary of wandering. He fell down upon the snow, and a dream carried him to a wide happy valley, filled with musical streams, where singing-birds and game were plenty. His spirit cried aloud for joy; and the 'Great Master of life' waked him from his sleep, gave him a dry coal and a flint-pointed spear, telling him that by the shore of the lake he might live, and find fish with his spear, and fire from his dry coal. One night, when he had laid down his coal, and seen a warm fire spring therefrom, with a blinding smoke, a loud voice came out of the flame, and a great noise, like thunder, filled the air, and there rose up a vast pile of broken rocks. Out of the cloud resting upon the top came numerous streams, dancing down, foaming cold; and the voice spake to the astonished red hunter, saying, '*Here the Great Spirit will dwell, and watch over his favorite children!*'"

GEOLOGICAL.

Dr. Jackson, in his report of New Hampshire, thus speaks of the White Mountains: —

"The White Mountains are the centre of a most interesting geological section. If a measure is applied to a correct map of the Northern and Middle States, taking the White Mountains for a centre, and measuring south-west and north-east, it will be noticed that the secondary rocks are nearly equi-distant from this centre of elevation, on each side of the axis, and the beds and included fossils will correspond in a remarkable manner, indicating that when the strata were horizontal, they formed a continuous deposit, effected under nearly the same conditions.

"If we estimate the strata of Vermont and Maine as horizontal, by imagining the primary rocks which separate them to be removed, and the lines of stratification brought to coincide in direction, it is evident that the whole of New England would be regarded as sunk far below the level of the ocean, and a space would still remain between the ends of the strata where the primary rocks had been removed. Now, since the strata were formed when the present rocks were beneath the sea, we may suppose the whole of the primary unstratified rocks to have been below the stratified deposits, and, by a sudden outburst and elevation, to have been more or less broken up, altered in composition, and included between masses of the molten gneis and granite. Thus, we may account for the loss of a portion of the disrupted strata, while we also explain the intercalation of masses of argillaceous slate in the primary series, and the metamorphosis of the sedimentary deposits by igneous action. A heaving sea of molten rocks, probably bearing on its surface the sedimentary strata, elevated, overturned, and effected chemical changes in them, the results of which we behold along the line of junction of the two classes of rocks.

"The reader would be able better to conceive of this state

of things, by the contemplation of the breaking up of a volcanic crater, or may figure the scene in his mind by imagining a frozen lake, with successive and thick layers of snow and ice, to be broken up by an earthquake, and the whole mass suddenly frozen while in the highest state of disturbance. This, however grand the scale, would not give a sufficiently enlarged idea of the vast movements of the earth's crust, nor of the changes which the materials must have undergone in the immense periods of geological time; for the action of a comparatively moderate heat for ages effects changes in the position of elementary particles which are not duly appreciated. This hypothesis will appear more plausible to those who will take the trouble to go over the ground from one end of the section to the other, noting the changes which are manifested in the order of strata, and considering the known causes of chemical action on the ingredients of rocks. It will be observed that the sedimentary deposits have all been disturbed by upheaval, and that portions of strata are included in the unstratified rocks, showing their posterior eruption, while, in some places, the fracturing of strata has been still more remarkable, a complete breccia being formed with their comminuted fragments, and the thick pasty rocks of eruption.

" Occasionally, the mechanical power of elevated granite is manifested by the complete overturning, or doubling back of large sheets of mica slate, and its chemical effects are seen in the remarkable induration of the rock along the line of junction, those slabs, when not bent, being chosen by the quarrymen, on account of their superior firmness.

" The geological features of Mount Washington possess but little interest. The rocks in place consisting of a coarse variety of mica slate, passing in gneis, which contains a few crystals of black tourmaline and quartz. The cone of the mountain and its summit are covered with myriads of angular and flat blocks and slabs of mica slate, piled in confusion one upon the other. They are identical in nature with the rocks in place, and bear no marks of transportation or abrasion by the action of water."

Sir Charles Lyell, the eminent English geologist, thus writes concerning these mountains: —

"The flora of the uppermost region of Mount Washington consists of species which are natives of the cold climate of Labrador, Lapland, Greenland and Siberia, and are impatient, says Bigelow, of drought, as well as of both extremes of heat and cold; they are, therefore, not at all fitted to flourish in the ordinary climate of New England. But they are preserved here, during winter, from injury, by a great depth of snow, and the air in summer never attains, at this elevation, too high a temperature, while the ground below is always cool. When the snow melts they shoot up instantly with vigor proportioned to the length of time they have been dormant, rapidly unfold their flowers, and mature their fruits, and run through the whole course of their vegetation in a few weeks, irrigated by clouds and mist.

* * * * * * * * *

"If we attempt to speculate on the manner in which the peculiar species of plants now established on the highest summits of the White Mountains, were enabled to reach those isolated spots, while none of them are met with in the lower lands around, or for a great distance to the north, we shall find ourselves engaged in trying to solve a philosophical problem, which requires the aid, not of botany alone, but of geology, or a knowledge of the geographical changes which immediately preceded the present state of the earth's surface.

We have to explain how an Arctic flora, consisting of plants specifically identical with those which now inhabit lands bordering the sea in the extreme north of America, Europe, and Asia, could get to the top of Mount Washington. Now, geology teaches us that the species living at present on the earth are older than many parts of our existing continent; that is to say, they were created before a large part of the existing mountains, valleys, plains, lakes, rivers and seas, were formed. That such must be the case in regard to the island of Sicily, I announced my conviction in 1833, after first returning from that country. And a similar conclusion is no less obvious to any naturalist who has studied the structure of North America, and observed the wide area occupied by the modern or glacial deposit before alluded to,* in which marine fossil shells of living but northern species are entombed. It is clear that a great portion of Canada, and the country surrounding the great lakes, was submerged beneath the ocean when recent species of mollusca flourished, of which the fossil remains occur more than five hundred feet above the level of the sea, near Montreal. I have already stated that Lake Champlain was a gulf of the sea at that period, that large areas in Maine were under water, and I may add that the White Mountains must then have constituted an island, or group of islands. Yet, as this period is so modern in the earth's his-

---

* "Some of the concretions of fine clay, more or less calcareous, met with in New Hampshire, in this 'drift' on the Saco river, thirty miles to the north of Portsmouth, contain the entire skeletons of a fossil fish of the same species as one now living in the Northern Seas, called the capetan (*Mallotus villosus*), about the size of a sprat, and sold abundantly in the London market, salted and dried like herrings. I obtained some of these fossils, which, like the associated shells, show that a colder climate than that now prevailing in this region was established in what is termed 'the glacial period.'"

tory as to belong to the epoch of the existing marine fauna, it is fair to infer that the Arctic flora now contemporary with man was then also established on the globe.

"A careful study of the present distribution of animals and plants over the globe has led nearly all the best naturalists to the opinion that each species had its origin in a single birthplace, and spread gradually from its original centre to all accessible spots fit for its habitation, by means of the powers of migration given to it from the first. If we adopt this view, or the doctrine of 'specific centres,' there is no difficulty in comprehending how the cryptogamous plants of Siberia, Lapland, Greenland and Labrador, scaled the heights of Mount Washington, because the sporules of the fungi, lichens and mosses, may be wafted through the air for indefinite distances, like smoke; and, in fact, heavier particles are actually known to have been carried for thousands of miles by the wind. But the cause of the occurrence of Arctic plants of the phænogamous class on the top of the New Hampshire mountains, specifically identical with those of remote Polar regions, is by no means so obvious. They could not, in the present condition of the earth, effect a passage over the intervening low lands, because the extreme heat of summer and cold of winter would be fatal to them. Even if they were brought from the northern parts of Asia, Europe and America, and thousands of them planted round the foot of Mount Washington, they would never be able, in any number of years, to make their way to its summit. We must suppose, therefore, that originally they extended their range in the same way as the flowering plants now inhabiting Arctic and Antarctic lands disseminate themselves. The innumerable islands in the Polar seas are tenanted by the same species of plants, some of which are conveyed as seeds by animals over the ice when the sea is frozen in winter, or by birds; while a still larger number are transported by floating icebergs, on which soil containing the seeds of plants may be carried in a single year for hundreds of miles. A great body of geological evidence has now been brought together, to some of which I have adverted in a former chapter, to show that this machinery for scattering plants, as well as for carrying erratic blocks southward, and polishing and grooving the floor of the ancient ocean, extended in the western hemisphere to lower latitudes than the White Mountains. When these last still constituted islands in a sea chilled by the melting of floating ice, we may assume that they were covered entirely by a flora like that now confined to the uppermost or treeless region of the mountains. As the continent grew by the slow upheaval of the land, and the islands gained in height, and the climate around their base grew milder, the Arctic plants would retreat to higher and higher zones, and finally occupy an elevated area, which probably had been at first, or in the glacial period, always covered with perpetual snow. Meanwhile, the newly-formed plains around the base of the mountains, to which northern species of plants could not spread, would be occupied by others migrating from the south, and perhaps by many trees, shrubs and plants, then first created, and remaining to this day peculiar to North America.

"The period when the White Mountains ceased to be a group of islands, or when, by the emergence of the surrounding low land, they first became connected with the continent, is, as we have seen, of very modern date, geologically speaking. It is, in fact, so recent as to belong to the epoch when species now contemporaneous with man already inhabited this planet. But, if we attempt to carry our retrospect still further into the past, and to go back to the date when the rocks themselves of the White Mountains originated, we are lost in times of extreme antiquity. No light is thrown on this inquiry by imbedded organic remains, of which the strata of gneis, mica schist, clay slate and quartzite, are wholly devoid. These masses are traversed by numerous veins of granite and greenstone, which are therefore newer than the stratified crystalline rocks which they intersect; and the abrupt manner in which these veins terminate at the surface, attests how much denudation or removal by water of solid matter has taken place. Another question, of a chronological kind, may yet deserve attention; namely, the epoch of the movements which threw the body of gneis and the associated rocks into their present bent, disturbed, and vertical positions. This subject is also involved in considerable obscurity, although it seems highly probable that the crystalline strata of New Hampshire acquired their internal arrangements at the same time as the fossilferous beds of the Appalachian or Alleghany chain; and we know that they assumed their actual strike and dip subsequently to the origin of the coal measures, which enter so largely into the structure of that chain."

CHAPTER XXII.

TEMPERATURE OF THE WEATHER AT THE MOUNTAINS.

THERMOMETRICAL TABLE. — SYNOPSIS OF THE WEATHER. — COMPARISON OF WEATHER WITH LONG ISLAND WEATHER. — EARTHQUAKES. — THUNDERSTORMS. — WIND. — COLD AND FROST. — CLEARNESS OF THE ATMOSPHERE. — LENGTH OF DAYS. — SPRINGS.— COMBUSTION.

FOR the following statement of the weather on the summit of Mount Washington, we are indebted entirely to the record of Mr. Nathaniel Noyes, of Boston. Mr. Noyes commenced a residence on the summit of Mount Washington, on the 7th of June, 1853, which he continued until noonday of the 16th of September,— one hundred consecutive days (with the exception of an absence of one week),— during all which time he kept a record of the temperature of the atmosphere, from observations with a thermometer, commencing with the 8th of June, at sunrise, noon and sunset, and continuing these observations three times daily until the 15th of September.

It has been found by comparison that the temperature of Mt. Washington is more even than that of any other place at which a record has ever been kept. Before many years have elapsed, physicians, without doubt, will recommend to patients who require an even and cool temperature, a residence at the summit of Mt. Washington during the summer months.

THERMOMETRICAL TABLE.

JUNE, 1853.				JULY, 1853.				AUG., 1853.				SEPT., 1853.			
Day.	Sunrise.	12 M	Sunset.	Day.	Sunrise.	12 M.	Sunset.	Day.	Sunrise.	12 M.	Sunset.	Day.	Sunrise.	12 M.	Sunset.
8	32	40	34	1	43	55	45	1	42	59	50	1	41	51	47
9	31	45	40	2	32	46	38	2	49	51	49	2	45	58	55
10	38	52	48	3	44	53	48	3	48	58	49	3	50	58	55
11	44	47	43	4	52	60	54	4	49	54	48	4	52	55	54
12	32	48	44	5	42	51	42	5	45	54	53	5	50	58	57
13	43	56	47	6	39	48	39	6	51	60	49	6	57	59	56
14	48	60	55	7	29	47	37	7	46	53	48	7	56	49	45
15	53	59	55	8	38	50	49	8	49	58	48	8	30	40	36
16	54	62	55	9	41	49	45	9	50	52	52	9	33	44	41
17	54	56	52	10	45	50	45	10	48	59	57	10	37	40	32
18	43	48	40	11	45	54	48	11	52	62	59	11	28	29	27
19	39	49	42	12	40	52	45	12	52	60	59	12	24	29	30
20	50	66	58	13	38	49	45	13	59	60	56	13	32	36	39
21	48	57	50	14	42	59	49	14	58	60	50	14	38	46	42
22	54	58	55	15	52	62	51	15	45	57	53	15	45	50	47
23	58	60	55	16	51	56	52	16	50	56	55	16	38	42	
24	56	42	35	17	44	49	37	17	49	62	55				
25	30	36	32	18	39	55	48	18	48	58	51				
26	24	37	30	19	52	53	50	19	33	37	33				
27	32	44	38	20	42	50	41	20	30	35	36				
28	34	43	35	21	38	45	46	21	36	46	45				
29	45	64	58	22	42	60	56	22	39	40	35				
30	54	61	53	23	50	66	56	23	33	43	42				
				24	54	64	59	24	37	46	45				
				25	52	63	55	25	44	42	36				
				26	50	51	45	26	31	47	42				
				27	43	59	49	27	42	47	47				
				28	39	47	45	28	34	35	32				
				29	44	59	54	29	31	46	43				
				30	49	59	56	30	38	51	50				
				31	50	59	49	31	46	49	46				

SYNOPSIS OF THE WEATHER.

The following is a synopsis of the weather during each month:

JUNE, 1853.

Average temperature at sunrise,   43.3 degrees.
Average temperature at 12 M.,   53.5 degrees.

INCIDENTS IN WHITE MOUNTAIN HISTORY.   293

Average temperature at sunset,   45.7 degrees.
Thermometer stood lowest, 26th day,   24   "
   "   "   highest, 20th day,   66   "
   "   below freezing at sunrise, 6 days.
   "   "   "   at sunset,   2   "

The greatest change in any day occurred the 24th, when the thermometer fell twenty-one degrees from sunrise to sunset; and twenty-six degrees in twenty-four hours. It snowed for several hours, covering the ground, or rather the rocks, several inches in depth.

JULY, 1853.

Average temperature at sunrise,   43.5 degrees.
   "   "   "   12, M.,   54.2   "
   "   "   "   sunset,   47.7   "
Thermometer stood highest, 23d day   66   "
   "   "   lowest, 7th day,   29   "

There was no snow during the month, but plenty of frost, and some ice.

AUGUST, 1853.

Average temperature at sunrise,   44   degrees.
   "   "   "   12, M.,   51.5   "
   "   "   "   sunset,   47.5   "
Thermometer stood highest, 11th day,   62   "
   "   "   lowest, 20th day,   30   "

On the eighth of the month there was a severe tempest, accompanied with hail, which fell to the depth of several inches on the northerly side of the mountain.

SEPTEMBER, 1853.

Average temperature at sunrise,   43.2 degrees.

25*

Average temperature at 12, M., 46.8 "
" " " sunset, 44.2 "
Thermometer stood highest, 6th day, 59 "
" " lowest, 12th day, 24 "

At sunset, the tenth day of this month, the thermometer stood at the freezing-point, and a snow-storm commenced during the night, which continued through the whole of the next day, and until late in the evening, covering the surface to the depth of nearly a foot. I have seldom, if ever, witnessed a more severe storm in the winter in any place, than the storm there so early as September 11th. It blew a perfect hurricane at times, prostrating a telescope stand belonging to the proprietors of the Summit House, which was intended to be of sufficient strength to withstand the hardest gales.

The following comparison of these records with records of hourly thermometrical observations made upon Brooklyn Heights, Long Island, near the level of the sea, was taken from a small circular, prepared by E. Merriam, Esq., of New York, together with the thermometrical observations made at the summit:

"It will be seen, by the annexed tabular statement, that, in the last twenty-three days of June, the greatest change during the twenty-four hours, on the summit, was twenty-one degrees; while on Long Island, during the same term, the greatest change was thirty degrees, a difference of nine degrees in favor of the summit. In July the greatest change on the summit was eighteen degrees, and on Long Island twenty-five degrees; making a difference in favor of the summit of seven degrees. The month of August was still more equilibrious, the greatest change on the summit being but seventeen degrees, and, on Long Island, but twenty-two degrees; being five degrees in favor of Mount Washington. September, from 1st to 15th, the period named by both records, was still more equilibrious than August; the greatest change on the summit being thirteen degrees, and on Long Island eighteen degrees; difference in favor of the summit, five degrees. It therefore most clearly appears that the temperature of the summit of Mount Washington is not subject to such sudden and great changes as the temperature of Long Island.

"The highest temperature on the summit, during the hundred days, was sixty-six degrees, which was at noon on the 20th of June and 23d of July; and, on Long Island, during the same time, the highest was ninety-seven degrees, and was on the twenty-first of June.

"The lowest temperature on the summit in June, was on the 24th of that month; twenty-four degrees, or eight degrees below the freezing-point; in July, on the 7th, twenty-nine degrees; in August, on the 20th, thirty degrees; and in September, to the 15th, twenty-four degrees on the 12th. On Long Island, the lowest temperature in June was forty-four degrees on the 9th; in July, fifty-eight degrees on the 18th; in August, fifty-five degrees on the 29th; and of the first fourteen days in September, fifty-one degrees on the 12th.

"During the hundred days, the temperature on the summit of Mount Washington fell to and below the freezing-point on seventeen days, viz., six in June, two in July, four in August, and five in September.

"During the hundred days, earthquakes occurred on five days, viz., on the 17th and 20th of July, at Portland, Maine; on the 28th of August, at New Madrid, Mississippi river; on the 8th of September, at New Bedford, Mass.; and, on the 11th of September, at Biloxi, Louisiana. These shocks of earthquake, each and all, reduced the temperature of the atmosphere upon the summit of Mount Washington as follows:

"The two shocks of earthquakes at Portland, Maine, between five and six, A. M., of the 17th of July, reduced the temperature on the summit from forty-nine to thirty-seven degrees, or within five degrees of the freezing-point; and the shock at the same place, on the afternoon of the 20th of the same month, reduced the temperature of the summit from fifty to thirty-eight degrees, or within six degrees of the freezing-point. An earthquake at New Madrid, on the Mississippi river, on the 28th August, reduced the temperature at the summit from forty-seven to thirty-four degrees, or one degree below the freezing-point. On the 7th of September, the shock of an earthquake was felt at New Bedford, Mass., in the evening, which reduced the temperature at the summit from fifty-six to thirty degrees; and a shock at Biloxi and along the lake coast, near New Orleans, on the 11th of September, at five P. M., reduced the temperature on the summit from forty-nine to twenty-six degrees. Thus it appears that of earthquakes occurring on or east of the Mississippi river, on two days in July, one in August, and two in September, and all that we have accounts of occurring within that district within that length of time, all produced the same results in refrigerating the temperature of the atmosphere on the summit of Mount Washington."

THUNDER-STORMS.

On the eighth of August, at four P. M., there was a thunder-storm, attended by some hail, on the summit; and at the ledge, about one mile below, on the eastern side, the hail fell to the depth of several inches. The thunder was heavy, and the lightning vivid; and the crash followed the flash so quickly, that it seemed difficult to distinguish any perceptible difference between the light and the sound. In the evening lightning was seen in several directions.

A thunder-storm was experienced at the summit on the 13th of August, at one, and again at six, P. M.; and on the 14th of the same month, at two P. M., was the heaviest thunder-storm Mr. Noyes had witnessed during his residence thus far on the summit. The lightning appeared the most active at the south-east; the rain fell in torrents all day, and during the thunder-storm, at two P. M., the wind was very severe.

The sound of the thunder at the summit is peculiar, resembling the quick discharge of a cannon, and the sound of but short duration.

The wind blows steadily with great pressure on the summit, and not in gusts as in other places. He thinks the winds are stronger than in the valleys.

COLD AND FROST.

White hoar-frost is occasionally seen on the summit of the mountain, but not often.

CLEARNESS OF THE ATMOSPHERE.

Mr. Noyes remarks, that he has never taken particular notice how many mornings in a week the sun rises clear; but he thinks not more than three mornings in a week on an average; and, immediately preceding the 13th of August, it had been nearly a week since they had been favored with a clear sunrise or clear sunset at the summit, the atmosphere having been foggy.

Objects can be seen at a greater distance after sunset

than during sunlight. Mr. Noyes remarks, that he could distinctly see the Glen House, situate at the foot of the mountain, which he computes at two and a half miles distant in air-line, at nine P. M., about sixty-five minutes after sunset.

LENGTH OF DAYS.

The days are about forty minutes longer on the summit, that is, between sunrise and sunset, than on the sea level in the same latitude.

A person hallooing from a position below the summit can be heard by a person standing on the summit a greater distance than the same hallooing upon the summit could be heard down the mountain, evidencing that the sound ascends.

SPRINGS.

A living spring of delicious water, about thirty rods below the house, on the northern side of the summit, supplies water abundantly; and while towns in the neighborhood, near the sea level, were suffering for water, the spring continued its uniform supply. Water from such a spring must be of the very best.

THIRST.

In reference to thirst at the summit, Mr. Noyes says: "I am well satisfied, from my own experience, as well as remarks made by my wife, and other members of the household, that persons are much more thirsty here than below. I have drank double or treble the quantity of water here that I should have required in Boston, although it is much colder here than there."

Almost every one who ascends the mountain is very thirsty, not only here, but drinking at every little rivulet on the way up; and these little mountain streams are very plenty.

COMBUSTION.

Mr. Noyes, in his letter of September 3d, says: "I have watched repeatedly to see if smoke ascends here; but have never seen it two feet above the ventilator. It always beats down around the house. When the air is still, wood burns very slow on the summit, and seems to burn more like wood in a coal-pit, where it is not allowed much air."

CHAPTER XXIII.

CONCLUSION.

BEFORE we leave these mountains, around which we have so long detained the reader, let us earnestly invite him to visit them. If he has already made their acquaintance, let him come again, and often. Not too often can he drink in the inspiration of these noble hills. If he has never yet stood beneath their mighty shadow, he cannot do so too soon. New sensations yet await him. Come from the thronged cities and dusty streets, and refresh yourselves yearly in the clear atmosphere of these "Crystal Hills." Says the eloquent Webster: "We believe and we know that its scenery is beautiful; that its skies are all healthful; that its mountains and lakes are surpassingly grand and sublime.

"If there be anything on this continent, the work of nature, in hills, and lakes, and woods, and forests, strongly attracting the admiration of all those who love natural scenery, that is to be found in our mountain state of New Hampshire. It happened to me lately to visit the northern part of the state. It was autumn. The trees of the forest, by the discoloration of the leaves, presented one of the most beautiful spectacles that the human eye can rest upon. But the low and deep murmur of those forests, the fog rising and spreading and clasping the breast of the mountains, whose heads were still high and bright in the skies, — all these indicated that a wintry storm was on its wing; that the spirit of the mountain was stirred, and that, ere long, the voice of tempests would be spent. But even this was exciting,— exciting to those of us who were witnesses before, and exciting in itself as an exhibition of the grandeur of natural scenery. For my part, I felt the truth of that sentiment applied elsewhere and on another occasion, that

> 'The loud torrent and the whirlwind's roar
> But bound me to my native mountains more.' "

Come; and when you come, come prepared to stay, to study, to feel them. Select some home beneath their broad shadows, and each day roam over and among them until they are yours — their image and their might indelibly fastened in your memory. " These old settlers are somewhat tardy in forming intimate acquaintanceships. With them ' confidence is a plant of slow growth.' Their externals they give to the eye in a moment, on a clear day; but their character, their occasional moods of superior majesty, their coy loveliness of light and drapery — all that makes them a refreshment, a force, a joy for the rest of your years, they show only to the calmer eye — to a man who waits a day or two in order to unthink his city habits, and bide their time. It is utterly impossible to know what the White Mountains are by whirling through Conway, and Glen, and Notch, and Franconia, in a week. Use the week at some one central point. Spend the same money at one spot that is to spread over the lengthened journey; take the proper times for driving out to the best positions, and the mountains will come to you, which, it is said, they refused to do for the author of the Koran."

Bring not the cares and anxieties of Wall-street and State-street, but shake off the very dust of them from your feet as you set your faces northward to these summer resorts. Freedom is an essential element in the air of these mountains, — freedom from the brain-ache and heart-ache attendant upon this money strife. Dollars and cents do not count in Tuckerman's Ravine, and their jingle is in harsh dissonance of the fall of the Thousand Streams. Calculation of percentage, as one sits and sees the

"Mysteries of color daily laid
By the great sun in light and shade,"

on these rugged, craggy heights, is impossible. Stocks are valueless when standing at the sources of those mighty rivers, which carry fertility, and wealth, and health, to all New England. Freedom from political prejudice is here found. Washington and Jefferson suffer no political strifes or ranklings beneath their shadows. Whigs and democrats go toiling up their steep sides together, and northerners and southerners, side by side on the same summit, look off on the same wide prospect below them. Americans and foreigners, descendants from the fathers of the Revolution and exiles from the iron rod of despotism, all bow in reverence and acknowledge willing allegiance to

"This family of mountains, clustering around
Their hoary patriarch."

Freedom from the thousand petty annoyances and restraints of city and village life is here the bliss of the traveller. Does the exhilarating air stimulate? Go out, and, to the full capacity of the lungs, wake the echoes of the hills. The chest all bare, breathe in the pure mountain air, until your deep tones shall awaken the talk of the hills, peak answering to peak in the far-off distance. Is the dress of fashionable life too restraining for climbing over the rough and broken places? — throw it off, and, clad in freer, looser garments, run, and walk, and ramble, the livelong day. No gossip should be whispered in the beautiful glen; no petty etiquette should be observed while standing on the ruins of the terrible avalanches.

Worshippers and followers of the same great Author of these mountains may forget their different sects, and bow in unison around these mighty "altars."

> "Not vainly did the early Persian make
> His altar the high places and the peak
> Of earth-o'ergazing mountains, and thus take
> A fit and unwalled temple, there to seek
> The Spirit, in whose honor shrines are weak
> Upreared of human hands. Come, and compare
> Columns and idol-dwellings, Goth or Greek,
> With Nature's realms of worship, — earth and air,
> Nor fix on fond abodes to circumscribe thy prayer!"

Come, and amid the works of God study the words of God. "The Bible came out of a mountain country. The book of Exodus, which, for poetic sublimity, makes the coloring of the Iliad pale, should be read, if one would get the true commentary on it, as Dr. Robinson read the sublimest passages of it, a few years ago, among the cliffs of Horeb, overlooking the plateau where the gathered wanderers saw the mountain quake and blaze. 'Job' must be studied by an imagination that can conjure Idumean landscapes and skies. There are passages in the prophets which no annotations could interpret to men that had lived on prairies all their days. And the Psalms, especially, which are dyed in the spirit of all kinds of scenery, as well as in the most intense and varied experiences of the soul,— which interweave with their rapturous piety imagery and colors caught from the pastures of Bethlehem, the forests of Horeth, the caves of Adullam, the wilderness of Engedi, and the mountain fastnesses of Ziph,— cannot yield the riches of inspiration to a formal reading, but must, many of them, be set under influences of nature kindred to those which helped to kindle them, before they will glow and sing themselves anew. The twenty-third should be read once in sight of the Connecticut meadows ; the nineteenth, on a hill overlooking a desert ; the eighteenth, during a thunder-shower ; the eighth, under a sparkling, frosty night sky ; the sixty-fifth after a rain that breaks the drought ; then the power of poetry, as well as of piety, that is in them would be manifest."

> "Lo ! in softened grandeur far, yet clear,
> Thy battlements stand clothed in heaven's own hue,
> To swell as Freedom's home on man's unbounded view ! "

Mountains are ever favorable to liberty. They abound with the very elements of its life and vigor. Survey the objects they embrace, and you must see the truth of this remark. These are all free and active in their movements. No fetter constrains them, no shackle confines them. Its streams all murmur the tones of freedom as they flow in their courses. Its eagles all scream of liberty as they wheel their flight about its romantic slopes, and over its more towering elevations. The note of every other bird, too, is in keeping with these. They all chirp exemption from enthralment, as they line its green valleys, or flit along its beautiful hill-sides.

Mountains are especially favorable to the cause of human liberty. When driven out from other portions of the world, she has always found an asylum in her mountains. There she is cherished. Nature comes to the protection of her votary, and throws around him the bulwarks of its rocks and precipices. These, wherever he comes to them, check the tyrant in his progress. This has been the case in all past time. "The inhabitants of our New Hampshire mountains were, it must be confessed, from the first, rather inclined to a mutinous spirit. I believe that is common to mountainous regions in most parts of the world. Scotland and Switzerland show the example of hardy, strong men in mountainous regions, attached to war and to the chase; and it is not unfortunate in our New Hampshire history that this sentiment, to a considerable degree, prevailed."

May liberty never be driven to our mountain passes. May we never be forced to these retreats, and the "patriot group" see tyrants marshalling their troops in these valleys. O, the voice with which those hoary peaks would almost speak! O, the anguish of Washington!

"I know the value of liberty. I helped pay a large price for it in the sweat I expended on the field of Monmouth; in the cold and suffering I endured at Valley Forge; in the dreadful suspense I had on the banks of the Delaware previous to the battle at Princeton; and now how can I bear to see it lost?

"I have stood here with my compeers, for a long time, watching the movement of things on the broad territory for whose good I toiled, with the feeling all the while in me that, if its inhabitants perpetuated the freedom I helped give them, I should be well compensated for my sufferings. But, if they barter it, and ever succumb to a tyrant, either temporal or spiritual, I could never wish to see the sight, but would gladly cover my head with an unbroken thick veil of cloud, as I have sometimes done with passing ones, and never again look on a land of vassals and slaves.

"As I have once said, I say again : I know the value of liberty, and never, never while I have strength to stand here as firm as I do, while the vigor is in me still that has enabled me to buffet so many storms as I have, never, never will I barter it away. My head shall always be free from the badge of a slave, towering up toward heaven in a significant speaking adoration to the God that has formed me."

No oppression, certainly none sustained by law or custom, can ever exist around the White Mountains. This is a cheering reflection. No slave can ever live on them, or near them. They are consecrated to freedom. They are suited to produce a race of vigorous freemen. We have loved them in times past. We love them still.

"Where'er our wandering footsteps roam,
 To thee our fond affections cling ;
Land of our love ! our childhood's home !
Land of the cliff and eagle's wing !

How proudly stands the mountain height
 That overlooks the vales and streams !
In youth it shone to bless our sight ;
In age it lingers in our dreams.

'T is in the mountain that the heart
 Resolves its thought and purpose high
To act the just, the noble part
 For God, for truth, and liberty.

How oft has freedom, in the days
 Of grief and war's disastrous shocks,
Her shattered banner dared to raise
 Once more upon the mountain rocks !

> Enthralment cannot climb that height ;
> Slaves cannot breathe that upper air ;
> Emblem of freemen, — 't is the flight
> Of eagles only that is there.
>
> We love thee, land of rocks and rills !
> Land of the wood, the lake, the glen !
> Great in the grandeur of thy hills,
> And greater in thy mighty men."

We say, then, in a few words to close, all ye inhabitants in this broad land, all ye in every part of her wide domain, visit these mountains as ye have done, and in larger numbers; breathe their air; bathe yourselves in their atmosphere, made rich and refreshing with bud and blossom; trace their rivers, and make closer acquaintance with their inhabitants, and you will get stronger, deeper energies to do life's great work. And you, inhabitants of the mountains, prize the privileges you enjoy, the blessings of your birthplace and home; trace your way up often to God through some of his grandest works. Through all your life, in full sight of them, serve him and your country well; and then, when life is done, from the very midst of them you may go up to occupy those higher delectable mountains, the very sight of which captivated the soul of Bunyan,— those everlasting hills on whose shining summits the people of God from every clime will swell the anthems of eternity.

FINIS.

Adams 167 Isaac 223
Agiocochook 14
Albany 181
Alden, Pres 14
Alexander, Herr 245
Allard, Stephen 182
Allen 133 David 188
Alpine House 262
Amariscoggan River 54
Ames, Moses 190
Ammonoosuc River 31 35 68 87 278
Anderson, Wizard 245
Andover 208 268
Androscoggin River 16 34 54 68 222 223 244
Applebee, Zebedee 278
Assacumbuit 50-52
Aston, Abiel 208
Atkinson, Theodore 244
Austin, 239 Hope 238 248 252-254 Judith 253 Mr 255 256 Mrs 238 252 254 Peter 237
Ayer, Ebenezer 208

Bald Mountain 246
Bald-face Mountain 166 167
Baptist Church 186
Barker, Mr 126
Barnett, Lemuel 278
Barron, Elias 208
Bartlett 26 71 105 119 125 147 164 166 167 169 173 175 187
Basin, the 39
Bean's Purchase 244
Bean 226 Mr 225
Belknap, Dr 14 31 32
Bellow's Clearing 263
Bethel 125 233 234
Bethlehem 279-281
Biddeford 216
Bigelow 286
Billerica 208

Black Mountain 167 175
Blue Mountains 246
Bond, Prof 17
Boston 159 259 291
Brown, Titus 74
Brydone 26
Bunker Hill 235
Bunyan 307
Burbank, Abraham 224 Barker 251 Ebenezer 177 Eliphalet 223 George 223 Mr 247 Susannah 224
Burton 276
Byron 139

Cambridge University 99
Camel's Hump 25
Campbell, Caroline 273 Cornelius 272 274-276
Cannon Mountain 36 38
Carroll 96
Carthage 246
Casco Bay 16
Castine 260
Chadbourne, Dr 118 Thomas 74
Chamberlain 213 218 John 208
Chapman, Eliphalet 223
Chatauque 186 209
Chatham 157
Chaucer 173
Cherry Mountain 69 70 72 91
Cherry Pond 25
Chocorua 53 54 271 273-275
Clark 195 241 Benjamin 236 Col 259 Jonathan 235 239 Mr 242 Mrs 236
Coffin, Peter 223 Stephen 223
Colebrook 76
Concord 190 208
Congregational Church 184 224

Connecticut River 16 25
  31 35 58 78
Conway 45 46 129 135 147
  152 165 169 173 175 177
  180 184 186 187 209 249
Conway Corner 181 186
Conway House 186
Cook, Amos J 198 Mr 199
Coos Co 58 244 Hill's
  opinion 59 climate 60
  town shapes 60
Coos River 58 111 112
Copp, Benjamin 167 Hays
  D 269 270 Mr 168
  Nathaniel 269
Cowper 60
Crawford House 98
Crawford 79 112 144
  Abel 96 Erastus 97
  Ethan 87 98 Ethan A 29
  45 Ethan Allen 80 97 Mr
  74 81 83 85 89-93 95 99
  145 Mrs 84 97 T J 98
  Thomas J 96
Crocker's Point 46
Cromwell 272
Crusoe 77
Crystal Falls 35
Culbane, Thomas 270
Cummins, William 207

Dana, Prof 276
Dartmouth 69
David, Allen 124
Davis 214 215 216
  Eleazer 208 Josiah 208
  212
Derby 59
Devil's Den 33
Dinsmore, Elijah 177
Doloff, John 177
Double Head 164
Double-head Mountain 175
Dover 154
Drake 50 206 271
Dundy Mountain 164

Dunstable 205 206 215
Durand, John 62
Durham 177
Dwight, Dr 60 143

Eagle Cliff 36 38
Eastman, Abiathar 184
Eastman, Mr 186 Noah 184
  Richard 184
Echo Lake 38
Elkins, Daniel 172
Ellis River 31 34 35 149
  164 166 167
Ellis River Valley 164
Emery 148 149 178
  Enoch 150-152 Humphrey
  150-152
Evans, John 190 Jonathan
  248 Simeon 248

Fabyan Road 28 29
Fabyan, Mr 98 99
Farmer 61 J 218
Farnham 277
Farrah, Jacob 208 Joseph
  208
Farrar, 214
Farrington, Capt 195
  Stephen 194
Farwell 205 214-217
  220 Josiah 207 Lt 212
  221 Melvin 224
Fessenden, Rev Mr 193
  William 199
Field, Darby 15 44 177
Flume, the 33 40 41
Fort Ticonderoga 235
Fort William Henry 190
Foster, Daniel 178
Fox, Daniel 149
Franconia 26
Franconia Mountains 36
Franconia Notch 36
Franklin Co 246
Freeman, George W 229 Mr
  230 Mrs 229-232

Freewell Baptist Church 172
Fryburg 47 48 189 190 193 194 196 199 204 205 209 217
Fryburg Academy 196-198
Frye 214 215 Jonathan 208 220 Joseph 190 Mr 211 216
Fryeburg 26
Fulham, Jacob 208
Fullam, Mr 212
Furber, Mr 46

Giant's Grave 19 79
Giant's Stairs 164
Gilead 222 237
Gilson, Joseph 208
Glen Ellis Falls 35
Glen House 63 263 265 267
Glines, Israel 70 John 70
Goffe, John 69
Goodhue, Daniel 224
Gorges, F 15
Gorham 244 258 261 262
Goulding, 270 John 269
Grafton 76
Granny Starbird's Ledge 246 247
Great Gulf 29
Great Haystack 36
Green Mountains 25 67
Groton 208 213
Guildhall 77 79 80
Hagkins 54
Hall's Stream 256 257
Hall 256 Joseph S 264
Hanes, Hannah 76
Hark Hill 255
Harriman 149
Hart's Location 74 80
Hart's Looking Glass 187
Hart, Richard 74
Harvard University 196

Harwood, Ens 212 John 207 218 219
Hasaltine, Samuel 125
Haverhill 84 208
Hegan, Tom 258 260
Hegon, Tom 192
Hidden, Samuel 224
Hight, Mrs 72
Hill, Henry 113 Isaac 59
Hubbard, Mr 50
Hurd, Marion Lyle 200-202

Indian relics 46
Indian unrest 205 234 253 258 274
Indians, Anasagunticooks 54
Indians, Lincoln's interest 55
Indians, Pequawkets 192
Indians, marriage custom 56
Indians, Skokies 47
Indians, superstitions and traditions 42 282
Ingalls 239 Benjamin 248 Daniel 248 254 H 224 Moses 246 250 251 Mr 249 Robert Fletcher 250 251
Iron Mountain 164
Israel's River 25

Jackson 25 147 149 164 166 167 169
Jackson City 164
Jackson, Dr 282
Jefferson 25 60 69 88 105
Jefts, John 208 212
Jericho 148
Jilly, Paul 149
John, Peter 255
Johnson, Icabod 208 Josiah 208 Noah 207

Jones 214-216 Josiah
  208
Josselyn 16 50

Kan Ran Vugarty 14
Kearsarge 25 175
Kenison, Spenser 161
Kennebec River 16
Kidder, Benjamin 207
Kies, Solomon 208 215
Kilkenny 62 69
Kimball, Phineas 223
King, T Starr 176
Kingfield 246
Kittridge, Jonathan 208
  212
Knight 260
Knight, Artemas 278 279

Lake of the Clouds 31
Lakin, Isaac 208
Lancaster 25 58 60 74
Langdon, Mr 198
Langdon, Paul 196
Langdon, Samuel 196
Lary, Joseph 223 Joseph
  Jr 223
Lee 149 177
Leland, Rev Mr 233
Lincoln, Enoch 55
Lingfield, Edward 208
Lisbon 278
Long Island 294 295
Lord's Hill 280 281
Lovejoy, Abiel 184 Mr
  130 Mrs 120 Mrs 120
Lovell 26
Lovell, Capt 68
Lovewell's Pond 205 206
  209 217 221
Lovewell 47 48 210-212
  218 220 221 Capt 206
  John 205 207 219
Lower Coos 84
Lower Falls 47
Lyell, Charles 286

Macomber, D O 264
Madbury 167-169
Madokawando 50
Maine 55 190 222 244 258
  284
Mansfield Mountain 25
Mason, John 223 John Jr
  224
Massachusetts 75 76 223
Mather 49-51
Maupertuis 109
Mears, Roswell 186
Melvin, David 208
  Eleazer 208
Merriam, E 294
Merrill's Intervale 46
Merrimac River 31
Merrimack River 207
Meserve, Clement 168
  Jonathan 168 Mr 172
Messer, Moses 248
  Stephen 229
Monadnuc 76 77
Monro 190
Montcalm 190
Montgomery 256
Moore, J B 218
Moose River 68
Morristown 278
Morton 48
Moses' Rock 246
Motes 175
Mount Abraham 246
Mount Adams 17 25 29 63
Mount Bigelow 246
Mount Clay 17 29
Mount Clinton 17
Mount Crawford 164
Mount Crawford House 29
  102
Mount Franklin 17 26
Mount Jackson 17
Mount Jefferson 17 25 29
  63
Mount Lafayette 26 36
Mount Madison 17 20 25

29 63
Mount Monroe 17 26 29
Mount Moriah 245
Mount Pleasant 17 26
Mount Pliny 70
Mount Washington 17 20
 24 28-30 157 186 263
 264 279 285-288 291 295
 296
Mount Washington House
 35 112
Mount Webster 17 19 20
Mount Willard 33
Mount Willey 19 26
Mountain Pond 164

Nancy's Bridge 102 103
Nancy's Brook 102 104
Nash 18 73-75 79 96
 280
Nataluck 55
Neptune, Jo Merry 261
 John 260 261
New Bedford 296
New England 30 31 48 106
 284
New Hampshire 13 35 58
 59 70 76 111 223 287
 290 305
New London 171
New Madbury 167
New York 294
Nickerson, David 125 188
Norridgewock 235
North Conway 115 175 186
 187
Notch House 122 123 129
 130 135 136 139
Notch Valley 79
Notch, the 17-19 36 68
 74
Noyes, Mr 297 299
 Nathaniel 291
Nutfield 207 208

Oakes' Gulf 29 164

Oakes 23
Ockett, Molly 259 260
Old Crawford House 81
Old Man of the Mountains
 37
Old Philip 192 193
Ompomponoosuc River 87
Osgood, Benjamin 177
Osgood, James 177
Osgood, Samuel 190
Ossipee 46
Ossipee Fort 215
Ossipee Lake 46
Ossipee Pond 48 207

Page, David 249
Pages, D P 32
Passaconaway 27
Passamaquoddy 261
Paugus 68 208-213 217-221
Peabody River 31 34 68
Peabody's Patent 222 237
Peabody's River 268
Peabody, Mary 224 Mr 229
 Oliver 192 227 228 268
 Thomas 223
Pegwagget 15 177
Pemmasawasset River 36
 39
Pendexter 138 John 152
 Mr 153 Mrs 153 Patty
 154
Pennacook 258
Pequawket 175 235
Pequawket Mountain 157
 164 175 187 204 217
Peter, John 255
Pettengill 237 238
 James 253 Mrs 238
Pettingill 195
Philbrook, Betsey 224
Philbrook, Henry 223
Pilot Mountain 61
Pinkham Road 168
Pinkham's Grant 269
Pinkham, Capt 170 Daniel

168 Joseph 168 Joseph D
168 Mr 169
Pitcher Falls 35
Plato 239 241 242 254
Pleasant Mountain 246
Polan 52
Pool, the fall into and
  the escape 41
Poor, 239 Peter 248 254
Porter, Dr 185 186
  Nathaniel 184 248
Portland 25 111 296
Portsmouth 152
Profile Lake 38
Profile Rock 37

Randolph 62 63
Randolph Hill 63
Rattle River 244
Rattlesnake Mountain 175
Richardson, Henry 224
  Thomas 207 Timothy 208
Rindge, Capt 239 242 254
  256 257 Jonathan 248
Robbins 214 Jonathan
  207 Lt 212
Robinson, Dr 303
Rocky Branch 148 149 164
Rogers, Maj 193
Rosebrook 29 112 Capt
  74 76-80 280 Eleazer 75
  Hannah 76 Mr 83 264 267
  Mrs 78
Rouse, Thomasin 50
Rouville 51 52
Royce, Vere 149 171
Rumford Falls 258
Russell, Thomas 184

Sabatis 192-195
Saco 47 191 216
Saco Pond 208
Saco River 15 16 18 26
  31 34 46 47 68 148 149
  155 164 166 177 178 186
  187 189 204 206 209

Saco Valley 164
Saddleback Mountain 246
Salmon Falls River 205
Sanford 191
Sawyer's Rock 73
Sawyer 18 73-75 79 96
  280
Searle, Edward 278
Sebago Pond 25
Segar 234 235 239
Segar 193 194 254
  Nathaniel 253
Sewall, Jotham 224
Shelburne 223 234 244
  248 250-253
Shelburne Addition 244
  261
Shelburne 193
Silver Cascade 32
Slide, the 68
Smith, Nathaniel 190
  Richard Ransom 186
Snow, Mrs 159 160
  Nathaniel,280
Solmond, Capt 261
Souther, Mr 160
Souther, Rev Mr 159 161
Spring, Jedediah 190
Spruce Mountain 167
Squando 49 50
Stalbard, Mrs 88
Stark, William 149
Strickland, Frederick 98
  George 99
Stuart, Esq 87
Styles, Rhoda 224
Success 244
Sudbury 234
Summit House 264 267 294
Susup, Peol 260 261
Swanson 193
Swarson 192
Swift River 186
Symmes, Rev Mr 207

Tamworth 224

315

Tarumkin 54
Temple 246
Tenth Turnpike 111
Thom Mountain 167 175
Thompson 119 J M 265
Thorn Mountain 167
Tin Mountain 164
Toby 207
Tomer, Jo 261
Tomhegan 235 239
Trickey, J 166
Tuckerman's Ravine 29 34
Twitchell 236 Capt 194
　Eleazer 235
Tyng, Col 217

Umbagog 55
Umbagog Lake 246
Upper Bartlett 149 150
　159 175
Usher 214 Robert 207
　212

Vermont 59 67 284
Vines, Mr 15 49

Wahwa 212 217
Wakefield 205
Walker, Nathaniel 194
　Timothy 184
Warner 171
Warren, Jonas 280
Warumbee 54
Washington 305
Waumbekketmethna 14
Webster 300 Daniel 13
　198
Wentworth, Gov 73 74
　Mark H 244 Mrs 254
Weston 208
Weston's Bridge 209
Wheeler, Amos 281 Nathan
　280 Samuel 223 Thomas
　Green 248
Whipple, Col 71 72 103-
　105 Joseph 70

Whitcomb, Maj 77
White Hills 111
White Horse Ledge 187
White Mountains 13 16
　24-26 36 42 70 111 147
　149 157 186 283 284 286
　287 289 290 Indian
　inhabitants 45 Willeys'
　first ascent 86 animal
　traps 155 auroral
　display 106 bears 92
　172 180 225 beaver 277
　birds 22 bridle-paths
　87 carriage road 73 263
　carriages 264 cats 90
　192 cattle 276 central
　cluster 17 dangers of
　guideless trip 99 dead
　trees 23 early
　settlers 75 early
　visitors 15 extent and
　location 13 height and
　visibility 13 in
　moonlight 23 in storm
　23 in winter 24 insects
　22 maple sugar 179
　mineral resources 166
　247 278 moose 165 279
　origin of Indian names
　13 public houses 112
　railroads 262 salt
　scarcity 76 170 schools
　182 slides 24 113 129
　141 148 224 spring
　sources 31 summits 20
　teamsters 111 travel 84
　turnpike 111 valleys
　163 vegetation 20
　weather 291 wolves 91
　255
White, Henry 224
Whiting, Samuel 207
Whitney, Samuel 211
Whittier 52
Wight, Ephraim 223 224
　Seth 223 224

Wild River 223
Wildcat Brook Valley 164
Willard Mountain 61
Willard 62
Willey House 113
Willey Mountain 113
Willey 68 Ben 154
  Elbridge G 188 Eliza
  Ann 188 Hannah 154
  James 131 Jeremiah L
  188 Martha G 188 Mr 154
  Polly L 188 Sally 188
  Samuel 149 154 Samuel
  Jr 188
Williamson 190

Willis 245
Windham 52
Winnipiscogee Lake 205
  207
Winnipiseogee Lake 246
Winthrop 15
Woburn 208
Woods, Daniel 208 212
  Thomas 208
Wyman 221
Wyman, Ens 211 215 Seth
  207 219

York 226
Young, John 168

www.ingramcontent.com/pod-product-compliance
Lightning Source LLC
Chambersburg PA
CBHW050430240426
43661CB00055B/2337